JONATHAN DARK

PRIVATE INVESTIGATOR

SNOWBALL IN HELL

A Jonathan Dark
Detective Mystery

by

Roland Hopkins, Sr.

BRANDEN PUBLISHING COMPANY

Boston

Library of Congress Cataloging-in-Publication Data

Hopkins, Roland.
    Snowball in hell : a Jonathan Dark detective mystery /
    by Roland Hopkins, Sr.
      p. cm.
      ISBN 0-8283-2040-3 (alk. paper)
    PS3558.06363S66 1999
    813'.54--dc21   99-19641
                                    CIP

Branden Publishing Company
17 Station Street
Box 843 Brookline Village
Boston, MA 02447

PROLOGUE
Boston Post, front page headline,
December 17, 1945:
TIRE RATIONING ENDS IN THE U.S.A.

L ou Mills, my *Boston Post* photog buddy, borrowed a pair of snowshoes from the Stowe hotel. When we left, I checked the second story window across the street and thought I detected movement of the curtain. Maybe it was just my suspicious imagination. I felt kind of jumpy. Must've been from lack of sleep.

We rode up the mountain in the first chair-lift, another semi-crowded day but the temperature seemed to be cooperating. Twenty degrees. The wind was five miles per hour with a bright sunshine. Next week, Christmas vacation, the resort would be packed.

Do our worst fears ever come true? I couldn't help look back each time the chair-lift reached the next high tower--some of them over sixty feet above the terrain.

"Don't be such a 'fraidy cat," Lou teased. "What can happen? Stowe is the first mountain in the country to use chair-lifts. They're all brand new."

I shivered as we reached one tower at least seventy feet high, slowed down and stopped. "That's what I'm worried about, Lou. We're Guinea pigs for this ski lift operation. What happens if the thing goes backwards?"

Lou grinned and poked me in the arm. "They have safety brakes for that eventuality, stupid. Don't worry so much."

I felt my heart jump into my throat as the chair began to slide back towards the little house we began in--about two thousand yards straight down. "When do they apply those breaks you told me about, Lou?" my shaky voice pierced the icy air.

4 ROLAND HOPKINS, Sr.

We were early enough in the day so that only every other chair was occupied. Maybe thirty to fifty people. I noticed some of the skiers on the lower chairs closer to the ground had already bailed out--maybe six to ten feet above the snow. Lou and I were still over fifty feet high. I knew I couldn't fly and I didn't want to break my good leg. "Tell me when to jump, Lou," I called through the rushing wind hitting our faces.

For the first time Lou's face appeared concerned as he squinted and tightened his body. "See that next tower?" he asked, as we approached. "The towers are high and the dips lower. After that one, it looks like we'll only be about twenty feet above the snow at the lowest decline. If the brakes haven't kicked in by then, we'll bail. Okay?"

As we speeded up, out of control, anything seemed better than the thought of crashing into that house at thirty or forty miles per hour.

We slowed down as we reached the top of the tower, then sped up again like a roller coaster. "Get ready to drop your skis," Lou yelled--"and your poles. You don't want to get skewered."

I was ready, lifted the safety bar, and felt scared shitless. Do tough detectives display fear? I wouldn't tell Lou.

Just as we approached the lowest dip in the cable, maybe twenty feet above the trail, the chair-lift came to an abrupt halt. "Told ya," Lou forced a smile. "Great safety breaks."

We sat for about two minutes, freezing our asses off before the chair-lift began its climb back to the top.

God, I hated skiing.

Lou and I agreed that he'd go ahead and I'd stay at the summit to make sure no one followed. Lou would get as close to my client's brother's chalet as possible--then snap pictures through his telescopic lens, hoping to get something worthwhile.

"If I'm not back by three-thirty, that means I failed," Lou scowled. "But, I'll be back long before then."

He strapped on his skis and was gone over the first hill toward the two-mile-away chalet in the blink of an eye.

I stood and watched for several minutes, then spied a binocular contraption affixed to a tripod that invited the insertion of a nickel. It was aimed at New York State--I don't know how many miles away. I pushed and pulled and twisted. It budged, then slid around just enough to catch the corner of the chalet where I hoped our prey was hiding. I put in another nickel and immediately saw Lou climbing a small embankment with his snowshoes. If I had enough nickels, I could probably follow his progress almost to within a half mile of his destination.

I checked my watch. Ten o'clock. I decided to ski down the easy trail marked by green. Two hours of lessons from Lou yesterday didn't make me an expert quite yet. The brochure informed me that blue was harder and black the most difficult. I planned to avoid those, retrieve lots of nickels and hesitantly ride back up the lift. I wouldn't be gone more than an hour, depending on the lift lines. What possibly could happen in sixty short minutes?

It took a ten spot to bribe a ski patroller driving a snow tractor to take me back to the top. I decided chair-lifts weren't my thing, and if I never rode one again, it would be too soon. "Did you hear that fifteen people had to be taken to the hospital?" The ski patroller said, "Someone monkeyed with the breaks last night. Looked like some kind of kid's prank."

"Sabotage?" I mumbled under my breath. Obviously, I had an apprehensive one-track mind on another train of thought than the ski patroller. Could someone have already known our plans?

"The war's over, sir," he said, apparently hearing me.

For him, maybe, I thought, but didn't respond.

I arrived back at the summit at exactly eleven-thirty. Someone was using the binoculars. Then someone else. Then my turn. I inserted my nickel and turned the contraption back toward the chalet.

Nothing.

I watched for at least a half hour, feeding the thing furiously with nickels.

Still nothing.

I walked over to the spot where Lou had put on his skis and left me that morning.

Something wasn't right. Something had changed. I spotted Lou's parallel ski tracks. But, right beside them were another set of tracks, not present earlier. We'd been the first people to the top of the mountain, so they couldn't have been there before. Someone had followed Lou's tracks and I didn't need many guesses who that was.

6 ROLAND HOPKINS, Sr.

The person behind the curtain across the street from our hotel rooms.

There were several people milling around the platform. One older gentleman was sitting with his back against the building wall, sunning himself. "Excuse me," I said, touching his side with my pole. "How long have you been up here?"

He opened his eyes, squinted into the sun over my shoulder and grunted. "Who wants to know?"

"My name's Jonathan Dark," I answered. "I'm a private investigator from Boston. A friend of mine went off toward Mr. Averly's chalet early in the day. I wonder if you saw anyone else go off in that direction?"

The older gentleman seemed to be checking me out. Was I okay? Was I really a private eye? Did he care? Finally he must've decided I was acceptable. "A ski patrol guy with a heavy accent. Tall, blond, all black outfit. Hans is what I think his name is. He hung around for awhile, then took off over there after looking through a small pair of opera glasses." The older man pointed in the direction of the chalet. "Funny, though," he said, "he carried a pair of snowshoes and a long leather case. It looked like a fishing pole to me. I can't recall there being any lakes or streams over that area."

"Thanks," I said. "Sorry to interrupt your sunning."

I reached under the back of my parka. Damn. I'd left my pistol in the hotel room. Great detective. Actor Dana Andrews in the movie *Laura* wouldn't have forgotten his weapon. On the other hand, he had the advantage of reading the movie script. I hadn't.

Gunless, I began to follow the double tracks, praying I wouldn't be too late. I didn't think our ski patroller was going on a fishing expedition. More than likely his leather case concealed a rifle. Hell, I had no snowshoes. Plus, I was a lousy skier with a bum knee.

Before arriving at the first incline, I'd fallen at least a dozen times. I could see where each man had changed his skis to snowshoes and back again.

Four indentations.

I removed my skis and walked in the snowshoe tracks, which had been partially matted down. Sometimes, I sank down almost to my knees.

At the top of the next hill I put on my skis and pushed as fast as possible. This time I trekked at least another thousand yards and only fell three or four times. I was definitely improving.

The next hill was steeper and harder to maneuver. The snow was deeper. But, I made it. From the top I could see the chalet. I must have traveled at least a full mile. But I still couldn't see any signs of life.

Neither Lou nor Hans.

I clamped on my skis and off I went. Faster and fewer falls. The next incline appeared almost impossible. I crawled on my hands and knees over most of it. When I arrived at the peak, I noticed that the snowshoe tracks changed direction. There was a flat terrain for about five hundred yards. Lou had gone one way, Hans another. I figured that the shortest distance between two points was straight ahead. Did I invent that theory? Then I figured that Lou had gone directly toward the chalet. That's what I'd have done. Hans must have determined he was getting too close and decided to circle around. I put on my skis again and pushed forward. Not up and not down. Just straight. I made pretty good time for a change.

Between the bright sun glaring off the white snow, my total exhaustion, and the violent pain in my knee, I began to feel frustrated and useless. I couldn't ski, walk or crawl another hundred yards. I possessed an empty holster and maybe was lost. I actually began to miss the boring divorce surveillance cases I was used to working on.

Suddenly I saw a tall, lean man dressed entirely in black standing behind a three-foot wall of snow, aiming something that glittered in the sun. It wasn't a fishing pole. Apparently he had built a snow fort and hid in it to observe something--most likely Lou. I estimated his position about two hundred fifty to three hundred feet away.

I could yell at the top of my lungs, attract his attention and maybe get shot at.

I removed my mittens and tried to form a snowball, but the day was cold and the snow fluffy.

One chance. Wet the snow.

With what?

I contemplated. No brooks. No canteens. What?

Ahh. I had it. Piss.

8 ROLAND HOPKINS, Sr.

I lowered my pants, froze my ass and pissed as fast as I could. My dink almost became solid; but luckily, the liquid didn't. Must have been the alcohol from the previous evening's scotch. I quickly rolled up a yellow snowball, reared back, took aim and threw, recollecting my numerous throws from center field in the Boston Park league, nailing many a surprised runner at home plate.

Bullseye.

The snowball hit its target somewhere on the man's face as I noted the ominous black figure go down behind the snow drift, the crack of his upset rifle splitting the Vermont wintry silence, hopefully alerting Lou from wherever he was hiding.

My knee may have been shattered, but my arm never seemed to fail me.

Chapter 1
MY HUSBAND IS MISSING
Boston Post headline,
Tuesday, December 7, 1945
NUREMBERG WAR CRIMES TRIAL BEGINS
SUPREME COURT JUSTICE ROBERT
JACKSON NAMED CHIEF PROSECUTOR

S he smelled like my kind of angel. Sexy. And she was tall. I had to squint to see her outline against the sun. I laid before her, eye level to her runty white dog. The mutt wore pink foo-foo ribbons and danced in place like it wanted to attack me, but didn't know how.

I ignored the canine. It hurt to crank my head around to glimpse, so I settled for staring at those delicious legs growing out of shiny high heels. I swear, if my left hand wasn't stuck in my glove, and if my right arm wasn't pinned somewhere underneath me, I would've grabbed her and stroked her just to see if I was awake--like pinching yourself.

"You're Jonathan Dark? Your secretary told me I'd find you back here."

In my heaven, angels purr like sex kittens, just like this one. "I was when I checked in at eleven this morning." I mumbled, feeling mighty foolish laying on my stomach after falling and missing a baseball bouncing off the brick wall in the alley. Maybe I hit my head and was dead. I cranked my neck and rolled onto my back, viewing a forest of two straight, beautiful legs towering over me as I relaxed in my bed of cinders and gravel and broken glass.

"Does this happen often?" she asked.

"Oh, sure. Some little boys never grow up."

"Well, I rescued your ball," the angel said awkwardly.

10 ROLAND HOPKINS, Sr.

"Thanks, whoever you are. Rose wouldn't have sent you out here unless she thought you were someone important. Are you?"

I continued to lay there, glancing up her skirt. I'm still human even after a bad fall.

"Do you need some help, Mr. Dark," she asked, reaching down with a thin, silk gloved hand.

Rose arrived just in time, grabbed me by the shoulders and brought me to a sitting position. "Mr. Dark used to play with the Boston Red Sox, before joining the Boston police force. He still loves to play, so he invented kind of a one-man baseball game back here. He throws the ball off the walls, plays the angles, works on his speed and accuracy--that kind of stuff. Kind of a stickball gym."

"How clever," said the lady.

Even I was impressed with Rose's line of bull. I might even have to pay her this week. I'd had two tryouts with the Red Sox. Excelled in both, but never quite made it. It did make for good baroom talk and I came closer than most jocks.

Jeeze. Now two women with beautiful legs were talking over me like I was a corpse. What the hell. I snatched a fast look up both their skirts. Wouldn't those legs be fun to climb?

"Yes, he does fall occasionally," Rose said. "He's very competitive. Sometimes playing with himself is just too much for him."

The lady chuckled. That cheap shot was uncalled for, I thought. Why do women get along so well right away?

Minutes later, Rose had me brushed off and limping up the stairs. We walked the short, seedy hallway to my office. The angel and her dog followed. The letters on the door somehow seemed like a label for someone I'd never met. *Jonathan Dark, Private Investigator. Boston's Best.* Under the circumstances, even I felt a little embarrassed. The best what?

The odor of the place revived me. Stale cigarettes, hot coffee, and Rose's perfume, laced with a hint of diesel smoke from the train yard across the street. And money. The smell of money was new. It must've been coming from the angel as I turned to meet her, because it wasn't comin' from either of us.

"Welcome to our humble office, Miss..." Had I heard her name, but forgotten it?

"It's Mrs. Averly." She smiled a gracious smile, a classy smile, and her eyes looked directly into mine. This person came from the world of crystal goblets, thick carpets, and chandeliers. Probably silk sheets, too.

"Mrs. Averly was on time for her appointment, Jonathan. I think you owe her an apology for being late."

Rose hadn't advised me of any appointments which had led to my back alley workout. But after all these years, we covered for each other's mistakes. Besides, I owed her a month's back pay.

"Sorry, Rose. It completely slipped my mind. We've had an awfully busy caseload lately." I turned to Mrs. Averly. "I'm so sorry, madame. Can you ever forgive me?"

I took Mrs. Averly's elbow and steered her into my inner office. Mouthing a silent "get lost" to Rose, I could tell we were both smelling money.

"I am sincerely sorry for forgetting our appointment," I said as a weak attempt at gallantry. "It's hard to regain my dignity after a lady has seen me lying in an alley in my grubby playclothes. I usually wear a three-piece suit and tie." My fingers were crossed behind my back.

"Forget it, Mr. Dark. I'm grateful you are able to see me on such short notice." She held my baseball while her tiny dog watched it intently. Would she throw it for the little fella?

Well, batter up. It was time to get serious. I limped to the other side of the desk and dropped into my chair. It squeaked, like it was as old as I felt. I waved her to sit down on the other side of the desk. She neatly brushed the seat of the straight-backed wooden chair and looked at her glove. Luckily, it was black. She sat down, her skirt hiking up to reveal shapely, familiar knees and enough thigh to start a pulse somewhere below my belt. I was beginning to enjoy looking at her heavenly body.

"So you used to be a ballplayer?" she said with slight interest.

"Still am, up here." I jiggered my finger at my temple and gave her my best tough-guy smile, but I decided to save the war stories for later. If there was going to be a later.

"And you're Boston's best? Like your ad says?"

"It all depends on what we're talking about." I tried to sound flip. A psychologist friend of mine said it covers up my insecurities.

12 ROLAND HOPKINS, Sr.

The only insecurities I have are a pile of unpaid bills, two months unpaid rent, and the ten bucks I owe Detective Red Kelly from last week's visit to the race track. Jim Kelly's my best buddy. Yes, cops bet on the ponies, too.

"I need the best for an assignment." She perused my office, the dust, the old furniture, the crooked picture frames hiding the tattered wallpaper. "I expected--well, I guess I thought--well, I'm just glad you could see me today."

I turned on the desk lamp and studied the nervous woman. If she were a hooker, she certainly displayed a lot more class than I was used to. I get hookers as clients and many battered wives. Hey, a guy's got to make a living. This doll's aroma was almost strong enough to fill the room. Sweet. Expensive. She resembled movie star Gene Tierney from *Laura*--young, same full dark hair, same sophistication, and all the rest. I never told anybody, but I had a picture of Gene Tierney in my wallet. What's the difference from all the GIs who hung pictures of Betty Grable's legs on their barrack walls?

Mrs. A's clothes fit her slim figure perfectly. A long, furry mink, head and all, draped her neck. And the jewelry--an extended strand of pearls rested on her perfect breasts, diamonds hung from her wrist, and several rings sparkled in the midday sunlight filtering through my crooked blinds. I decided I liked her.

"I always seem to be available at this time of year," I said. "The fall and winter holidays are slow times for a private detective. People don't want to spoil the festivities with murder and mayhem." Actually, every month had been slow for a long time. The war was finally over, but business was still in the dumper. Maybe people were too busy getting their lives started over to get into trouble.

My small two-room office was located only three blocks from Boston's classy Copley Square, three floors up, across the street from the dirty Back Bay railroad yards and just beyond the high rent district. But, the sound of the trains embarrassed me now. The smell of the cigarette butts overflowing in the coffee can ashtray embarrassed me, too. Luckily, the bathroom was down the hall, or that aroma would also have embarrassed me. Jonathan Dark, Private Investigator's office wasn't composed for any hoi polloi client.

"So you do have time for a case?" she asked.

I wondered about her legs again. I'm an incurable leg man. I'm also a bust man. And come to think of it, I'm also an ass man. I guess I just appreciate people of the opposite sex. She fluttered her mascara eye lashes. Little did she know how she was affecting me. Or, did she?

"I've got only one other case at the moment, and it's a lulu. It's a special case from the police department. Confidential".

That much was true. It was a bizarre string of dog killings. I got the caper from Red Kelly. He came through for me occasionally when he noticed I wasn't eating regularly, throwing me a bone or two in a moment of charity. And, it paid.

"Here's a bone the department doesn't have time for," he said last week. Great play on words. "It's not much, but you can send the city an inflated bill. Besides," he winked, "it's got everything you like. Dogs. Fleas. Death. Depression."

Hell, I needed the work. Butchering family pets is still a crime, even if it is penny-ante.

"I'm impressed, Mr. Dark" she said, gazing at the photographs adorning my dismal walls. I'd framed my PI license, high school diploma, a letter with an eagle seal from the United States government informing me I was 4-F, several winning circle pictures from Suffolk Downs racetrack with my friend, Bob Wise who handles their publicity, and my yellowing letter from the Red Sox inviting me to Spring training in 1930. I let her be impressed. Why not?

"Mrs. Averly, is there something I can help you with?" I finally asked and fired up a cigarette, inhaling deeply.

Apparently she wasn't ready to spill the beans. She looked down at her lap, seemed surprised she was still holding the baseball from the alley. I wanted her to put it down. It had been autographed by Ted Williams. She studied it, squeezed it, felt its hardness, fondled it. I watched her play with it, while her dog watched her play with it. This was getting interesting.

"Cigarette?" I pushed a simulated silver cigarette box across the desk. It was engraved: J. DARK FROM THE BOYS OF 1933 over the design of a baseball. Another memento to impress people. That was the year I led my Park League team in batting.

She reached into the box and pulled out a wrinkled Camel. She frowned, put it back, and searched until finding a filtered tip--a

Herbert Tarryton. I scratched a match against my thumbnail, leaned over my desk, and lit the cigarette she held daintily between her long, well-manicured fingers. Hell, the war was over, rationing ceased--she probably had plenty of fresh cigs in her pretty little purse. Maybe she didn't want to hurt my feelings. If she only knew that every Wednesday night I played poker with these cigarettes as the stakes. On a good night, a guy could win 30, 40, sometimes 50 stale weeds--all brands. I felt lucky to have extra cigarettes around during wartime conditions when they were sometimes as scarce as nylons, steak, and gasoline. The war might be over now, but this was another thrifty habit that persisted for the needy.

I reached in and found a Chesterfield. Strong and manly. John Wayne advertised them.

I tried Mrs. Averly again. "Maybe you should start at the beginning. Why did you call this morning?"

She stared right through me, as if trying to make a big decision. I put on my most professional look.

"Are you familiar with the Averly Brewery?" she asked.

Of course I recognized the name. Averly Brewery was a big producer in South Boston. The company had somehow managed to thrive during the war, despite shortages, barriers to importing and exporting, red tape, and whispers about the Averly's German connections. They also owned a brewery in Berlin.

"Averly Beer was my father's brewery. My brother Richard and I ended up with it when my dad died two years ago. Richard runs it. I just sign what he tells me to sign and stay out of the way."

I recalled reading about her father's auto accident. He'd some-how lost control of his car on a bridge between the city and South Boston and flipped into the river.

I hoisted an imaginary toast. "I don't know how many times I've stopped at Jake Werth's for lunch and ordered wieners, sauerkraut, and Averly black German beer," I said.

She finally smiled a beautiful, embracing smile.

"So what does a pretty, rich dame like you need with a poor shamus like me?" I attempted to blow a smaller smoke ring through a larger one that floated over my desk, heading for the unrevolving fan on the ceiling. It had been broken since the middle of last summer.

She dragged deeply, then snuffed out her stale cigarette in my already-filled coffee can. She smiled with those puckered Gene Tierney lips. Probably a Vassar or Radcliffe girl.

"My husband's missing."

I thought about that for a long second. "I don't do missing husbands," I said in a firm but polite voice, wondering all the time why I was saying it. Hell, I needed the business. Any business. This was no time to be noble."

"Why not? I would think you would take any kind of assignment. I mean, look at this place." She thrust herself forward with an intensity I didn't expect, and I saw a hint of contempt toward me like how dare I even consider turning her down. The effect on me was compelling. Damn. The rich really can get away with being different.

I hated the fact that she was right about my needing the dough. "I just don't take missing husband cases because nine out ten turn out to be missing by choice. Understand?"

She squinted her lovely eyes and stared deeply into my unlovely ones. "Then my case falls into the tenth category. My husband loves me and I support him well. He'd have no reason to stay away. Especially since he couldn't afford to."

I thought about that remark. Rich wife, poor husband.

Rose burst in. For someone who erased sixty words a minute, her timing was flawless. "I'm heading out for a quick bite, Johnny--I mean, Mr. Dark. Can I get anyone anything?"

What bull. Rose had less money for snacks than I did for cigarettes. The truth? Rose had nose trouble. I looked at Mrs. Averly and tried to imagine her eating a sandwich or hot dog from Joe & Nemos. Bad idea. "No food for us, thank you, Rose."

"And this note just arrived for you, sir." She exited as quickly as she'd entered. I unfolded the sheet of paper she'd deposited on my desk.

TAKE THE CASE! WE GOT LOTS OF UNPAID BILLS!

"Do you still play ball?" Mrs. Averly said. "I mean, beyond your imaginary ballfield?" She was really giving that ball of mine a workout in her lap. The saliva drooling out of her dog's mouth helped me to hope she wouldn't throw it for him.

"Weekends in the summer. But a bum knee curtailed any real career." I immediately regretted telling her about that. Who the hell wants to hire a private eye with a bum knee?

"Can you still chase bad guys?"

"Is your husband a bad guy?"

She flashed a small grin. I grabbed another cigarette. A mentholated Kool. Willy The Penguin Says Smoke Kools. I hated Kools. "Missing husband cases are bad business," I insisted. "Not ever worth it when the client finds out that the husband left for another dame. I end up getting the blame. Sometimes, don't even get paid. It's not fair, if you know what I mean."

She faked a pout. Cute. I could easily fall in love with this woman if I ever allowed myself to fall in love with any women-- which I didn't.

"Oh, poor boy. Did your mommy and daddy tell you life was supposed to be fair?"

Now she was trying to be flip, maybe charm me, or bait me. I faked a smile. She reached into a leather handbag and dropped a thick envelope on my desk.

"What would it take to change your mind?" she asked.

I opened the envelope and started counting a lot of one hundred dollar bills. I tried to look unimpressed.

"Money is the least of my worries," she said. "Right now, my missing husband is my main worry. Is five thousand enough to change your mind?"

I tried to hide a choking sound. "Five gees is more than I make in a year," I admitted.

"It's what I earn in a day, Mr. Dark," she said. "My father also owned a lot of real estate in the Back Bay and a brewery in Europe."

Strange feeling. My groin began acting up. What the hell did all this money have to do with sex? I'd ask my friend, Doctor Edge at the next poker game. He knew about all that Sigmund Freud stuff. The brain in my head and the brain in my pants signaled yes. So did the note from Rose. Take the dough.

"I'm uncomfortable taking that much money for a case," I forced myself to say. "It reminds me too much of a bribe. You see, my father was a cop. An honest one."

I blew another smoke ring and adjusted my chair so I could view her exposed thigh.

"An honest cop?" Her well formed painted eyebrows lifted. "If you say so."

"Let's just say that I'll consider your case if you promise not to blame me if you find out that he ran away with another meal ticket. Some mugs do that. Find a rich skirt, wine her, dine her, marry her, spend her dough, and take off. Gigolos. Hustlers. Heartbreakers."

A small tear formed in her right eye. A train whistle blew from across the street, and the building trembled slightly. I was used to it, but it seemed to startle Mrs. Averly.

"No earthquake," I assured her. "Just the trains in the Back Bay train yards. They leave fine black soot all over the place." I ran my finger across the blotter on my desk and showed her the stain.

I fumbled for another Chesterfield, couldn't find one and had to settle for a Lucky Strike. I hated them--gave me a headache. "Another cigarette?" I handed her the crummy case. She found the last filter.

We both knew I'd take the job. I had to. At least she had the class to keep quiet and let me salvage some of my pride by pretending that I had a choice. What the hell, it beat counting canine carcasses.

"I may have some time," I said. "Got a picture of him?"

She fumbled through her purse, putting a nearly full pack of smokes on the edge of my desk. Funny woman. Here she was smoking my old weeds when she had a fresh pack of her own. I'll never figure out the opposite sex.

She presented me with a black and white snapshot, head and shoulders of a handsome, dark haired, sharp featured Sicilian-looking face. I glanced up at her from the picture and detected new tears forming in both eyes.

I handed her my handkerchief. Lucky for her, I changed hankies every Monday and this was Tuesday.

She dabbed the corners of her eyes. "When I met him he had no money," she began. "He was so handsome and so nice to me. Later on, he quit his job because of me. I wanted a companion. A friend. Someone to travel with--go out to dinner with--dance with--sl...sleep with." She stuttered and actually blushed, something I hadn't seen a woman do for a very long time. I didn't hang with dames who blushed.

"I loved him from the very start," she continued. "I loved to show him off to my friends. He's so beautiful. I know he didn't run away from me. We had our little spats like all couples do. But, he'd have no reason to stay away so long. He loves me, too. I know it. I'm betting five thousand that he does."

Now she was bawling her eyes out.

Rose appeared again. "Everything okay, Johnny--I mean, Mr. Dark?" she asked. "Can I do anything for you, Mrs. Averly?"

Mrs. Averly turned. "Thank you, Rose. You're too kind. Maybe a glass of water."

Rose placed her hand on Mrs. Averly's shoulder. Women seem to know what to do during tears; guys don't, especially tough detectives who never cry themselves.

Rose came back with a glass. Mrs. Averly drank it down without a pause.

"Thank you," she smiled at Rose. My busty blond secretary beamed and stuck her tongue out at me while Mrs. Averly wasn't looking.

"Yes. She's a peach," I said.

Rose grinned, then left the room--back to an embarrassing radio soap opera. Why didn't she turn on a symphony, just for appearances? I could hear the announcer saying: "Can a woman of thirty-five still find happiness? Blah, blah, blah..." Hell, I was thirty-five. Could I still find happiness? How about some respectability, some honor, a true love with a true lover? I'd even settle for some dinner money.

I returned my attention to my beautiful client. "How long has your husband been missing?" I asked, removing a small black notebook from the upper drawer of my desk.

She sniffled as she spoke. "On Saturday, at lunch, we had a little tiff, and then he didn't return from his workout at the University Club. He played--I mean, he plays squash there and swims several times a week. We live on Beacon Hill."

Of course, I thought.

"Louisberg Square, actually," she said. "So it's an easy jaunt down the hill in his new sneakers, across the Common, through Copley Square over to the club. Maybe a half hour."

Damn. The rich even play differently. This year, my Park League team would be lucky to get a few new balls and bats. Forget about spikes and uniforms.

"So you haven't seen him since about noon on Saturday?" I attempted to do the math. I checked my wrist watch. It was just past noon.

"Seventy-two hours ago" She said.

"What was the argument...I mean the tiff about, if I may ask?"

She sat up straight and smoothed out her skirt, cheating me of my sexy view. "Nothing of importance," she snapped, showing me a flash temper.

"What did the police say?"

"They're idiots. They'll list him as missing and begin an inquiry soon," she said, still sounding angry. "Imagine, after everything we've done for this jerkwater community. I know they think this is just a tempest in a rich bitch's teapot."

Her lapse into coarse language surprised me. I tried another approach. "What did they say at the club?"

Mrs. Averly attempted a smoke ring and failed. I was secretly pleased that there was something a poor slob private eye could do and a rich bitch debutante couldn't. "He got there at about two o'clock, and he left at around five," she said. "He always stopped off someplace on his way home for a drink, so I never expected him until nearly seven. Before we had our fight, we made reservations at the Ritz for eight-thirty. He never came home, and he never showed up at the Ritz."

I scribbled as fast as she talked, attempting to appear competent. "Any reason you kept your maiden name? Things like that can affect a male ego," I suggested.

She crossed, then uncrossed her legs. Was she nervous? Doctor Edge would say so. I decided I liked her nervous because I enjoyed the view.

"Tony didn't have a male ego like most of you...you men," she said. "He and I discussed it at length and agreed that Boston society wouldn't accept Mr. and Mrs. Coraloni as easily as Mr. and Mrs.

Averly. We're members in good standing at the Longwood Cricket Club, the Country Club in Brookline, and of course, Tony belongs to the University Club."

Her magnificent face took on a snobbish aura, nose turned up. "Understand?" she asked, not expecting an answer.

I understood only too well. I came by my awe and disdain for snobs honestly, learning chapter and verse from Uncle Bill, my 69-year old house mate. To him, the working man was the heart and soul of this country, and aristocratic attitudes were just plain un-American. For example, he and I could never understand why the Red Sox didn't employ Negro baseball players, especially since I'd played against some pretty talented ones in school. Apparently it was an unwritten law that no team hire one. When I tried out for the Red Sox this past season, all the colored guys outhit, outran, and outhustled us on the field. Hell, if they'd signed a few, they could've won some games. The Red Sox didn't even employ Italians.

I reached into my cigarette box for anything other than a Lucky or a Kool. After fumbling around I found a Camel. "More people smoke Camels than ever before"--that was the commercial on the Jack Benny Program. One of my bad habits was smoking. I blew a large ring and watched it float toward the ceiling, then pushed two small ones through it. Mrs. Avery appeared impressed. That's why I practiced it so often. "What else can you tell me about Tony's habits?" I asked. "In my business, the devil is in the details."

Mrs. Averly studied me. "Any more filters?" She picked one up, read the label and made a face before dropping it back in the box. "Where do you get these awful stale things, anyway?"

I decided I'd already been too honest with this lady. "I buy them on the black market along with steaks, nylons and butter."

She smiled. "We don't need to do that anymore," she said. "Now that the war's over, there's plenty to go around for everyone." She looked down and fussed with her skirt. Jeeze, she was attractive. "If you take my case, you'll be able to afford fresh cigarettes and a cleaning lady for this filthy office. Maybe even a new shirt."

I self-consciously brushed my shoulder, remembering the pothole in the alley that tripped me as I stretched for the catch.

She took a new cigarette from her own pack. I lit it for her, striking a wooden match with my thumbnail, another impressive talent. She dragged deeply, never taking her eyes off mine. "He grew up in Revere, the Italian section," she said. "Still has family there. Not the highest caliber, mind you."

I got her drift. Mr. Coraloni was Sicilian, below her caste.

She smoked and spoke. "I think he dropped any friends he may have had when he met me. They didn't fit into the places we frequented."

"Did he--does he--have a favorite watering hole?" I asked.

She looked puzzled.

"A regular drinking spot. A hangout where he knows the owner, cook, or a favorite waitress. A place he feels comfortable, away from home, where he can make an ass out of himself without anyone judging him. All guys have them."

She didn't wince when I said ass.

"Maybe," she said. "Maybe he had a place like that somewhere between home and the club. I know it's only about a half hour's walk, but he always took at least an hour and a half. That leaves a missing hour. So, you're probably right. Tony must have had a watering...a watering what?...watering hole, but he never said anything to me."

She began to cry again. Either she was a good actress like Gene Tierney, or she really did love her husband. The room shook as another train passed. She wiped her eyes with my hanky, staining it with black mascara, then blew her pert nose, proving to me that even high class snobs have snot. She probably farted, too. What the hell. Now I was forced to change my routine and get a clean handkerchief tomorrow.

"What's your usual fee?" she asked. She was playing with me again, and she tried to blow a smoke ring. This one resembled an egg.

"Want me to teach you how to do that?" I asked and lit up a brownish, tainted Old Gold I found buried between some Pall Malls.

She nodded and recrossed her shapely gams, her skirt riding up a bit.

I took a deep inhale, rounded my lips like an O and blew haltingly three times that produced three perfect rings.

"Try it," I said. "You have to make your mouth round like an O. I'm sure you can do it."

She made the O. Pretty mouth. Full lips. I felt a tightness in my pants. I could become a gigolo for a woman like her.

She blew. Three times. Out came an oval of smoke. Almost round. Then another and another. She cracked a genuine smile. Probably the first genuine thing she'd done in a long while.

"Not bad for an amateur," I said.

She watched her ovals disappear into the broken ceiling fan. "You didn't answer my question," she said.

I didn't know what difference it made, but answered, "Twenty dollars a day plus expenses. Sometimes less if a person can't afford it and I like the person."

She smiled again. This time not genuine. "Do you like me?" she asked, rounding her mouth again and blowing.

I decided not to answer.

"What happens when people can't pay?" she asked. She was admiring a horrible painting I had hanging in the far corner of my office. It was a Picasso look-a-like. Eyes, ears, and noses all messed up in the wrong places. It looked like nothing to me.

"Barter," I answered. "If someone can't pay, I take something from them that they can afford to give. Like my car. It's a real shiny 1936 convertible with a rumble seat. I got it from a used-car dealer friend of mine who was being robbed on a regular basis. Hired me to find the culprit. Paid me with the car."

"Who was robbing him, if I may ask?"

"His mistress."

She frowned. "What about the painting over there? I like it."

"A struggling artist was being blackmailed. I helped him and he gave me the painting. I don't understand it and hate it."

"Who was blackmailing him?"

"His mistress."

She frowned again. "Is there a moral to these mistress stories?" Then she blew a perfect smoke ring.

I stood up and blew one right through hers, then wondered what Doctor Edge would say about that phenomenon--everything has something to do with sex according to Freud. A male ring through a female ring. My, my.

"I guess people can get away with cheating on their legal mates, but it's hard to cheat on a mistress. Maybe that's the lesson. I really never thought about it till you asked."

She nodded like she accepted my analysis. "Have you ever shot anyone?" she asked, leaning closer to the desk as though I was about to reveal some deep, dark secret for only her ears. I had half a mind to just pass on some stories I had read in Uncle Bill's Dashell Hammett books. But maybe Mrs. Averly had read the same stuff, so I decided to tell the truth. "Look, lady, sorry to disappoint you, but private eyes in real life aren't like the ones in movies or books or on the radio. I'm no Mr. Keen, Tracer Of Lost Persons or Humphrey Bogart or Ellery Queen. I do mostly security work, sometimes cleaning up after the police. Once in awhile I guard a second rate personality who blows into town. I only shoot my gat at the Berkeley Street Precinct shooting range with the permission of my friend, Detective Red Kelly. I follow a lot of boring people, spy with opera glasses and never attend the opera. I've never investigated a murder case and never pulled my trigger on duty and don't know any private dicks who have."

Her face seemed to drop. "Okay, okay, so you're not a hero. Although you do sort of resemble those movie detectives. You must work hard on your athletic build," she said. "I mean, you're tall, dark and even handsome, in a rough sort of way. And your voice is deep and...well...you know."

I didn't, but it sounded like a compliment. A movie star, heh? Like her husband Tony. I looked back at his picture. Yes. He was handsome, but appeared a little on the effeminate side. Well, so did Allan Ladd, and he was the number one box office draw in Hollywood.

"If it'll make you feel any safer, Mrs. Averly, I think of myself as an everyday hero with the simple people who rely on me to help them out of their humble jams. I don't pretend that my purpose in life is to save the world. Hell, I didn't even serve in the war. And, maybe I can't even save myself. I just do whatever I need to do to stay in the game. Sort of keep pitchin' every day."

She stared at me for a long second. "That's really quite deep, isn't it, Mr. Dark? I thought you were an outfielder." She tossed my baseball back to me. I caught it with one hand.

She removed a check from her pocketbook and proceeded to write it for twenty dollars. "Heavens sake, I don't want to offend you in any way by overpaying. This is for today. I'll compensate you weekly upon receipt of an itemized bill. I'm sure Rose can handle that menial chore. Here's my card. I expect you to report in every day until Tony is found. And you will find him, won't you?"

It wasn't a question.

"I'll try, Mrs. Averly."

"Just keep pitching, Mr. Dark. Hard, every day, until we find Tony. Please." She held my eyes with hers. I thought she was going to start crying again.

"One more question," I asked. "Why me? You can afford to hire Pinkerton, or Wells Fargo, or a dozen companies with nicer offices and reputations than mine."

She flashed another genuine smile that melted my heart. "The truth? I need a real man. Maybe this will get rough, or public. Maybe there is a mistress--but I truly have my doubts, as you will find out in your search. All the investigators I ever met in real life resemble bank clerks or school professors and don't seem to have an appreciation for the darker side of life." She shrugged. "I looked in the Yellow Pages and liked your ad. Small, but effective. The Dark Man, I thought. And your ad said you're the best. I like confidence and conceit. Now we'll see, won't we?"

She rose from her chair, picked up her ugly midget dog under one arm, crossed the room and removed the ugly painting from the wall, exiting without another glance my way.

"Keep the five thousand," she said over her shoulder. "It's for the painting."

Well, well, I thought. Some days it pays to come into the office.

Chapter 2
HARD LESSONS
Boston Post headline,
Tuesday PM edition, December 7, 1945:
ST. LOUIS BROWNS RELEASE PETE GRAY,
ONE ARMED OUTFIELDER

I had to hurry. Dammit, I was the best in Boston and I was going to make the most of this windfall. I can't believe the St. Louis Browns. Pete Gray was the inspiration of so many paraplegics and the inspiration of my trying out for the Red Sox a second time. Me and my gimpy leg. And I almost pulled it off, too. I've got a great arm and can still hit the horsehide over the Fenway left field wall. But I've got no left leg. Hey, Pete Gray had no right arm. The fuckin' Browns. The war's over, the stars are returning and they cast off poor Pete Gray to the scrap heap. Well, at least he can say he made it to the bigs. More than I can say. Maybe he'll become a private eye and compete against me.

I had to forget baseball. The pace of my world just picked up speed, thanks to Mrs. Averly. But I had to clean up a few old messes first before finding her loving husband. There were a lot of places to go and people to see. I didn't envy my task. Confucius Say: He Who Dig Hole Must Either Dig Himself Out Or Fall In. I don't really know if he said that, but I did.

I made it to the bank, the bookie, and the bakery, in that order. Along the way, I ducked in and out of some seedy hotels and rooming houses. I was looking for Shoeshine Eddie's sleeping quarters. He was my favorite snitch. Of course, he did his best business in the better areas of town--like the financial district downtown, or Copley Square uptown.

Just so no one would get the wrong idea, I planned to change a few of the hundreds for small bills when I visited the bank. I didn't want to attract attention to myself. I knew I looked like a guy with somewhere important to go, and that was like a magnet for trouble in this neighborhood. But I couldn't help it. It felt good to have the moola. Like those times I wound up out in center-field in the Sunday Park League. They didn't complain about my limp, then. I'd peg a guy out at home plate. Dead on. A perfect strike in midair. Nothing like that rush. Nothing.

I didn't have to worry. It was late afternoon in a busy, chilly winter city. People were bundled up and looking down, thinking about their own problems. Funny how we might pass within inches of politicians, murderers, actors, bums, even people who could make us wildly happy for the rest of our lives, but we would never know. All those lives, close together, but never intersecting. If Tony Averly wanted to lose himself, and he had half a brain, he could do it in any big bustling city of the world.

I had one close call with a muscle-head who did part-time collection work for the liquor store. I don't drink a lot, but I drink on credit when I'm broke. Which is all too often. It's a little trick I have--if I can't charm my way through to another fifth of scotch with Fat Annie, the owner and head clerk at the bottle shop, I know I'd better lay off the sauce for a while. Hell, a guy in my profession has to live by his wits, which means he fails when the bullshit don't sell.

Anyway, this muscle-head recognized me when I went to the john in the back of the pub. He followed me in, then stepped up to use the urinal next to me. Funny how you can get a guy's undivided attention under certain circumstances.

"Well, this's my lucky day. Johnny Dark's blessed us by stoppin' by to perform the porcelain baptismal ritual with us."

I forget his name. Moose or Bubba or something like that. He'd failed in a tryout for the Chicago Bears--all two hundred fifty pounds of him. At this vulnerable moment, I still had most of the five gees cash in the inside pocket of my overcoat. My bill at Fat Annie's was seventy-five bucks.

"You want me to piss on your leg?" I figured my best chance was to make my anger bigger than his need to see my money.

It worked.

"Slow down, Darkman, slow down. I was jess makin' conversation. Jess wanted to see you close up, make sure you was still healthy. Jess's friendly concern," he said. "I'm only doin' what I get paid to do."

I wasn't in the mood. "You'll get your money, ass-hole. It's ten days to the end of the month, for those who can't count."

He laughed. He knew I wouldn't dare to really insult him. "I'm not leanin' on you today, Darkboy. I know I'll get my turn. Besides, it looks like you already been mugged once."

I checked myself in the mirror. True enough. With my trench coat open, I could see the dirty torn shirt worn by the little boy who got caught playing baseball in the alley.

"Fuck you, Moose."

Before he could punch me, knowing that I had now dared insult him, I handed him a hundred dollar bill. "Keep the change, friend. But don't forget to give the seventy-five to Fat Annie."

He smiled, revealing a lack of several front teeth. He must've occasionally run up against deadbeat ex-football players who had made the team.

I headed straight for the bank, depositing four thousand of the five in my minus bank account. Now Rose could pay herself and the back bills. We wouldn't be evicted this month.

My next stop was to visit Jimmy The Geek. the bookie holding Uncle Bill's problem. He's mean and his collector's a full-time gorilla who flunked charm school. Uncle Bill's got the bug and uses the bookie on the days we don't travel through the tunnel to Suffolk Downs, which is once or twice a week. Uncle Bill would spend every day at the track if he wasn't crippled by arthritis. He brought me up after my dad died and now I take care of him.

I thought about Uncle Bill sitting up late last night in his wheelchair, listening to mysteries on the radio and smoking his smelly pipe. I could tell he was worrying, but he didn't say anything to me. He never talked to me about his gambling like it was a problem. We just dealt with it.

Jimmy the Geek sat at his favorite table in his favorite bar. This was his office, too. At least his smelled better than mine. And it had more dames.

I waved and walked over. "You comin' to see me?" He fixed a beady snake eye on me. Damn, I hated this crook.

"Yes, sir." I fed him the humble pie shtick. "My Uncle Bill? Bill Dark? Says he owes you some money. Sent me down to pay you."

"You make a living telling lies like that?" Jimmy sneered.

Oh, oh, I thought. Something was wrong. The gorilla was grinning from cauliflower ear to cauliflower ear. "Save your bull, kid. We paid Billy Willy a visit an hour ago. No way he could've sent you."

Instinctively, my hand was reaching for the dusty gun hidden in the holster strapped to the small of my back. The one I'd never used in combat.

"SAVE IT!" Jimmy screamed, slamming the table with his fist. His ferocity startled me and I stopped in mid-reach. "I don't want your lies, your threats, your excuses, your promises, your crap about your poor uncle and his disability. Nothing except cash. This is a business. If you've got cash, we can talk."

The gorilla and I sized each other up. We were each about one syllable away from making idiots out of ourselves in a quick-draw match with coats on. I gave him my best too-crazy-to-care look.

"When I see Uncle Bill again, will I like what I see?" I asked.

The snake glanced at the gorilla, then me. "Yeah. He's okay, for now. We just had a financial planning meeting, you know, trying to figure out how he could square his account. Besides, do you think we'd cripple a cripple?"

I didn't honor the silly question with a silly answer as the two baboons broke up with laughter. "I'm here to pay up. How much?"

"Five fifty." The snake didn't blink.

I thought about that. Mugs got killed for a lot less. Uncle Bill would be seventy next summer. Not exactly a customer with a future. Suddenly, I just wanted to be finished with these clowns.

"I'm going to give you all of it." I counted out the bills carefully. "But if I don't like what I see when I get home..."

"Yeah, yeah, I know the drill," Jimmy said. "You'll track me down like a dog and cut out my worthless excuse for a heart." He drew some stubby papers from his pocket, scribbled on one and threw it my way. "Nothing personal, y'understand. Just business."

A half minute later I was phoning Uncle Bill. It rang and rang, and I began to imagine the worst. I looked back at Jimmy and the gorilla. They were returning the stare. I was calculating how many seconds I would need to get my gun out. Not that I would.

"Hello?" It was him.

"Uncle Bill? I'm just checking in. Everything okay?"

"Sure, sure," he said. "Are you all right?"

"I'm flush. I just saw your bookie. I bought your marker."

Uncle Bill was quiet and I thought I heard him sucking on an orange. He had a habit of using a syringe, filling a whole orange with vodka and sucking it out during the day. W.C. Fields taught him the trick. It worked, because Uncle Bill always seemed sort of bombed. So did W. C. Fields.

"Thanks, Johnny. I'll pay ya back."

"I'm not worried. I know where you live. You sure you're all right? Jimmy the Jerk made it sound like he roughed you up."

"That bum. I fought in World War One, remember? It takes more than what he's got to scare me."

"Good. Say, I might be in late tonight, okay? Don't hold supper."

"Yeah, okay, we'll talk whenever. That's three nights in a row you haven't been home. Finally met a nice girl, son?"

I wished I could've said yes or even maybe, but steady solid dames weren't on the menu for cops or private dicks. I could never imagine living in a little suburban cottage surrounded by a white picket fence, a wife, and a couple of brats. What guarantee could I give the family that I'd ever return home from work or even bring home a paycheck? Not fair to them or me. My cop friend, Red Kelly, felt the same way.

It was getting colder and windier out on the sidewalk. Now I could focus on finding Shoeshine Eddie. He was one of those characters who made a few extra bucks here and there by keeping his ears open. Sometimes it backfired.

I took the scenic route back towards the office, trying to think like the loser Shoeshine Eddie. Where would he be shining today? He found me first and yelled to me from across a busy street in Post Office Square, just before he was hustled into an alley by two figures in letterman jackets. By the time I reached him, the bullies were gone and he was on his knees, holding his gut with one hand and his lip with the other.

We assessed the damage in a restroom at the First National Bank building. His lip was split, and he wouldn't be shining any shoes for a few days, but he'd live. We'd known each other since high school. He was a small guy with thick bifocals and an apologetic smile. In other words, a born victim.

"I'm going to be sorry I asked, but I'm concerned, Eddie. What's this all about?" I handed him some more toilet paper for his bleeding mouth. I would've given him a real towel, but the attendant was watching us like we were a couple of low-lifes that had no business at the classy bank.

"Awww, it's nothing, Johnny. Coulda been, though. Lucky for me you came along when ya did. Those guys wanted to beat the crap outta me. Imagine, all that fuss over me just passing on some simple information."

I decided not to pursue it. "Well, I was looking for you anyway. Maybe you can help me find someone."

"Maybe."

"Tony Coraloni. Married to Helen Averly. You know, Averly Beer."

"Everyone knows the Averlys. You can find them at a different swank party every night. They're in the book, ya know. Louisberg Square on The Hill."

"He's missing. His wife's my client."

"Nice gig." He lit the remains of a cigarette and gingerly took a drag. He leaned against the sink and looked me up and down. "You look like a mess, too, Johnny. What's your excuse?"

"Occupational hazard." I decided not to tell him about my one-on-one baseball game. Eddie was one of those guys who got uncomfortable with silence, so he'd talk to fill the spaces if I just shut up for awhile.

Eddie shrugged his slight shoulders. "I'm good at low-life information, Johnny, but the upper crust don't usually open up much to me. So why you askin'?"

"I reached into my pants pocket, removed a C-note and folded it into a tight little ball. Then pressed it into Eddie's meaty hand. Everyone has some natural gifts and Eddie's was money instincts and sharp ears. He didn't have to unfold it to know what it was.

"You know things," I said. "Or can find out things."

Eddie wiped some blood off his mouth. "For you, my friend, and for the bill, I'll find out what I can. Gimme twenty-four hours."

I patted him lightly on his sore back. "Thanks. I knew I could count on you. Mrs. Averly wants to keep this strictly low profile, if you know what I mean."

He nodded.

My stomach informed me it was lunch time. I had dough so invited my disheveled friend to the city's snobbiest restaurant, Locke-Ober's, just walking distance from the bank.

"Will they allow me in?" Eddie asked, brushing dirt off his jacket and pants.

"Not with your shoeshine kit," I laughed. "But they know me there. Not that I frequent it much. I'm friendly with the cook. Her husband takes a powder on occasion and she retains my services to find him. I always do and she rewards me with a free meal."

Eddie and I reconvened in the bar. A double scotch on the rocks for me and a Pepsi for him. He was already loopy, judging from his glassy eyes.

"I wasn't always a rumor monger," Eddie rambled. "I used to work for one of the Boston dailies as a reporter."

I remembered. Eddie was starting his career as a writer at the same time I was trying to break into the majors in baseball. He saw me during the tryouts with the Red Sox at Fenway Park in 1930, and he gave me three glorious inches of copy in his column. The Sox liked my arm and they liked my bat. Both better than anything they had under contract in those days, several years after they'd sold Ruth to the Yankees and dropped from first into last place to stay for what seemed like forever. After fifteen years, Uncle Bill still treasured that faded yellow scrap of newsprint taped to the side of our ice box.

"Hey, we both had talent, Eddie. What happened to us?"

"Bad timing. You ruined your knee and I drank myself out of a good job. Forget the past, Johnny. Let's deal with the now. Tell me about Tony Coraloni."

I set the picture of the Italian in front of him. "This guy lives in the shadows of his wife and her family. He doesn't seem to mind. Suddenly, he has a row with the little woman and he's a foul ball, out of the park. What do you think?"

Eddie studied the picture. "How's your sex life, Dark?" He shot me a I'm-with-it look. "The last pictures I saw of Tony weren't so pretty."

"I don't get it."

"None of us get enough of it." He smiled at his own joke.

I was losing my temper, and I heard a hard edge come into my voice. "Eddie, if you can help, come across. You're nothing but a rumor ragman, washed up and squeezed out. But it's not my fault. It's your turn to do some good."

Eddie turned his glassy eyes toward me. "Lemme make a phone call. Then I think I can throw some light your way. I'll be right back. Got a nickel?"

I flipped him a couple of nickels, waited and sipped my scotch. It went down smoothly and I could feel it starting to do the job.

Eddie was back in less than five minutes with a shiteater look on his puss. "Tony was into some pretty serious sex stuff. Kinky. So was his wife."

"Helen?"

"Whatever. After her father died she came into oodles of dough. She and her husband had a ball spending it--but not fast enough and couldn't quite find enough jollies. Tony had that smooth Sicilian style--he was the perfect guide into the wild side. Something new, different and exciting. They had the dough and the freedom. They were like kids in a candy store. Or sailors in a brothel."

"Who's feeding you all this garbage? Is he reliable?"

"The newspaper society editor." he whispered. "An old drinking buddy of mine. I shine his shoes every day for free. You know, one shine deserves another."

"Yeah, yeah. So what's all this sex stuff got to do with anything? They're all consenting adults, even married consenting adults--what's to skip town for?"

Eddie lit a fresh weed, or half a one. "Lemme spell it out for ya, Johnny. The Averlys started throwing sex parties. Real carnivals, lasted for days. This city's high society got into it big time, like a fad. Lots of swapping, gals with gals, guys with guys, even some leather and studs. Playtime for everyone. My pal even attended one party--but didn't write about it."

"Interesting that she left all that information out," I said as a tuxedoed waiter poked my shoulder and asked for my order. "Liver and bacon," I said and turned to Eddie. "It's good here. They don't overcook it. That tends to make it like shoe leather."

Eddie nodded. Hell, the check was on me. "I'll have the same and another Pepsi."

I ordered another double scotch. Two always got the job done for me. Anymore after that didn't seem to register.

"Everything was fun for about six months," Eddie continued. "Then, about a year ago, things started falling apart. The parties were getting too rough. My friend heard they went too far one night, and someone almost died. A freelance working girl brought in to fill one of the beds. It was sort of like that Fatty Arbuckle affair. The girl was found almost dead with a Pepsi bottle up her...well you know where. That freaked out Mrs. Averly--Helen--and she made Tony promise to stop the craziness. I guess he tried, went cold turkey celibate. Maybe that's what this really is all about--Tony's fallen off the fidelity wagon and he's shacked up somewhere. Mrs. Averly's seen him in action--she knows he's got a huge appetite for sex, and she's probably going crazy wondering if he's eating out again, only this time without her."

A small warning light began flashing in my brain. I decided I needed to ignore it for a little longer.

"This would be a damn profitable story for your friend, Eddie. Why haven't I read anything about this scandal in the papers?"

"My old paper wouldn't print it and the Hearst papers don't know about it. I told you, my friend attended one of the soirees. He's happily married, got kids, a good job, and respect in the community. He's not spillin' the beans."

"Good thing for Mrs. Averly," I said, chewing on my ice cubes.

Eddie cradled Tony's picture like a baseball trading card in mint condition, barely holding it by the edges. "You know how I have a sixth sense about dough? Well, I also have one about murder. I don't like this picture."

I looked over his shoulder. It was just a simple snapshot of Tony, laying on a long chaise, smoking a pipe. Very aristocratic. "It's just a photo," I said.

"Look closely in the corner of the couch," he said.

I did, holding it up to the dim barroom light. Something long and thick lay on a pillow. Upon closer examination it seemed to be a dildoe. "Shit," I said. "Is this what I think it is?"

"I'm no expert on sex toys, but it looks mighty like a dildoe to me. Could Tony's disappearance have anything to do with pictures? Lemme make another call."

Eddie left the room. I dug into my liver. It melted in my mouth like only Loch Obers can cook it. I glanced around the room. If successful businessmen were ever recognized like athletes and movie stars, this place would be even more famous. I noticed the president of a large insurance company, the publisher of a daily newspaper and the mayor. How many of these people frequented the Averlys' sex parties?

Eddie returned, chewed on his liver and washed it down with a Pepsi. "They did take pictures," Eddie said. "Just for the fun of it, mind you. But a few of them mysteriously got misplaced. What do ya think?"

"A few compromising misplaced pictures of some of the people who frequent places like this could be quite damning," I said. "Too bad we can't find out who's in the pictures that vanished. There may even be some blackmail involved in this caper."

"I don't know, Johnny. Are you sure you haven't bit off more than you can chew? Can't you stick to mild divorces and murdered dogs?"

"Oh, even you heard about that case."

"Yeah. Everybody did. Hey, a day's pay is a day's pay."

I swigged down the last drops of my scotch. "What else did your pal say?"

"He says that the friggin' Averly mansion in Louisberg Square has so many rooms and beds and mirrors, no one could keep track of who was snapping pictures of whom. Everybody just thought it was one a big joke. And they all smoked a little dope. That might explain the looseness."

My imagination had already started to paint different pictures of Mrs. Averly and her playboy husband. She had conveniently left out the story about parties and drugs. Those things usually lead to no good. And apparently this did too.

"How about this scenario?" I asked Eddie. "Tony, an emasculated husband, decides to make his own money--takes one of those revealing pictures and blackmails the wrong person? What do you think?"

"Sounds like a good mystery novel. But you've got no proof."

"Then again, he could've done all those things, collected the ransom and he's on a plane to Rome right now."

"All that could be true, Johnny, but my friend says that Tony had no shame or pride and liked spending Mrs. Averly's funds. She didn't emasculate him because the guy was born emasculated. I'd cross out the idea that he's discontent. Sorry."

"Does your pal have any ideas, Eddie?" I asked, waving at the waiter for a check.

"If he does, he's keeping them to himself, Johnny. I think he's hoping none of this scandal ever gets out. It could cost him his job. My part of town doesn't need another shoeshine boy."

The waiter brought the check. It was marked paid and a note saying I OWED YOU ONE. I guess this was an ante-up day.

Chapter 3
TIMING
Boston Post headline,
Wednesday AM edition, December 8, 1945:
PRESIDENT TRUMAN NAMES
IKE EISENHOWER CHIEF OF STAFF

T he sweet smell of the pillow was the first thing that woke me up the next morning, and the strong aroma of fresh coffee was the second. I felt guilty again, just for a moment, because I knew I was in Rose's bed, naked as a bad alibi.

I opened my eyes slowly. The yellow country flowers on the cheap wallpaper were a few inches away. I was aching for a whiz. The bright wall pattern along with the several scotches we'd shared the night before made my head throb. So I closed my eyes and forced myself to relax until the spinning stopped. Whirly beds? I had them.

Rose had gone through her half-hour jealous routine after Mrs. Averly left. I put up with her antics just about every time an attractive woman hired my services--not that it was often enough. Rose knew that most of the women who retained me were hookers having trouble with their pimps or pre-divorcees trying to get something on their husbands. She also knew that quite often I bartered, leading her imagination down unchartered alleys not healthy for our relationship, professional or otherwise.

Mrs. Averly was no common streetwalker--and women have a sixth sense about their sisters' motives. I will admit, and Rose knows, that unlike. my horny compatriot Red Kelly, who'd screw anything that wasn't already nailed down, I'm sort of a romantic. I have to be attracted to the person before barreling in. I think I have to feel something down deep inside. Not love necessarily--but compassion or passion or something like that. Silly, isn't it. No whorehouses for me. I've never paid for it yet. Something about those kind of tramps give me the creeps.

I put up with Rose's fussing because, well, maybe I half deserved it. Besides, if it helped her to blow off a little steam, I can take it. She's a good kid, mid-twenties, just trying to get her life started after returning from a long trip to the West Coast. She's from Revere, the home of big families. Family is a big thing with Rose. She'd be married now, raising a passel of little brats while baking pies in some sodbuster's kitchen, except something happened and she came to work for me instead. I figured someday she'd reveal her secret. So, I never asked.

Right after Mrs. Averly left, Rose had rushed into my office and demanded to know everything about her. I made a crack about people looking through keyholes, then dramatically shook all that money out of the envelope. She literally dropped to her knees, grabbed two fistfuls, and inhaled it. "And the best part is," I teased, "I also get twenty bucks a day and expenses."

Rose came to her senses real fast and turned on me with righteous indignation. "What on God's green earth does she want you to do for this kind of money? Father her child? Father ALL her children?" I laughed, stooped my six feet down to her five and shushed her with a tender kiss on the forehead. "I'd do that for free. I'll tell you all about it at dinner. Hold the fort until I get back from the bank and a few other financial errands. Get the checkbook out of mothballs and start paying our backbills. We can afford it now. Also give yourself a raise. Five dollars a week. You deserve it, sweetheart."

We wanted to celebrate after our long dry spell. The cash was like a sudden gulp of fresh air. It was freedom. It was hope. It was also perfect timing--one of the very few times in my life off of a baseball field when my timing worked for me. Usually, my timing was lousy. Except when I was throwing out a guy at a base from the outfield or pitching woo to a prospective lady friend. Then, I was perfect. Unstoppable. Then, everyone got exactly what I wanted them to get.

I guessed Rose got what she wanted. "You were a real man, Johnnykins...I mean, boss," she said, sitting on the edge of the bed and combing my neck hairs with her nails.

"Service with a smile." I managed to turn and escape to the bathroom over the end of the bed. I always kept a straight razor and toothbrush in her medicine cabinet.

"You don't really think Mrs. Averly is as pretty as me, do you, Honey Pie?" she called at me with her favorite baby names. Great. She wanted to play.

I diplomatically grunted an affirmative into the soap foam covering my face. While Rose had had little schooling and was often treated like a dumb blond, I knew better. She possessed an abundance of common sense, which I've always found came in handier than all the so-called brainpower passed out with school diplomas. Her sweet-bawdy humor helped keep both our spirits up--no matter how bad things got.

I finished my shave, brushed my teeth, and returned to the bedroom. I jumped onto the bed, propped myself up on my elbow and looked into her fluttering eyelashes. "You're much prettier, sweetheart. And I found out from Shoeshine Eddie that Mrs. Averly is a sex fiend. How you like them apples?"

She vaulted over me, bulbous breasts bumping across my nose, and bounded bare-ass to the nook that passed for a kitchen in the small studio apartment. Every part of her short frame was a sensual curve, farm-fed and strong. She was still baby-fat busty, cute and alluring in a fresh and honest way, not often seen in the big city-- especially the part of the city I hung out in. I often found myself acting crazy around her, but only dropped over when sloshed. We both agreed that office romances only led to doom and heartache.

I threw on my slacks, a T-shirt, socks and shoes, then admired my naked cook as she set about pulling breakfast together and putting it on a tipsy table. She worked with grace and joy, shamelessly, a silhouette of man's desire against the morning light. I ignored another pang of guilt. I wanted her in the worst way, but wasn't in love. In lust, yes. And I had nothing to offer. She deserved better than an irresponsible Darkman with little future.

"My stomach's not hung over, anyway. Are those waffles I smell, sweetkins?" Two could play at the childish name-game. "Something smells almost good enough to eat." I eyed her backside and fantasized.

She brought on the steaming breakfast stacks with margarine and Aunt Jemima maple syrup. Neither of us had enjoyed butter or real maple syrup since the beginning of the war. Too many ration stamps for the unneeded delicacy.

As I dug in she put her arms around my neck and nipped my ear. "You can eat Rose's petal for dessert," she promised in a husky whisper.

I had to slow this down or Mrs. Averly wouldn't be getting a full day's work from the Jonathan Dark Detective Agency.

We sat down at the tiny table, she still buck naked, grinning at each other, with our knees touching.

"One of the dates you fixed me up with," she said pointing to hard-to-find bacon. "He plied me with wine, bacon, and nylons. I accepted all three."

"Did they work?"

Silence.

"Oh, oh. Fun's over."

"What?"

"Did they work?" I repeated. Damn. It was too early for a fight. Judging from her downcast look, she was not to be teased, but I started it, so I drove forward, pretending not to notice that we weren't fooling around any more.

"You mean to ask me if his sacrificial offerings led to him having his way with me? Did he get me into the sack? Did he use me as a slippery sheath for his big, gorgeous...well you know?"

Good. She was talking slutty, so I guessed we were playing again. I didn't remember much about the previous night, but I remembered a couple of huge, juicy steaks and lots of wine which can creep up on you. She had thanked me for paying her back-three-week's wages, and the raise. That's one of the great things about Rose--she's willing to wait for her paycheck. In this business, that's a big deal. I'm smart enough to know I need her. She does a good enough job with my feast-or-famine cases, works cheap, and is loyal. She also has a mad crush on me, which I try not to encourage. I introduce her to young, eligible males, which she dates, but rejects when things get too hot and heavy. As I said, we only sleep together when I've had too much to drink. Unfortunately, I don't drink enough too often. But, when I do--it's way too much. I don't even remember if we had any fun last night. I might have passed out--and probably did.

"The answer is yes," she said quietly.

"Yes, what?"

"Your question. Did he get me."

My fork stopped midway to my mouth. Rose actually did it with one of those guys? I looked into her eyes, and I saw that it was true. I felt a crack start in my heart, then quickly slipped behind my mask of indifference. What did I care, anyway? Wasn't it happy news? Wasn't that what I wanted for her?

"Well, great. So where is this Ralph or Timmy, this guy who stole you from me?"

"Do you care?"

"Okay, okay, I care--in a brotherly sort of way."

"Oh, brother," she quipped. She went back to her food, letting me twist in the silence. She definitely had the home field advantage.

I surrendered without a fight. "I give up. Tell me all about it."

"It's sooooo sad. He's gone. Gone away to fight in the big war." She batted her eyes at me like an underage innocent. "An' li'l ol' me, barefoot and pregnant." Her voice trembled just a bit.

My heart split again. "My God, Rose, you're serious?" I sat back, my head starting to swim again. But the fuckin' war was over. This little damsel was pulling my leg. Then I saw the smile tugging at the corners of her oh-so-kissable lips.

"Gotcha," she whispered.

I got angry. Two can play this game. "You lied to me. You violated our sacred employee-employer relationship! I ought to fire you, and cast your sweet ass out into the cold street."

"Did I say he got into me? I did not," she giggled, almost out of control. "He tried, though. And I would've let him. I even tried to help him. We were over there, right in that bed, wearing nothing but each other's sweat--but he couldn't do the deed."

"You're kidding!"

"Not this time, my semi-private dick. I was a very, very bad girl."

"Okay, I'll bite again--why were you a very, very bad girl?

"I laughed at him."

"You what?"

"I laughed. You know how I like to yuck it up, get pretty loose-- well, his thing looked so small and cute, like it was a little boy trying to puff up for a man's job. I think you've spoiled me for other men."

"You laughed at his...thing? Jeeze. You're lucky he didn't kill you. Dames aren't supposed to laugh at a guy's thing. That's the lowest vanity blow of all. You should know that."

Her face became serious. "He almost killed me. Remember that day I came in with a shiner?"

I did. "Yeah, I recall. You said you walked into a door."

"He popped me good. But he shouldn't have done that, Johnny. Sex should be fun. You men can get so weird, sometimes."

She was telling the story like it was a runaway train.

"What did you do then?

"I hit him the way you taught me. His dong wasn't the only thing that was limp when he left." Her voice had turned hard.

I thought about her story. She was crying soundless tears. Maybe I was somewhat at fault. I'd fixed her up with the jerk.

"Johnny, I was so ashamed. I just wanted so badly to have someone all to myself to love."

I mumbled something like how much I cared, and it seemed to help. She apparently felt better with the telling of the story, but I wasn't sure.

We polished off our breakfasts. I swallowed two more aspirin and finished getting dressed. I really wasn't in love with Rose--but I did love her. Was there a difference? I guess so. I didn't want to stand in the way of her finding happiness with someone else. I really didn't. Even though I admitted to being jealous. What's that all about?

I dried the dishes after she washed. She was still naked and it took all my willpower not to go back to bed. Ten minutes later, we were saying good-bye at the door, just like a normal couple. It was nice, but why did I suddenly feel the need to bust out for some fresh air?

"You open the office and I'll check in at noon," I said. "Don't take any new cases. I think this Averly thing's going to be full-time for awhile."

"What about the dead dogs? You did accept a check."

"Maybe you can make a few phone calls. Maybe to a few loony bins. Ask if they recently released anyone who had it in for canines. That may give us a lead."

"And you?"

"I've got to find a hangout between the University Club and Beacon Hill. Mrs. Averly's husband stopped off somewhere every evening for about an hour or so."

"You say he's Italian?" she asked.

"Very."

"How about something like an Italian restaurant?" she suggested, using her common sense again..

"I'll keep that in mind. Couldn't be too many spaghetti joints on a straight line between Stuart Street and Beacon Hill."

"While you're doing that, I'll call the hospitals and check the morgue for anyone matching his description," she said. Rose wasn't anywhere near as naive as she pretended to be.

I threw on my black trench coat and snap brim black felt hat, kissed her forehead and left on foot. Her apartment on Commonwealth Avenue wasn't far from Copley Square and the fresh morning air helped clear my fuzzy head. Too many scotches and wine. At thirty-five it now took me two days to recover. The drinks seemed worth it at the time, but not the hangovers. Maybe the entire drinking exercise was a weak excuse to shack up with Rose, as though I needed an excuse. Maybe it was an excuse to feel sorry for myself and for my missed opportunities. Baseball. Two tryouts and two misses. Shit. Uncle Bill still encouraged me. "Maybe next year." It's always next year, but not with my wrecked knee. Next year will never come.

I owe Uncle Bill a lot, though. I've lived with him since I was thirteen, which is when my dad died and my mom got so sick she had to go away. Uncle Bill taught me to play baseball, read the racing form, shoot a pistol, control my temper, and blow perfect smoke rings. He also loved baseball, purchased the same two front row box seats at Fenway Park every year for as far back as I could remember and knew all the stars by their first name--even the Babe. I promised myself I'd dial him up in a few hours. Uncle Bill, not the Babe.

It was brisk and windy, and I soon felt better. A fine December day and good to be alive in Boston. But right on schedule, the cold started to chisel into my torn up knee, making me gimp like a war hero. Terrible pain forecasted rain or snow. I ducked into a drug store to buy some aspirin. I was waiting for the light to change at the corner when a pretty woman pushing a baby carriage touched my sleeve. I turned and looked into soft brown eyes that hinted of hot suppers and tender kisses by the hearth.

"Excuse me?" she said haltingly. "I just want to say thank you. For going. For being there."

I must have looked puzzled.

She continued. "You know, your leg. I'm glad you made it home alive. Her daddy didn't..." She drifted off with tears in her eyes.

She reminded me that the war was over and I'd never been a part of it. The limp that she mistook for me being in battle was the reason I'd been kept out. The euphoria of D-Day had faded and the city's streets were filling up with the wounded, the jobless, the crazies and the brokenhearted.

I was glad the young mother didn't wait for me to respond. Women weeping make me feel helpless and frustrated. What would I say? I missed my chance to go to war? Missed my chance to play baseball? Missed my chance to save my mom and dad? No, my stories were nothing compared to her world of hurt. As I limped toward Copley Square, I promised myself again, for the thousandth time, I would do my bit if I ever got the chance. I'd change the first words in the Bible from 'In the beginning' to IN THE BIG INNING. My big inning--the one that never came--yet.

Maybe I'd ask about timing again at my regular weekly card game tonight. Doctor Edge knew lots of reassuring things to say. And, besides, he drank more scotch than I.

The University Club was near the train station in the Back Bay, two blocks behind the Copley Plaza Hotel. A three-storied nondescript building, the Club surprised people with how much bigger it looked inside. It featured squash courts, handball, a swimming pool, and a large badminton room the size of a basketball court that doubled for business and party functions. It also sported a nice restaurant-and-bar combo, well attended by members for lunch and dinners. Very swank. Too exclusive for a Sicilian like Tony unless he was Mrs. Averly's husband.

It was about eleven when I arrived. Glasses clinked as waiters set up for lunch. A few elderly, saggy-eyed gentlemen were already taking their places at the bar. I flashed Tony's picture to the elevator operator, a short, muscular man. Given the quick ride to the top of the Club, I tried the direct approach. "I'm looking for this mug. Tony Coraloni. He's been missing since Saturday. Anything you can tell me about him would be appreciated."

He fingered Tony's picture, but said nothing.

Two dollars was the going rate for street information in a war economy. But the war was over and this case was different. I figured if two dollar bills usually did the trick, a fiver would do it now. How about a ten? Five times the chance he'd sing a pretty tune. Good math, if you ask me, and I never graduated from college.

I handed him a twenty.

He looked up and smiled, revealing some gaps between brown front teeth and less than enchanting breath. It was probably a week's pay. "Nice man," he uttered in a slow way. I wondered how many times this guy had been hit on the head and how much garlic he plowed into his food. "Never stayed after his workouts," he continued. "Always talked to me on the elevator about sports. The Red Sox. The Braves. The Bruins. The Football Yanks. They stink, you know."

I knew.

"And mostly the dogs and horses," he said.

I stopped him. "What do you mean? Did Tony play the ponies?"

"Sure," said the operator. "It's The Sport of Kings, is it not? It's the sport for little guys like me, too. I used to be an exercise rider. Feel this arm."

I reached out and touched his muscle. Hard like steel.

"Horses weigh more than a thousand pounds and these little arms got pretty tough holding onto the reins when they'd run over thirty-five miles an hour," he continued with a dreamy look. He obviously loved it and he missed it, like an ex-rookie baseball player I knew. "When Mr. Coraloni found out I was an ex-jock, he became my buddy."

"Did he win or lose?" I knew it was a dumb question. I never met a gambler who told himself the truth, much less an elevator operator.

"Win a few. Lose a few. Nothing wrong with a little bet now and then, especially if you can afford it like Mr. Coraloni. He always flashed wads of dough. Tipped good, too."

"Ever set him up with a bookie?" It was a wild shot, considering bookmaking was against the law and my relationship with this guy was only as thick as a twenty dollar bill.

Someone buzzed the elevator, so I knew the interview was over. "Ask Louis. The bartender," he whispered. "Thanks for the lettuce. Can't exercise horses anymore since I was thrown on my head." Then the door slid closed and he was gone.

Louis the bartender was bald and fiftyish. Was it a rule written down somewhere that all bartenders had to be bald and fiftyish? He also wore thick bifocals. He smiled as I took a seat at the far end of a long, glass-topped bar. I placed my hat and coat on the stool beside me and waved. He approached.

"Hi, Louis. Bloody Mary?" I asked.

"Celery?"

"Yep."

He squinted through his glasses, then realized he didn't know me. "You a new member?" he asked, his smile gone. "I know everyone around here. I don't recollect your face."

"How about Andy Jackson's face?" I slid a twenty dollar bill and my card under his nose.

He squinted again. "Oh. Mr. Dark. Of course. Bloody Mary coming right up."

A few of the stodgy old members lifted their eyes out of their drinks to cast me a glance.

I smiled.

They looked away. They didn't recognize me either. I wondered how they'd treat a black jew. Bunch of bigoted old farts, I thought. But then again, who was I to judge? They were American bluebloods who belonged here, and I didn't. If I could afford it, wouldn't I leave my drab life behind and join a club like this so I could swim, play badminton and squash and swap lies with other elitists? Fortunately, I'd never get a chance to find out.

Louis brought my drink, which I downed with one gulp. It seemed to work better on my hangover than the orange juice and aspirin I'd consumed at Rose's a few hours earlier.

"Nothing like wagging the tail of the dog that bit ya," Louis said.

"How'd you know?" I asked. "And don't mention dogs to me."

"Tell by a man's eyes," he answered. "Don't drink myself. How long do you think a bartender who drinks would last on this job? About as long as a jockey or trainer who gambled on horses."

I slid him a quarter. "How about a pack of Chesterfields? And another Bloody?"

When Louis returned, I lit a cigarette with a wooden match and my thumbnail. "Speaking of horses, Louis, can a guy get a bet down around here?" I began sipping my second drink and offered him a cigarette.

He seemed to study my face for awhile before answering. "You're not a cop, are you?"

"My father was a long time ago. He also played the ponies. I'm a private eye and only buying some information."

He studied my face again, took the cigarette and placed it behind his ear. "I guess you're okay."

I dropped Tony's picture in front of him. "Ever call in any bets for this guy?"

Louis hesitated.

"It's all right. His wife hired me to find him. Been missing since Saturday. She's worried," I said.

Louis looked at the picture again. "That's Mr. Tony. Swell guy. Everyone who wasn't snooty really liked him. He only had one hangup."

"What was that?" I asked.

"The ponies. He'd bet every day. Right here. Through me. He'd buy the Telegraph, sit here between squash and swimming, and handicap the races. Didn't play every race like some fools. Just picked what he thought were sure things. Actually, he played too many favorites. You can't make no dough playing chalk. I tried to tell him that. He bet a lot. Sometimes he'd hit. Hit big. Like a thousand or two. More often he'd lose. Then he'd double up. He'd get behind two thousand, four thousand, eight thousand, sixteen thousand. But, he always paid. Somehow he always came up with the green. I like him, but I couldn't keep up with his action. Sometimes he'd give me a live one. You know. A horse that couldn't lose. And sometimes I'd bet ten or twenty. And sometimes they'd hit. And sometimes they'd lose. You know the game. Tony's a nice fella. I like him a lot. Sorry if he's in any trouble. Maybe I should feel sort of responsible if it's because of the bets."

I finished my drink and my cigarette. "Uncle Bill, he's my mentor, he taught me that we're each responsible for our own actions. No one else is to blame. If I drink too much, it's me who pours the drinks down my throat, not the bartender. If I gamble too much, it's me who picks the winners and tells you who to call. Nope, Louis, you're not to blame for anyone's actions but your own."

Hell, I was lecturing a man twenty years my senior. It should've been the other way around.

A big smile crossed Louis's weathered face. He liked the philosophy. It got him off the hook for Tony, and maybe off the hook for a lot of drunks who drove home unsafely late at night after last call.

"Maybe you're right. If I hadn't called the bookie for Tony, somebody else would have. Or, he would've just gone to the track."

The rich fragrance of steaks and seafood met my nostrils. Lunchtime had arrived and my stomach was clearing up. But I wasn't here to enjoy myself. I couldn't--not at these prices. Any minute, Louis would get too busy to talk.

"Tell me about last Saturday afternoon," I said. "Did Tony act differently? Was he behind any more than usual? Did he mention leaving town? Anything you can remember might help me find him."

Louis was my confidante now. We were pals, bonded for a few minutes with a shared concern for a fellow traveler. He'd answer any questions I asked, if he could. He removed the Chesterfield from behind his ear and put it to his lips. I lit it for him with a wooden match, broke the match and flipped it on the floor. Two stodgy aged members noticed, pointed and frowned.

"Now that you mention it, Tony left earlier than usual." Louis said. "He didn't even bet that day. Strange. I didn't think anything about it then. But come to think of it, Tony bet every day. Saturday was different. He didn't bet and left early. Almost like he didn't care if he never put another bet down."

I pushed another twenty in front of Louis. "I know you can't give names or numbers, but how about me making a bet?"

Louis hesitated. He looked down to both ends of the bar as if to see if someone was watching or listening. "Good idea," he said. "It's just a telephone number anyway, and then every Thursday this big tough looking guy comes in and I pay him or he pays me. Whichever. I get a split of any losses. Not a lot. But every bit helps. You know. If I didn't do it, someone else would. Isn't that what Uncle Bob says?"

"Uncle Bill."

The bartender pushed my twenty back to me. "I don't know no names anyway. They don't like it that way. And they don't worry about you paying. Everything's done on credit. They know you'll pay. And they always pay if you win. Reputation, you know. Good and bad. No one dares not pay."

I knew what Louis meant. Personal experience. I wondered if Tony had gotten in too deep and had used a loan shark. He wouldn't be the first cocky gambler to be transferred from the Bad Bet Department to the Bad Loan Department, slipping ever deeper into a nightmarish web of relentless harassment and endless payments. It took a strong will and some moral backbone to stand up to these guys and keep them away from you. Tony didn't strike me as the type. He appeared to be a lover, not a fighter. On the other hand, his wife hadn't mentioned any money problems and neither had Louis.

"Maybe I know your runner. Does he have a couple of chewed up ears?"

Louis started nodding carefully. I smiled. "And does he have this goofy grin?" I mimicked Jimmy's gorilla.

More nodding.

"You do get around, Dark."

"It's my job, Louis. It's my shitty job."

"Sorry, kid. Anything I can do to help."

"Make me a bet, Louis," I said. "Any bet. You pick it and I'll share the winnings. Twenty bucks. No. Hell. Make it a hundred. I'll drop by Thursday. Maybe I'll have found Tony by then and he'll be with me."

"I hope so, Dark," Louis said, sounding like he meant it. "I hope so."

The midday sun was beginning to duck behind clouds and a cold rainy wind whipped down the streets between the office buildings, forcing me to turn up my collar and pull my hat down tightly, making me look more like a hoodlum than an honest private eye. My knee had been right about the weather again.

I stopped at two dives on Stuart Street, one on Clarendon and one on Berkeley, having a dimey in each, trying to quiz the patrons efficiently and quietly. About two hundred dollars lighter, it occurred to me that I was asking the wrong people. Barflies are creatures of habit, and Tony's habit was to walk through this neighborhood after work, late in the afternoon. I changed my strategy, asking only the barkeepers and waitresses.

Still, no one recognized Tony's picture. The beers were beginning to bloat my hungry stomach. There was only one Italian joint in the vicinity, and remembering what Rose suggested, I checked it out. The manager recalled seeing Tony on several occasions, but not regularly. He said he thought Tony lived somewhere in the neighborhood, but didn't have an address. The food smell finally engulfed my brain and I ordered a bowl of spaghetti with meat balls, then continued my quest on a full stomach and clearer head.

I put in a call to Rose from a corner booth. She actually sounded like a real secretary. Funny how money in the pocket gives people a new attitude. She told me that no one matching Tony's description had turned up in any of the emergency rooms or the coroner's office.

I told her to widen her search to include suburban hospitals.

"Already started," she said. "And you were right about checking on sanitariums. A crackpot escaped just last week. Guess what the guy eats?"

I didn't dare guess, but knew. "What, sweetheart. Dog food?"

"Close, she said. "Dogs. He's a sort of cannibal. But doesn't eat people. At least not yet. He eats dog meat."

I felt heated saliva gathering on my mouth. "Can we change the subject?" I said. "Write up a report, sign my name and send it to Red Kelly."

"Okay, boss. Any luck finding Coraloni?"

"Closing in, kid. Closing in."

50 ROLAND HOPKINS, Sr.

I heard her kiss the phone. I wondered if that was sanitary. Then she rang off.

I called Mrs. Averly. No kiss. She wasn't taking calls, which was fine with me since I had nothing to report. I left my office number with a huffy manservant. At least she'd know I was earning the twenty dollars. I tried to imagine her face with her eyes closed, completely surrendered to a moment of pure physical pleasure. Do the rich moan differently, too? I fantasized. "Thou shalt not fantasize." Was that in the Bible or did I make that up?

I called Uncle Bill. "Everything's fine," I said. "See you tonight for sure with the birthday cake." Uncle Bill loved police work because he hated crime. Just to make the old guy happy, I had tried following in my father's footsteps by joining the Boston Police Force. I quit after less than two years. The stress from the bureaucracy and politics nearly killed me. On the positive side, I was a top student in one of the country's best training programs for law enforcement.

Right and wrong was never that clear-cut for me, anyway. Private police work, which is what the P.I. business is all about, suits me just fine. I answer to no one. Get up when I'm ready. Work when I want, as hard as I like. I take only the cases that interest me, usually when my bills pile up too high. Doctor Edge, the head doctor in our poker game has a different theory every week about why I do what I do. He thinks I became a P.I. because I'm just plain curious about people. The problems I get paid to solve--when I get paid--are pretty damn interesting by the time they get to me. And, like I said, I get to call the shots, though sometimes I think I hired the wrong guy when I went into business for myself. I try to be honest with everyone, never make commitments I can't keep and stay footloose and fancy-free. Think of all the marriages sworn till death do us part in front of God, family and friends, then all the divorces, wrecked friendships, bad business deals, unloved kids, and other busted dreams that could've been avoided if people were just honest with themselves about what they really wanted.

My dad never figured that out, and it killed him. He stroked out at the age of forty-four because of stress. At least that's what the doc at the hospital said. My dad was an honest, God-fearing cop, always trying to do the responsible thing he thought other people expected him to do. He was nervous, uptight, righteous, toed the line, and always tried to save the world. At the impressionable age of thirteen, I promised myself that what happened to my father would never happen to me. So far it hasn't.

Uncle Bill also has a sweet tooth--so the weekly birthday cake. I wondered what would happen when all his teeth fell out. I'd find out sooner than we thought.

I turned down my collar and entered the back of the big Copley Plaza Hotel. It covered an entire block, so it warmed me to cut through from Huntington Avenue right into Copley Square. I walked across the plush lobby filled with potted plants and people. Just before I swung out of the revolving doors, I heard a piano playing my favorite song. 'Accentuate The Positive, Eliminate The Negative, Don't Mess With Mr. In-between'. What was all that about?

My watch said three-thirty. I didn't need a highball, but my feet changed direction and I entered the Merry-Go-Round Bar, one of the nicer watering holes in the city. It was actually a real merry-go-round without the horses. Tables, chairs, and booths rotated around the stationary piano player who sat in the middle. I hopped on and took a seat. I placed my hat and coat on the chair beside me and motioned to a waitress, who was dressed in black to go along with the room's lighting and decor. Dim.

"Can I help you?" she asked in a polite voice. I could smell the starch on her white collar. Better than smelling waitress' armpits in some of the joints Kelly and I hung out in.

"Some snacks, a scotch on the rocks, and some information," I said. "Ever see this guy in here?" I slid a picture of Tony into her hand. A false gas lantern sat in the center of the table. She placed it under the lamp, looked at it and then back to me.

"Who wants to know?" she asked, her voice not quite so pleasant.

I tried the twenty trick. Easy trick if you have a bunch of twenties to burn.

It worked.

"Tony Coraloni. He's in here every evening. What's it to you, bud?"

"Was he here last Saturday?" I asked.

The waitress checked me over. Head to toe. Then she said, "You look kinda honest, if a guy who looks good enough to eat is honest. Maybe you're okay. The twenty says you are. But, you'll have to ask Doloras. She's his friend. I don't know anything else. He just comes in here frequently and talks to Doloras. Tips good, too. Like you. Twenties."

"Can you send Doloras over when she gets a minute?" I asked in my most eatable voice.

"Sure, bud. Change your seat to the other side and she'll wait on you. See her?" The waitress pointed over the piano player's head. "The one with all the hair. Brown and bushy. And the big you-know-whats. But don't let her looks fool you. She's not what she seems."

I changed my seat. The piano player changed his tune and began a Glenn Miller medley starting with 'In The Mood'. Glenn had been missing overseas for almost six months now and was presumed lost. What a shame. Best band leader I ever danced to.

Doloras brought my order. She was tall, wide, and kind of tough looking, in a homely sort of way. She even had a few pockmarks on her cheeks. Her eyes were different than the rest of her. Deep. Soft. Caring. She resembled one of the Andrew Sisters. I wondered if she could sing. I'd soon find out.

"Askin' about Tony?" she grunted, planting her frame across from me. Her low voice was more like a man's. "Who the hell are you? Cop, FBI, friend, or what? And if you're any of the above, why do you need to be passin' out twenties?"

I gave her my card. "I hope a friend," I said. "His wife hired me yesterday to find him. You a friend?"

She studied the card, then my face. After a long minute of sizing me up she apparently decided to trust me. "You do look good enough to eat. But not my taste," she finally said. "Tony and I are good friends. And I'm surprised his wife hired anyone to find him. She was fed up, last I knew."

I sipped my chilled scotch and felt it light up my stomach. "That's not what she told me," I said. "She vowed she loved him and gave me a lot of dough to find him."

Doloras shot me a strange, doubting glare. "Look, shamus, Tony trusts me and talks to me. They had a bad fight. She threw him out.

The poor slob still adores her, but she was finally fed up with him. At least she was Saturday evenin', the last time I saw him. She advised him to take a hike. He was a mess."

I nibbled my snacks and washed them down with the rest of my drink. I could feel another forgettable night with Rose coming on. "Why was he a mess?" I asked. "And do you know where he's hiding?"

Doloras looked around at her other tables. The room was half empty, so she had time to talk. "I've known Tony for about three years, since '42," she said. "That's about the time he married that rich bitch. Pardon my French. Everythin' was hunkydory with them until two years ago when her old man checked out."

"And that's when her brother Richard took over the brewery. Right?" I filled in the blanks.

"She did confide in you, didn't she. Did she tell you that Tony couldn't stomach her brother--that's Richard--and he had several long arguments with him? Over what? I don't know. Tony never wanted to talk about it, and I didn't push. Like I says, we're good friends. Tony told me what he wanted, when he wanted to."

"Romance?" I asked.

Doloras broke out with a low laugh. "When you get to know me better, you'll know that's not possible. All I know is that last week he owed someone some big-time money. His wife always came up with the cake before, but not this time. This time she said no more. Finite. It scared the bejeezes out of him. But something else seemed to scare him even more."

Another customer waved to Doloras. The piano player segued into 'As Time Goes By' from the movie Casablanca. I'd seen it last month with an unknown date and she'd fallen in love with Humphrey Bogart. What chance did I have against that cool competition? Here's lookin' at you kid. Who's kiddin' who?

"I'll be right back, shamus," Doloras said. "Don't let me forget my train of thought. I like Tony."

I sipped the last drops of my scotch. Doloras was a good lead and seemed like a good person. Occasionally you run into genuine people like that in my business. But not often. She returned, carrying another drink. Maybe she was a mindreader.

"Sorry about that interruption. I gotta make a living, you know. Where was I?"

"Thanks for the refill. You were telling me that he owed some dough."

"Oh, yeah. I offered to lend him a few bucks I got stashed away. Anything for a true friend, you know. But he just laughed and said I didn't make enough in five years to pay what he owed. And besides, he told me he knew how to get the money without his wife."

"That sounds like a problem with gambling debts," I said. "What do you know about his gambling?"

Now that she was gabbing away with me and relaxed, I decided that Doloras was kind of attractive. Big shoulders. Bigger breasts. Square jaw, blazing eyes and an assuring voice. She'd make a good-looking man. Whatever that means.

"No big deal," she went on. "He bet with the books. Sometimes in the summer he went to Suffolk, Lincoln, Narragansett, or Rockingham. Even took me once. I lost all my week's tips. But, no big deal. He always had a major wad. His wife gave him loads of dough. He was never broke. And he loved the bitch. At least he tried to."

I decided the piano player looked like Dooley Wilson from Casablanca as he began playing some war tunes. 'When Johnny Comes Marching Home.' Johnnies were marching home all over the country now that the war was over. I should be, too. I always wanted to be a hero. Dammit.

"Appears like you guys were close," I said. "Mrs. Averly know about you?"

Doloras frowned. "It's not like that with us," she said abruptly. "We're good friends. Just friends. Nothing more. Males and females can be plutonic, you know. It doesn't have to always be sexual. He told me his troubles. I told him mine."

I reached out for Doloras's hand. "Sorry," I said. "I didn't mean anything. Mugs in my business have to check all the angles, you know."

She pulled her hand away like I'd burnt her, but smiled, then looked back at my card. "Okay, Mr. Dark. Maybe I can trust you. Maybe I can't. But all I can tell you is Tony's real scared of something or someone. He won't tell me. Says he doesn't want me to get involved."

I cupped my hand over my mouth and leaned forward. "Do you recognize that suspicious looking character over there who keeps looking this way?" I disguised my fingerpoint to a table about three away from us.

Doloras peeked, then shook her head. "Never seen him in here," she whispered. "But he sure does look shady, doesn't he? When's the last time you saw someone wearing a monocle?"

I studied his reflection in a mirrored decoration. This hood looked too sophisticated to be a bill collector or arm breaker like Jimmy's gorilla, Moose. Suddenly, I noted my hand shaking. Shit, I'd seen this same guy during my afternoon rounds. Two, maybe three times. I wouldn't have thought about it two seconds, but now I could feel him staring when he thought I wasn't looking. My sixth sense--the one for self-preservation--told me he was going to be trouble.

"We'll deal with him when the time comes," I said. "Go on with your story."

"As I said, things seemed to change in the Averly household after her father's death. They're famous for imported German beer, you know. But the loyalty laws forbade them from importing anything during the war. Until her old man died in that car wreck, that's the way it was."

"But that changed when the son took over?"

"Apparently. They own a brewery somewhere in Germany. Berlin, I think. Coincidentally, right after the old man's demise, Averly Imported Beer started showing up on the black market."

"Sounds like Richard had had enough of wartime limitations," I mumbled. "If he sold his European production in the States, he makes money on both sides of the ocean. Sounds like a greedy, unpatriotic son-of-a-bitch. Now you'll pardon my French?"

Doloras smiled. "You're not naive, Mr. Dark. You're old enough to remember prohibition. People found ways to get a drink then. Is drinking wartime German beer so different? No real harm in that. Do you think?"

"My Uncle Bill started needling oranges with vodka during prohibition. No one ever knew he was drinking hard liquor back then. They still don't. And I admit I bought lots of black market goods during the war when and where I found them and could afford them. So did everyone else."

Doloras nodded.

"How did Tony change after old man Averly died?" I asked.

"That's personal."

"True. But, Doloras, I agree with you--I think Tony's in a tight spot now, maybe in over his head. We should work together to help him, if we can."

Doloras seemed to debate with herself, then leaned forward and whispered. The stranger still hovered three tables away. "Tony's wife changed more than he did. She started throwing lavish parties, bringing more people out to the house as weekend guests."

"Was that unusual?"

"These parties were different. Very avant garde."

I wasn't sure what that meant, but I was willing to take a guess. "Sex?" I asked.

She nodded slowly.

"Were you one of the guests?"

She answered quickly. "Why would I be invited? I believe they would've seen me as one of the lower class."

"I didn't ask that. Did you ever attend?" My voice took on a firm edge.

She dropped her head as if she was ashamed. "Once. Only one time was enough for me. Mr. Dark--may I call you Jonathan? I lead a very private personal life. Frankly, I found it more than a little childish and dull."

"Guys with guys and gals with gals?" I asked, "and you can call me Johnny."

She covered her face. "I'd rather not talk about it."

I was sorry I asked because it was none of my business and Doloras had been so helpful. "Nothing personal, Doloras. I get paid to pry. Let's drop it."

"Don't worry about hurting my feelings, Johnny sweetie. I just wish I'd never gone."

"Did Tony talk to you about his wife?"

"Constantly. She was his number one problem, yet he still loved her the best he could. She complained they couldn't make it together-

-so the parties. Those kinky parties. They were her idea. Tony admitted she got off on group sex."

I checked on the alleged infiltrator. He was still watching us. Was I just being overly suspicious? Maybe this guy thought Doloras was cute. I doubted it. Maybe he thought I was cute. I hoped not.

"What about Tony? Did he get off?"

"I guess he did," Doloras answered. "But it eventually drove them apart. She wanted him to herself. Didn't want to share. But she also wanted it all. Crazy. Don't you think?"

"So Tony was trying to be a good host and keep everyone happy, while his lusty wife used the guests to pursue her own gratification."

"Essentially. That's how Tony explained it to me, anyway. But she was really just trying to get off with him, Strange way to accomplish that goal, I think."

I tried to clear my thoughts. "Tony's wife paid all his bills up to last Saturday," I said. "Then cut him off, threw him out. Now she wants him back. Does he have any other reason--or person--that would cause him to change his address? Another romantic interest?"

"I don't think so. Mrs. Averly's a bitch to live with, but he remains devoted to her alone, as far as I know."

"When did you and he last talk? Since he's disappeared?"

She waved her hands in front of her. "Enough. If I tell you where he is, will you help him?" she asked, placing her hand over her mouth.

I reached over and touched her other hand. This time she didn't pull away. "Scouts honor," I said and then couldn't remember the Boy Scout sign. "I promise," I said. "I'll do the best I can to help him out of any jam."

She took a pencil out of her pocket and wrote something on the back of the bill. "He's here. Don't let anyone follow you. He's scared shitless and you're probably right. I don't think it's gamblers who scared him off."

We both peeked at our observer. He was gone. But, maybe not far. Not far enough.

The front of the bill was for two bucks. I pressed a fiver into her hand. "Follow me into the kitchen," she said. "I'll show you the back way out. It'll take you at least four hours to drive to Tony." We walked quickly toward the kitchen. "I'll call him and describe you to him. Close to six feet?" She grabbed my stomach. "Tight, no flab. Hundred seventy-five or eighty pounds?" She ruffled my hair. "Full head of your own black hair--no toupee like Humphrey Bogart and Bing Crosby."

"I didn't know they wore rugs," I raised my eyelids in surprise. "I thought all the movie stars were perfect. Real hair, real tits, real beards, real everything. Am I as naive as I feel?"

"Alan Ladd stands on a box in his movies to look taller," she said. "You probably still put a tooth under your pillow for a dime."

"My Uncle Bill puts a dime under the pillow hoping for new teeth," I grinned.

"Keep your sense of humor," she said. "You may need it." She rubbed my chin. "Five o'clock shadow and a pleasant smile. Handsome and sexy in a tough sort of way. Sound like you?" she teased.

"Not my passport photo," I said. "But you're flattering. Write your telephone number on the duplicate bill and I'll stay in touch. And, by the way, thanks."

I attempted to slip her a friendly kiss on the cheek and she pushed me away. "Nothing personal, Johnny," she said. "Nothing personal."

Chapter 4
PROVINCETOWN
Boston Post headline,
Thursday December 9, 1945:
TRUMAN ANNOUNCES MEAT AND
BUTTER RATIONING ENDING IN USA

Route 3A runs south out of Boston through thinly inhabited towns along the South Shore and on towards Cape Cod. I felt good to be driving, my two-seater ragtop performing like a racer, and I relished every bump and turn.

I'd tempered my drinking the night before at Red Kelly's apartment. We broke up our poker game at about midnight and I slept on Kelly's couch. Our regular group featured a cop, Kelly; Doctor Edge; a physician, Doctor Hack; a stock broker, Pete Holdem; a public relations executive, Bob Wise; a newspaper photographer, Lou Mills; a plumber, Jerry Wirth; me and Uncle Bill, when it was my turn to host the table. We always played nickel-dime and only allowed three raises. The most you could lose on a bad night was about thirty bucks--it was also the most you could win. At the end of the evening, with about an hour to go, we always played for cigarettes, a habit we picked up when all of us were just getting started in our careers and were church-mouse poor. Last night I lost ten bucks and picked up twenty-two stale cigarettes. I was sure Mrs. Averly would be thrilled. Half of them were those filter-tipped things she liked so much.

I tried to remember when I'd last driven the Cape Cod route. It was early summer and Uncle Bill was with me. With the top down, the glorious sun made our joints feel young and tough. It was a day of high spirits and swapping dreams. We'd won three days in a row at the track. The Red Sox were hotter than ever. They'd won two in a row. Everything was possible as long as the road kept going.

Despite this morning's brooding sky and barren trees, I managed to hold that sunny picture in my mind.

I made a pit stop and called the office. Rose was disappointed I hadn't allowed her to tag along. On a different case, I would've closed the office and made this a great adventure. She was good company, and she could've been useful. Sitting next to a pretty girl for several hours was a guaranteed tonic for helping solve mysteries. But someone had to mind the office.

I could tell she didn't believe we were gonna find Tony. I guess she had him pegged as some kind of cut-and-run gigolo. Her instincts were usually pretty good, but I was betting against her this time.

It was Thursday. Tony hadn't been seen since Saturday afternoon, and I'd joined the search team on Tuesday. I felt a little proud of myself. After less than 48 hours on the case, I'd managed to scrape up a solid address for our errant fugitive and was homing in on him. If Tony was willing to patch things up with the lovely Mrs. Averly and return with me, well, maybe I could have this mystery put to bed by nightfall. When someone gives you five thousand dollars for a shitty painting, anything's possible.

The further I drove, the thinner the traffic became. According to Doloras, Tony had hidden himself in a small, ramshackle hotel on the tip of Cape Cod. Provincetown.

I always liked Cape Cod, especially as a kid, before they built the bridge, when the Cape was a real escape. I used to take my dates across the canal on the ferry and walk to the Sandwich sand dunes. Lots of privacy, which led to lots of other stuff. But since they completed the bridge ten years ago, cabins, hotels, gift shops, trailer parks, and all the other building blocks of little communities started springing up along both coasts. So, I have mixed feelings about the bridge. I remember that two workmen fell into the concrete in 1935 and their bodies were never retrieved. They didn't name the bridge after them, though. Did that mean their lives didn't mean very much? Or maybe no one wanted to commemorate two screw-ups. Hell, they gave their lives for the bridge, so didn't that make them some sort of heroes just like those soldiers who won't be coming back from the war? Anyway, despite the bridge, the Cape remains quaint, with Provincetown the quaintest of all. But it seems to my memory that I've been told that fairies congregated there.

True history says that the Pilgrims landed in Provincetown first. They weren't queers. The town boasted a tall monument to prove it. Then, the brave band of settlers traveled through the Massachusetts Bay into Plymouth Harbor, stepping off onto The Rock--and into the history books. Everyone's always let down when they see The Rock because that's all it is--a rock. No Canada Dry girl sitting on it with her tits exposed. What did tourists expect?

My car radio played one of Frank Sinatra's slow love songs, 'Put Your Dreams Away For Another Day'. Romantic tunes with happy endings. Real life? Maybe. The war had a happy ending for the allies. Being a cop for awhile had given me a taste of battle, but it was nothing like the hell the American GI Joe endured in the trenches of Europe. I read everything I could about the war and attended every movie. Maybe I couldn't be there, but I could sympathize.

Now it was Dick Haymes singing a love ballad. Every song, every movie, every novel had a happy ending. I turned the radio up and found myself thinking about the young mother who stopped me outside the drugstore yesterday. Poor kid. She'd survive, though, toughen up, maybe even fall in love again. But she'd be haunted by what might have been. She'd live another life, walk another path, in her mind. That other life would be with the man and the love that was stopped hard by an enemy bullet or mortar or whatever it was. It wasn't natural for a love to end that way, so suddenly, by something as stupid as a war. If someone got sick and died, well, that was different--that was natural, and you could say your good-byes, and put it behind you. But a violent death was different. Death wasn't supposed to come that way. So after it took away the one you loved, you spent way too much time wondering about what might have been.

I looked around at the passing countryside. Now that the long war had ended, a serene spell had fallen over the land. People were ready to be happy again. Besides, the radio newsman announced that I could buy butter without ration stamps. La di da. I was just learning to like margarine. But most people I knew missed butter and had grown tired of buying the white stuff that had to be mixed with a yellow coloring pill.

I lit a Chesterfield and allowed my mind to wander aimlessly. Doctor Edge said that was good therapy. I recalled the day I took my Army physical. Everything jelled. I wanted to get into the fight in the worst way. I even passed the cough test. Then the doctor asked me to perform a few simple deep knee bends. At least, that's what he called them. 'Simple deep knee bends.' They weren't simple for me. After three grunts and groans, my knee caved in and I fell on my face. The doc asked a crazy question: "Are you trying to fool us?" If a guy tries to skip the draft, he doesn't do it this way, I thought, angrily. The doc checked me out, then wrote in the official government report, right below the 4-F: "Lucky to be able to walk at all." The bad knee that had kept me out of professional baseball had now kept me out of the service. I stayed angry at the world for weeks afterward.

Most of the trees became pines as I approached the tip of Cape Cod. I could've made the trip in under four hours, but I added some time because I left the main route several times just in case I was being followed. That strange duck in the Merry-Go-Round still haunted me, monocle and all.

My watch read high noon when I pulled into the dirt driveway of a small hotel-and-restaurant combination. The Myles Standish--who'd of guessed? It was situated right on a sandy beach.

I rolled down the window and settled back for a smoke, something from last night's winnings. This was a Lucky. Uch. The strong salt smell lined the inside of my nostrils and the loud, whitecapped waves licked almost up to the wooden deck surrounding the building.

I counted four cars parked by the door.

I waited fifteen minutes.

No one followed me into the parking lot.

It was safe to enter.

And when I did, I was met with a cheap nautical motif barroom with dilapidated nets hanging from the ceiling, lobster pots hanging on the walls, and a large mirror behind the bar reflecting the ocean so the drinkers could look up over their drinks and see the view behind without turning around.

Smart decorator.

A fuzzy-faced bartender, more than middle-aged with a weathered complexion, was handing a sandwich to a dark-haired, handsome guy who resembled my picture of Tony Coraloni. Two younger men sat in a booth and appeared to be holding hands. Two tough looking dames sat on the far end of the bar, whispering, giggling, and occasionally kissing.

The aroma of beer, salt, and fried cooking filled my nose, something unattractive in the city, but very homey on Cape Cod.

Doloras' male mannerisms suddenly made sense. How many times during our conversation did she hint that she was different? And how many times did she cringe when I tried to touch her? Boy, was I naive. She must've been a lesbian. That also might explain why Tony had trouble satisfying his wife. Tony Coraloni was a homo. Birds of a feather.

I waited a few minutes more before making a move. I gazed out the window admiring the ocean, the sand, and the squawking seagulls' ballet over the waves. No one paid any attention to me. Good.

I took a stool right next to my picture boy and motioned to the bartender. "Beer with a shot," I said quietly. Tony Coraloni turned his head and gave me the once over.

"Close to six feet. One seventy-five or one eighty pounds and cute. She said you were cute in a tough sort of way." Tony had no lisp or limp wrist. So much for stereotypes. "You Dark?" he asked with a you-got-me smile.

Now I could see why Mrs. Averly was attracted to him. Tony Coraloni was not only handsome, he was pretty like a chorus boy on Broadway. Too pretty. "I'm Johnny Dark," I said putting out my hand to grasp his.

We shook. His grip was stronger than mine. Too much handball at the club. "Your wife hired me to find you. She wants you to come home."

"Yeah. I know," he said. "Doloras tipped me off. But it's not that simple. She wanted you to find me all right, but she didn't tell you the whole story."

"So what else is new? No one ever tells private eyes the whole story. Don't you ever go to the movies. We have to find out the hard way."

The bartender brought the beer and the shot.

I threw down the shot and chased it with a gulp of beer.

Tony noted my enjoyment.

"Report back to my wife that I'm here, I'm safe, and I still love her," he said. "But I'll go home when I'm ready. In any case, you've earned your dough."

I downed the rest of my beer, thinking about the five gees that I didn't honestly feel I earned yet. "I promised Doloras I'd try to help, even though your wife is paying the freight." I surveyed the room again. Very few people--all looked like locals. "I smell trouble around you, Tony. I can at least listen to your story."

Tony forced a smile. His eyes were ringed with red as though he hadn't slept well in days or was heavy into drugs. I didn't have any idea which. He fidgeted with his glass. He wore a diamond ring on his pinkie finger, twisting it around again and again. I'd questioned enough suspects to recognize someone who wanted to spill the beans, but wasn't quite ready.

I motioned to the bartender for more drinks. That usually loosened tight tongues. I pretended to be patient.

The bartender slowly slid two more beers and a shot down to us. I took a swig. Tony gulped his. I decided to attempt the shock routine. "I know about the wild parties and the photos," I said.

That seemed to break the ice. Tony stopped turning his ring and fidgeting with his glass. He had decided something. "Are you a smart enough detective to deduce that I'm a fairy?" he asked, staring at me, watching for some reaction. He got none.

I supposed it took a lot of guts for Tony to tell me straight out that he was so different. My poker face served me well. And, I really didn't give a shit. To me, people were all people first and whatever else second. Tony Coraloni was just people to me.

He seemed satisfied with my response--or lack of it--and visibly relaxed. I offered him a Chesterfield, or was it a Pall Mall or a Kool.

He declined.

I lit up and blew one of my famous rings. "Does your wife know?"

He threw his hands out to his side, palms open, very animated. "That's the whole problem between us. She knew it from the outset.

But she saw me as a challenge, in a sick sort of way. She was going to cure me. Can you believe that? Cure me. People don't cure queers."

"I wouldn't know," I honestly said. I didn't have any experience with queers. If I knew one, I didn't know it.

"Do you know that one out of every seven men is queer?" Tony asked.

I immediately counted my poker group. Nine guys. Did that mean one of them was queer? I wondered which one.

Tony kept talking. "She insists it's a disease. I don't think so. I've always felt this way." He was talking fast like a teletype, trying to make me understand before he thought about what he was telling me. "I've always preferred men. But she was so nice and persuasive. And she's a very handsome woman. And..." he sighed, "I couldn't say no after she offered me so much money when she found my Achilles heel."

"Gambling on the ponies?" It was a safe guess.

He nodded. "I finally gave in and married her. It wasn't really so crazy." Now he began to whisper. "I can't get it up for girls. But for awhile, we were very good for each other. I mean, we had a lot of silly fun trying to perform sex. She kind of became my challenge and I hers."

"Is that where the sex parties idea came from?"

He ignored my question. "I really liked and respected her father," he said. "He was a great gentleman and a real patriot. You know, he was one of the few people who was willing to accept me as I am. I just hated the idea of taking that much money from a woman who I could never make happy."

"But you stayed around and used her money for your gambling habit?"

"Yeah. I admit it. I used her. And I liked the sex parties. We both always got off--but with other people. So, you see, I wasn't a complete failure."

"Then what made you run away?" I asked.

He dropped his head. "I wasn't brought up to use people. I actually always thought I was a good Catholic boy. Even attended confession once a week."

"The Priest must have got a kick out of listening to your yarns."

"Well, at least he forgave me after a bunch of Hail Marys. But the problem was, I couldn't forgive myself. I started to feel like a frigging stud service. I hated myself for all my weaknesses, and I resented her because she used my weaknesses to control me."

"Why don't you just go back and explain? Maybe she'll understand and give you a break. Let you be yourself. I'm sure she still loves you. At least she told me she did."

He looked at me patiently and kindly, those dark Sicilian eyes flashing a look of lost innocence. "You can never go back, my friend. Once you've lost your virginity, it's gone forever."

"So what did you do--before coming here, I mean?"

"You mean, before running away?" he said. "Damn, I'm such a coward. You want to know what I did? I tried to become a real businessman. Really. I threw myself into the family's brewery business, telling myself I was finally carrying my fair share, doing my part. Turns out I'm a very good salesman. You'd be surprised how many homo clients we have."

"Yeah? One out of every seven?"

Tony laughed for the first time. Maybe there was hope to bring him back, yet. "I went to work every day--for myself," he said. "Not that we needed the money. But Helen hated it. She married me for a playmate, not a meal ticket."

"But the old man must have appreciated the effort."

"Damn tootin' he did. He saw some real value in me. Called me his 'second son', which drove Richard--that's Helen's brother-- simply wild. Richard came to loathe me more every day."

I blew several perfect rings. No one cared.

"For awhile, I was back to my strapping self again. I felt good, like a real man with a real purpose in life. Even became a boring customer for the priest on Saturdays. I had a direction, some self-respect. And I gave Helen some of the best loving she'll ever know. I still couldn't get it up, but there are other ways of bringing a woman satisfaction, you know."

I guessed I knew.

"But she felt threatened by my success. She felt she was losing her control over me--and she didn't believe her love, by itself, would be enough to hold me. Richard had the same fear in the family business, because his father referred to me with high praise just once too often. So, I was fighting Richard's insecurities all day in the office, and his sister's insecurities all night in the bedroom. They couldn't help it, I suppose. When you're brought up with a silver spoon in your mouth and someone threatens to take it away--well, I guess I could understand. I wasn't trying to take anything away from them. On the contrary. I was trying to add something and feel my worth. But then they both did exactly the wrong thing, looking for new ways to control me. My string was only so long."

"And you came to the end of it? So Tony the handsome Adonis and Tony the sales machine rebelled?"

"Richard was really starting to give me a rough time in the office, undercutting every idea I developed, telling anyone who'd listen that I was a fairy. He was cruel, an insecure child, and I was fed up. But before I could do anything about it, old man Averly died. In the weeks following his death, Richard out-shouted me and out-maneuvered me at the brewery, so I was cut off from work. Helen became an insatiable animal, setting up more of those self-demeaning parties."

Sweat was beginning to form on Tony's forehead. The telling of the story had taken its toll.

"Tell me some more about the old man," I suggested. "Why do they say he was such a great patriot?"

"His family came from somewhere in Europe. His father had set up a brewery in Germany long before the war. Mr. Averly hated the Nazis and refused to deal with them, even though it cost thousands of dollars in imports. It cost Hitler a few shekels, too, I'll tell you," he said.

The bartender brought two beers. I refused any more shots and flipped him a fiver.

"Did closing the brewery cause your stepfather any trouble?"

Tony's face flushed and his jaw dropped. He whispered. "It got him murdered."

I wasn't sure I'd heard him correctly. I, like everyone else, was under the impression that Mr. Averly had been killed in an auto accident.

The high-tide waves lapped against the deck just outside the large picture window facing the ocean. I motioned to the bartender again as my stomach hinted at lunch time. "Did you say murdered?" I asked Tony, not too loudly.

Tony blurted. "The bastards killed the poor old man because he wouldn't cooperate by importing the stuff bottled in Berlin. They wanted to sell it on the black market here in the United States. Richard was eager to do it, too. He knew the Nazis were running short of hard currency, and he was secretly a big fan of Hitler. By the time I discovered this, I was hip-deep in hock to my wife again. She almost literally owned me. So I kept my mouth shut as long as Helen covered my debts, thereby proving to myself again that I'm a cowardly lion--or a lyin' coward, all depending on how you want to look at it."

It was nice to realize that this guy still had a sense of humor. "So why are you here?"

"I'm breaking away, Dark. I'm scared to death and tired of trying to be something I'm not. I've finally been forced to face the fact that I'm not a man and I'm not a businessman, either."

Murder? Shit. I thought Tony was just over-reacting. I read about Mr. Averly's accident and I remembered Red Kelly discussing it. No signs of foul play. It was just a plain mishap. Icy bridge and alcohol on the old guy's breath.

I lifted my head and glanced into the long mirror. I almost fell off the stool. The monocle man from the Merry-Go-Round was seated at the end of the bar. Or was it another monocle man? I assumed all monocle men looked alike. Like hell. He'd followed me. Smart tracker. Smarter than this private dick. My mind raced in idle, trying to see the big picture. Maybe this was Mrs. Averly's plan all along. Hire a private investigator to find her husband, then move in and take what she wanted. Whatever that was. Maybe she wasn't after a loving husband, but something else that I was beginning to suspect wouldn't be very healthy for Tony or me.

"You got any proof that Mr. Averly was murdered? I asked, trying to avoid the monocle man.

Tony glanced right and left, then directly at me. "You check the accident report. It says that Mr. Averly's accident was alcohol-related. They kept that out of the papers so his daughter never even heard about it. But I did. I read the whole report."

"So what?" I asked. "The majority of auto accidents are related to alcohol abuse in some way or another."

"Mr. Averly was a teetotaler," Tony whispered. "He never touched the stuff--and that's the best kept secret in the brewery business. He didn't even drink his own beer. But they found two bottles of Russian vodka in the car. The entire front seat was soaked with it and so was he. That's twice as insane--because not only did he hate the Nazis, he also hated the Russians. He insisted they're not friendly with us and we'll end up being their archenemies."

The missing husband case was over, but a murder investigation was about to begin. All I needed was a client. Unfortunately, the liquor shots were beginning to take their toll. I needed substance in my stomach or my brilliant detective deductions would fog over just as the mist from the waves were fogging over the front window.

"And you never pushed it," I said, beginning to slur my words.

"I told you, I'm a coward."

I decided to change the subject. "What happened Saturday afternoon that got you so upset and caused you to come here?" I asked. "Your wife gave me a lot of dough to find you under the guise of true love. She seemed sincere enough to me and I deal with phonies every day."

Tony was silent for a long moment. I leaned forward so he could talk softly. Monocle man had ordered a sandwich and was munching carefully and observing intently.

"As a part of her 'cure' for my 'disease', she tried nearly everything to turn me on. Okay? Sexy underwear, sexy nighties, sexy pictures."

"That's why you took those photographs during the sex parties?" I asked.

He seemed a bit surprised I knew about the pictures, but dismissed it. "Right. We both found them erotic and stimulating. These people were our friends, and we loved them, so it didn't seem dirty. Kind of our personal pornography. She looked at the boys, and I looked at the...well, I looked at the boys, too. But even those photos became too threatening for her. She wanted me to love her, just her, in the traditional way."

The waiter checked us for an order. "Two hamburgs," I said. "What about you, Tony? You should eat."

He waved the bartender away. "I feel too sick about this whole thing. I think I'll just drink beer."

"Tell me about last week?" I prodded.

"Two weeks ago Helen was desperate. We were both miserable. I told her I was contemplating suicide. That was a mistake. She even went so far as to hire a guy to sleep with us."

How naive was I? Once in awhile Kelly and I bought dirty paperback books in Scollay Square. The stories were bizarre and kinky. Tony's story was better and real. I always thought the book tales were some sick author's wild sexy imagination.

"What happened next?" I was curious and suddenly felt like a newspaper reporter discovering an illicit exclusive.

"I got horny, all right. But I ended up fucking the guy instead of her."

I did everything in my power to hold back a laconic laugh. "And she watched?" I asked, thinking about Rose laughing at her date's midget penis and what happened to her.

"She watched for awhile, then stormed out of the bedroom. But it gets worse. Last Saturday, she surprised me with a nooner suggestion. She said she wanted us to eat each other for lunch. Or something like that. She'd bought some sex toys. I guess that's what you call them. Rubber things that you strap on. She strapped one on and made like she was a man. I wanted it to work. Oh, I wanted it to work. But it didn't. I mean, imagine a guy with long hair and tits. It just didn't look right. I couldn't even get it up for that show."

"I hope you didn't laugh," I quickly said.

"Yeah. How'd you know? I started to giggle. She looked so silly. The more I laughed, the more hurt and angry she got. She finally blew her stack, telling me to get out for good."

"I met her and experienced a bit of her temper," I said.

"Both she and Richard have violent tempers," Tony said. "The father was a teddy bear. It must have something to do with being brought up spoiled rotten. Don't you think?"

I didn't think I knew the first thing about psychology or being brought up spoiled rotten. Uncle Bill brought me up and spoiled me as much as he could afford--but not rotten. I'd check it out with Doctor Edge at next week's card session. "So all of this is over a love gone wrong?" I asked, not quite convinced he was telling me everything. "You could've gone back and tried to make up. Isn't that what all lovers do?"

He leaned his head back, opened his throat and downed his beer. "Please, Mr. Dark, believe me when I tell you I've tried, many times before. I tried so hard. Maybe too hard. I did love my wife. Still do--in my way. But she doesn't understand, much less love a big part of who and what I am. Now I'm trying just as hard to forget."

"You've got a plan?"

"Yeah. Stay alive. I owe the bookies a shitload of dough. If they catch me, they'll kill me." He scanned the room, seeming to spot Mr. Monocle. He began fidgeting again. "There is something else. Way bigger than my marital problems or gambling problems."

"Sure. The old man's murder. You want justice."

"No, no--much more important than that. But he was part of it. It's a conspiracy that stretches from here to Washington to Berlin. Old man Averly was killed because he became a threat. He was killed by his son, Richard, no less. The only reason I'm still alive is because I've got heavyweight insurance."

I glanced across the bar at monocle man again. He seemed to be pretending not to notice us. At least I knew he couldn't hear us. "Let me guess--a photo?" I said.

Tony nodded. "Some people call it blackmail. But I think it's keeping me alive--so far."

"It sounds like smart business to me," I said.

Tony snarled. He looked at the intruder in the mirror. Did he recognize him? "I can't tell you any more here," he said.

I scratched my head, hoping to wake up my slow brain. "Don't be too obvious, but take a look in the mirror," I whispered, cupping my hand over my mouth. "Ever see the mug at the end of the bar before? The blond with the monocle. Do you know him?"

Tony pretended to blow his nose into his napkin. "I think I've seen him around the Averly Brewery. Why? Maybe he's a fairy. There's more of us around than you realize."

"Yeah," I said. One out of seven."

"What?"

"Oh, nothing. Just a scientific calculation."

"I don't know who the hell he is. But I think he does some security for Richard."

"Well, you might not be concerned, but he's been following me all day. And all the way from Boston."

"You think my wife hired him?"

"I only know she hired me. Maybe someone else hired him. Any ideas?"

"Her brother would be my first guess. It's complicated, but since he now knows that I know the truth about what he's doing, he's got to be lying awake at night, just like me."

"Let's try and fool this guy," I said. "Pretend I'm your boy-friend. It may save our lives." I couldn't quite believe what I'd suggested.

Tony didn't hesitate. He cuddled up to me and began running his fingers though my hair. He played the part real well. I cringed. But I decided to act as though I was enjoying the physical attention. I had a bad feeling about the monocle man now that I knew he worked for Richard, and I figured it was in our best interest to ditch him, one way or another.

We got up off out stools, hand and hand. Tony led me out of the bar, through a small lobby and down a corridor lined with numbered doors. At 21 he took out a key, unlocked the room and we entered.

"Lock the door," he said, "and let's figure a way out of here."

"Is there more to this than I know?" I asked. "I thought this was just another silly missing husband case. We're safe here, Tony. That guy'll just wait."

Tony shook his head. "No. No, That guy's a professional. He was sent after me. He followed you to find me. Their plan worked. You fell right into their trap."

My mind began to work a mile a minute. "Who's they?" I asked. "You said Richard murdered your father-in-law. Do you have any proof? Is Richard trying to kill you for what you know?"

Tony's eyes bulged. Sweat poured from his brow. Fear was written all over his face. I'd touched a nerve. "What about the money you owe?" I asked. "Who else are you hiding from? Are you blackmailing someone with dirty pictures in order to raise dough? Are you sure your wife isn't trying to have you killed?"

Tony opened his mouth to answer my questions, but before any words reached my ears, there was a rap on the door.

Tony spun around. "Who is it?" he asked, stuttering.

A male voice answered, "Linens."

Sounded reasonable to me.

Tony shook his head, vigorously. He was obviously panic stricken. We were behind a locked door in a faraway room that no one knew the number.

"Don't need any," he said. "I'm busy right now. Come back later."

Before I realized what was happening, two shots splintered the door handle. It flew open and three more shots smashed into Tony's chest.

I instinctively drew my revolver from my back holster, unlatched the safety and fired.

The first bullet missed everything.

The second caught the intruder right next to his monocle. It was a lucky shot for me because his final shot was aimed directly at my midsection. He fired for the last time as he fell forward, the bullet driving itself into the floor between my legs.

I leaned over and felt monocle's jugular.

No pulse.

Then I felt Tony's neck.

He twitched.

I ripped open what was left of his shirt. Blood was seeping from everywhere. His chest had been blown away. "Tony," I said. "Can you hear me?"

"The key," he mumbled through bloody clenched teeth. The pain and shock was taking him quickly. "They killed me for the key."

Thick blood and mucous spewed out of his mouth.

Poor frightened Tony Coraloni had joined his confident assassin and his very dead but honorable father-in-law.

I stalled the crowd that gathered in the hall. I demanded someone call an ambulance and a policeman, then slammed the door in their faces, as if daring someone to disturb me. Fortunately, most of the guests probably had no desire to get involved in anyone else's trouble.

I searched our uninvited visitor's pockets. They were empty. No ID. No license. No anything. The only clue was the fact Tony had noticed he worked for Richard's brewery in security. I knew he wore a monocle and carried a pistol. A German Luger.

Tony's personal belongings didn't yield much more. His wallet produced ten bucks, a driver's license, a draft card and a picture of his wife. That was it.

I quickly scouted the room, desperately tossing the rug, feeling the top of the window frame, checking the bed, breaking open the back of the radio. Nothing. No key. Except...I returned to his wallet. In the secret compartment, where I never thought anyone ever kept anything, I found a key with a number 17. It was small and thin and looked like a locker key. If this was the key Tony died for, it must've been a key to something damn important.

I felt confused with frustration.

What was he talking about?

Why was he killed?

I heard the noise in the hall grow louder. I quickly slipped through the back window and crossed the parking lot to my car. I didn't have the time or the disposition to explain anything, especially since I didn't have all that many answers.

Less than four hours later I checked into my office. Rose had gone home, but left several messages. Only one interested me. It was from Doloras. I ignored it for the moment and dialed my police detective friend, Red Kelly. I confessed most of the highlights, leaving out the part about the key. Red knew I was familiar with police procedure and told me to come in for the paperwork.

I refused. "I got some checking to do first," I said. "My life may be in just as much danger as Tony's. I've gotta be free to wheel and deal."

He threatened to put out an all-points-bulletin on me. But I knew he wouldn't. And he didn't. Hell, he was my poker buddy and owed me six cigarettes.

I made a beeline to the University Club. It was supper time and busy. Other than the ex-jockey elevator operator, no one paid any attention to me.

"Find Mr. Averly?" he asked, letting me off on the locker room floor. I didn't get too close. My weakened and empty stomach couldn't deal with his strong garlic breath.

"Not yet," I lied and handed him two bucks. I wasn't buying much. "Which way to the lockers?"

"Down the hall to the left," he pointed.

The locker room reeked of sweat. The same sweat I remembered in high school. I guessed rich guys smelled as BO'd as poor guys.

Locker 17 was in the third aisle.

I tried the key.

Right side up and upside down.

It didn't fit. Shit. I knew it had to be a locker key. But not this locker.

I heard the heavy diesels in the Back Bay train station across the street. Maybe Tony used those lockers.

The station was packed with evening commuters. The bay of lockers was located in a back room that carried more soot than my office. I found locker 17 and forced the key into the lock.

No go.

It didn't fit.

Fuck. Another dead end.

I checked my watch. Six o'clock. Red Kelly had had time to confer with the Provincetown police. Soon, someone would be calling Mrs. Averly. I dialed her number. A male voice answered. I said, "Mrs. Averly, please. Tell her it's Johnny Dark, and it's urgent."

After several seconds I heard her voice. She sounded surprised to hear me. "Is this really you, Johnny?" she asked, her voice sounding out of breath or just frightened.

Did this dame expect me to be dead, too? "Do you have anything to report?" she asked.

I took a few thoughtful deep breaths. "I've found your husband," I finally said, matter of factly. "He's been shot."

Silence.

"Did you hear me, Mrs. Averly? I said your husband's been shot."

"Where are you now?" she asked with no emotion in her voice.

"Mrs. Averly?" I asked, "don't you want to know what happened?"

"I want you to come to my house immediately," she replied in a demanding tone. "I paid you enough money to do as I say. Don't you think, Mr. Dark?"

"You paid me to find your husband and I found him. Case closed. Unless you have another assignment for me," I said firmly.

I heard some muffled conversation. Then I heard, "I might have another assignment and it could be worth more. Are you interested, Mr. Dark?"

Did I explain how fast one's sweat glands open up when someone shoots a gun at you? I was only interested in taking a long, hot tub. "How about tomorrow, Mrs. Averly? I've had a long day and I'm sure you'll hear all the particulars from the Provincetown police sooner, rather than later."

"Provincetown?" she said. "What police? What was he doing in Provincetown?" She paused. "On the other hand, I should know. I didn't tell you he was a fairy, did I?"

"You didn't tell me a lot of important things, Mrs. Averly," I said. "If you had, maybe Tony would still be alive."

I heard a gasp, then a long stillness. "You didn't say he was dead. Is he dead? How do you know he's dead? Are you certain? Please tell me what you know, Johnny. Tony was my husband and I did love him."

I heard flows of tears. At least they sounded like tears would sound if tears made sounds.

"I'll call you tomorrow morning and set up a meeting place," I said. "Not my office or your house. If you have any more questions after you get the police report, or if you want to talk about another assignment for me, you can tell me about it then. However, I warn you, after talking to Tony, I don't trust you. It bothers me that you seem to be conferring with someone else in your room. It also bothers me that you seem surprised to hear from me. And it bothers me a great, great deal that you were not honest with me about the risks your husband was apparently facing--some of which appear to be put in motion by you. You'd better hope the police don't find me before tomorrow morning. If they ask me for a suspect, I'm naming you as number one."

More silence at the end of the phone line, then some muffled discussion I couldn't make out. Then, "I don't have the slightest idea what you're talking about, Mr. Dark," she said, sounding indignant. "Must you deliver such terrible news in such a hostile and accusatory manner?"

"No more lies, Mrs. Averly. Tony's dead. The monocle one is dead. Your father is dead and I was almost dead. No more fabrications, please, Mrs. Averly. They hurt people."

Silence again dominated the phone. She didn't hang up like I expected her to, but said nothing.

"Mrs. Averly--are you still there? Mrs. Averly?"

"I'm here," she moaned. "I'm here. I did love him. I tried so hard to change him. Oh, my beautiful Tony! What have I done? Oh, please, Johnny, forgive me. I'll meet you tomorrow and confess everything. Oh, what have I done?"

"You know the Public Gardens across the street from the Ritz Carlton?" I asked, assured she'd spent many a lunch or dinner at the Ritz.

"Yes. Everyone knows the Public Gardens," she said. "Do you want to meet there? Isn't it too cold?"

"Bundle up in your woolies," I said. "After being used for target practice I want as public a place as possible. I'll meet you where they dock the swan boats. I think the season's over, but lots of people wander around there summer, spring, fall and winter. I'll be the guy you don't see."

I heard a deep sigh. "What do you mean by that remark, Johnny? This is a serious matter."

"That's why I'll find you. Just show up at ten o'clock. Sit on a bench and I'll find you. Don't bring your friend!"

More sighs. "What friend are you referring to, Mr. Dark?"

"The one sitting beside you right now, Mrs. Averly. Remember, I said no more falsehoods or you can hire yourself a new detective."

I heard the phone click off. Now I wondered if I'd made the right move. I'd attempted to push her buttons for a reaction. What had I really learned? Was Mrs. Averly safe until tomorrow? Was I safe? Would she even show up? And who was her mysterious confidant that she denied existed?

I smelled like a locker room and needed a bath. I limped my sorry ass to a steam room and massage parlor in Scollay Square. No questions asked. No answers either. Kelly and I frequented it often for numerous reasons. This time I was there only for a simple massage and relaxation.

The last thing I remembered as I closed my eyes were Scarlet's words after Rhett dismissed her with, "Frankly, my dear, I don't give a damn." She simply said, "I'll wait until tomorrow. Tomorrow is another day."

Chapter 5
THE PICTURE
Boston Post headline,
Thursday PM edition, December 9, 1945:
BRANCH RICKEY SIGNS JACK ROBINSON TO MINOR LEAGUE BASEBALL CONTRACT, LEAGUE'S FIRST NEGRO PLAYER

The gray morning light was comforting. Everyone in my business suspected that the bad guys were bums who slept in while us good guys arose early, hit it hard, got to it, and generally corrected the poor field position we ended up with the previous day. Everyone knew that gangsters were lazy sons of bitches--that's why they made all the wrong choices and ended up losing. Maybe I was the exception to the rule--but I figured if the bad guys slept in, so would I. At least I didn't give them a head start.

I parked my old convertible between two sharp sedans on Commonwealth Avenue. No one had built a new car since 1941 so my '36 really wasn't that outdated. Our apartment sat on the first floor in an unelevated four story Brownstone. Uncle Bill already had the coffee and bacon on. It smelled great. He spun his wheelchair, shot me a broad grin, and saluted me with the spatula.

"Right on time, Johnny. I don't think I've laid eyes on you in four days. Remember the cake?"

I don't know how many people know someone who ate birthday cake and sucked oranges for breakfast. Fifteen minutes later I had shaved, showered and changed into clean clothes. I loaded a plate and joined Uncle Bill at the table.

"So, tell me--how are we doing?" Uncle Bill was retired, but still sharp. I unloaded, holding nothing back. He listened intently, letting me tell my story. I had had a few new thoughts while soaking in the bath last night at Red Kelly's.

"The key is my next step," I said. "It's my only step, actually."

"Have you considered just walking away? Whatever this cesspool Coraloni stepped into, does it have to become your grave?"

"I don't have a choice. I'm the next logical target. I have to assume the monocle man reported his movements and my existence to someone. If they want to continue their hunt for the key, they'll come after me next."

"Who do you think 'they' are?"

"Unemployed Nazis, working for someone who doesn't like their picture taken. I dunno. Civic fathers who were being blackmailed? Mrs. Averly? Richard Averly? Leg breakers? All of the above? None of the above?"

"Strictly speaking, you don't even have a client anymore."

"Strictly speaking, I'm not a threat to anyone. But Mrs. Averly wants to hire me again. I've got to at least look into it. I kinda feel a little responsible for Coraloni's demise. I am a detective and was on the scene."

"If you didn't get the five gees, would you be thinking different-ly?" Bill had given food for thought. Was it the dough? Was it Mrs. Averly's long, sleek legs? Was it the fact some prick I never even met put a bullet in the floor between my legs? "People are starting to die," I said, picking a piece of delicious bacon from my teeth. "I've got an obligation to protect my ass, your ass, Rose, Doloras-- maybe more. We're caught up in this thing, whatever it is. My fault, I know. But that's the score. And it looks like right now we're behind by a few runs. But I admit, without the money, it would be harder."

"So--how can I help?"

"Watch your back. Stay safe. If we had another place to go, I'd make you go. But I'm betting that they'll try the direct approach and attempt to deal with me first. They don't know what I know or don't know--only that I found Tony."

Uncle Bill wheeled himself to an old roll top desk, reached into the side drawer and removed what looked like an antique pistol. "I'll oil this guy up. I used to be a pretty decent shot in my day."

Other than the arthritis, Bill was healthy like any sixty-nine year old World War I veteran on disability could expect to be. Especially one who's been sucking vodka for most of his life.

"I just got sore feet," he laughed.

"You never walk on them," I said.

"That's what I mean. They're sore anyway. My ass is fine and I sit on that all day. Ahh, just sore feet."

I stood to leave. "Oh, here's something for the cookie jar." I tossed his gambling marker on the table.

"Thanks, again. I'll pay you back tomorrow."

"Not unless your pension check tripled. But no sweat--we're living on Averly money for awhile."

He shot me a look. "Wait. How much did you give Jimmy?"

"Eight-fifty."

"What?"

I repeated the figure.

"Damn. He ripped us off, Johnny. My marker was two hundred and change. Damn."

My detective sense always craved to ask the next question, even when it wasn't healthy. "Why would he do that? You're a good customer, aren't you? He must've figured we'd compare notes."

"He paid me a little visit a couple days ago. The day this case started. That chowder head of a goon--the one with the chewed-up ears--pushed me too far, and things got a little out of hand."

And I wasn't here for him, I thought. I was screwing my secretary instead. My jaw tightened. "Tell me. What did they do?"

Bill just nodded at his feet. Without a word, I dropped to one knee and gently removed a floppy sock. I saw the angry slash of a fresh blue bruise welting up from the bottom of his foot, and I leaned lower to see the heel. He'd been hit hard. Uncle Bill would not be even attempting to walk for weeks.

"It looks worse than it feels," Uncle Bill rushed to say. He sounded embarrassed. "I'm icing them, but that makes me cold, and it makes me stiffen up."

"I'll kill em both," I grumbled. "I know what it feels like to kill now."

Uncle Bill laughed, almost like the old days when I was a kid and he used to take me to Fenway.

"You've never shot anyone in your life," he said. " They sop up their pancake syrup with guys like you."

"Thanks. I thought you were my number one fan. Besides, I've got my first notch on my barrel now."

"You know what I mean. One shot in self-defense doesn't make you an accomplished gunslinger. This was just a minor enforcement action that went a little too far. Hell, ya gonna play, ya gonna pay. He probably just wanted to give me a reason to call him up and bawl him out. That's what I'll do, too. He'll probably give me a side bet to show me there's no hard feelings. If word gets out that they're soft on deadbeats, they're out of business. You and I both know that."

I hated to admit that Bill was right. He owed and knew the consequences. I'd figure another way to get revenge on those pricks. But now, I had to get going.

I stuffed my rage inside, promised to call Bill later, and walked briskly across town to Copley Square and the Merry-Go-Round at the Copley Plaza. I counted ten gongs from the church clock in the square as I slowed down and headed toward the fancy main entrance. A few Yellow Cabs picked up and dropped off well-dressed patrons.

The bar piano player tickled the familiar notes from Casablanca, 'As Time Goes By'. I pulled my ear-lobe like Humphrey Bogart, then spotted Doloras before she saw me and took a table in her area. She flashed me a big smile. Within a minute, she brought me a double scotch on the rocks.

"It's early, but you look like you need this." Good waitresses remember a patron's preference. Doloras surely earned good tips.

"Thanks for remembering," I said, gulping down my drink. It stung my throat, but settled warmly in my belly. "I'd like to be the bearer of better news."

Her face dropped into seriousness. "Tony?" she said. "You found him?"

I chewed on a piece of ice. It was cold on my teeth. Too cold. The best way to tell someone bad news is to tell them the bad news. At least that's what Doctor Edge preached.

"I'm sorry, Doloras," I said, not looking her in the eyes. "They found him and killed him. Almost killed me."

As I looked up, I noticed a small tear forming in the corner of her right eye. Tony had obviously been a very special friend.

"Can you tell me the whole story?" she asked. She aimed a look to another waitress, waved and sat down next to me.

I passed her my handkerchief--a clean one--and told her the entire story, leaving nothing out. Not like the story I told Red Kelly or Mrs. Averly. For some reason, I trusted Doloras. Her caring manner? I guess she was what you called 'real people'. What you sees is what you gets, or something like that.

"What do you make of it?" I asked.

Doloras was focused on systematically demolishing a paper napkin. I guess we all do physical things to bring ideas to the forefront.

"I told you that he kept things from me," she said, her voice taut. "I guess he felt that the less I knew about his troubles--the less trouble I'd get into. But I never expected this. Maybe the guy with the monocle was hired by Mrs. Averly to follow you, leading him right to her husband. That's a gruesome thought, don't you think? What does your friend on the police force say?" She blew her nose into my snot rag.

"He thinks I was a fool for leaving the scene of the crime," I said. "Why do you blame Mrs. Averly so fast?"

The piano player changed his beat. 'Chicory Chick Cha La Cha La'. Whatever the hell that means. Doloras looked down at the table with an almost shameful face.

"Not fair," she said. "I don't like the woman. But that's just me. Maybe she's okay. I don't know. All I know is that Tony's dead and he was afraid. Maybe it wasn't her. Tony hated her brother, Richard."

I reached over to comfort her. She instinctively pushed my hand away. "Don't take that personally," she said.

"I know. I don't. But you and I have to work together. I think between us we know things about this case we don't know we know."

I removed a new pack of Chesterfields from my coat pocket, shook one loose and offered it to Doloras. She waved it away. I lit it, breaking the match and neatly placing it in the ashtray. I then blew a great smoke ring that hung with all the other heavy smoke in the room, making it easier for me to blow two quick small ones through the larger one.

Doloras' eyes widened like a child. "I've never seen anyone do that," she said.

"I'm no magician," I confessed. "But it makes for good conversation or changes the subject."

"Can't your cop friend help you--I mean, us--find Tony's killer?" she asked, taking the hint. "Or at least help us find out why he was killed?"

"Provincetown's not his jurisdiction," I said. "I was a cop once and know how sensitive turf issues can be. Detective Kelly's not even close to the scene. But he'll help in whatever ways he can. Trouble is, I can only tell him so much at a time. Only facts. Not guesses. You and I are only guessing that Mrs. Averly hired the monocle man. Maybe we're completely wrong. Maybe someone else hired the hit. Maybe Mrs. Averly really did love her husband, in a strange sort of way. She seemed to cry real tears when I told her he was dead. Or at least it sounded that way."

"Actress," Doloras said under her breath, making a displeasing face.

"What?"

"Nothing," she said. "You're right. I'm not being fair. It's just that I don't trust that woman. Sex drives people to do things you'd never imagine."

"He told me the whole story," I said. "She pushed him so hard to change. And he tried. He tried everything she suggested: Head doctors, aphrodisiac pills. He spilled the beans about her trying to make him something he wasn't and it only frustrated him. Nothing worked. The harder he tried, the worse it got. The more insecure she got. Each thing she tried was weirder and more desperate than the one before."

"He told you all that?" Doloras said.

"Yeah. You should have seen us. Real buddies. We even left the bar holding hands. Trying to fool the monocle man."

Doloras let a few more tears escape. "Sounds like you didn't fool anyone except yourselves."

"Before the hitman blew Tony away," I said, "Tony was about to tell me about something else. Something important, something bigger than his marital problems or business problems or gambling problems. That's what the key's linked to. Whatever it is, I'm thinking that that's what got him killed."

She quietly shredded another napkin.

I decided Doloras hadn't told me everything. "Tell me about Provincetown. Why'd Tony pick that hotel? The Myles Standish."

She started to hesitate, then looked me straight on. "We met there. In case you hadn't figured it out, I'm just as queer as Tony. He liked the guys. I like the girls. So there--now I've said it."

I tried to smile a face that announced it made no difference to me. "How often did you go there?" My poker-face smile had the right effect.

"Every few months," she said. "His wife traveled to New York occasionally--shopping spree. Hell, she had the dough. Might as well spend it in the right places. Tony and I took advantage of her absences and went to Provincetown. He'd meet some guys and I'd meet some gals. You know. Nothing really wrong with it. To each his or her own. I mean, you like girls and so do I. I'm sure you can understand that attraction."

I decided it was too early in the day to discuss my feelings on the subject of homosexuals. Frankly, I didn't care one way or the other, as long as they left me alone.

"Did you take his car or yours?" I asked, wondering just how discreet they'd been.

"Neither," she said.

"Neither?" I asked, surprised. "How'd you get there, swim?" I could be flippant.

"Bus."

"Bus?" I asked, blowing another ring.

"Yeah. Bus. Convenient. Kind of fun. Right around the corner from here. The Park Street Station."

"Bus," I said again. A light went on in my dull brain. "Sometimes I don't look as dumb as I am."

Of course.

Bus station.

Locker.

Key.

I got up and dropped a fiver on the table. "I'll go the bus station and see if he used that locker. I'll check back with you tonight. Don't leave before we talk."

The early December temperature must have dropped more than ten degrees while I sat in the Merry-Go-Round, down to maybe thirty-five. I turned up my warm trench coat collar, covering most of my ears and hiding half my face. The bus station was two blocks from the Copley Plaza Hotel. I was careful to double back a few times, ducking into a few alleys and buildings to make sure I wasn't followed.

I wasn't.

I hoped.

The station wasn't crowded. I noted a few derelicts lying on the hard wooden benches. There were three young women on one side of the waiting room and two men on the opposite end. No one gave me a glance.

The lockers lined one entire wall. I placed the key in the lock of number 17 on the third tier. It turned. I opened the metal door, then looked around the station. No one was paying me any attention.

At first perusal, the locker looked empty, but I couldn't see the bottom. I reached in and felt around. My fingers touched an envelope. I picked it up and withdrew it from the locker. I quickly glanced around the room one more time. Still no one paying any attention to me. The large, dark brown envelope was sealed. No writing on the front or back.

I opened it.

I pulled a thin stack of eight-by-ten glossy photos out of the envelope. The top photo was a woman in an evening gown, her head thrown back on a pillow, eyes closed. Her dress was hiked up to her waist, her legs were spread, and both her hands were busy. Between her fingers, something disappeared into her that looked like a string of pearls. The photo aroused me. I turned the picture ninety degrees.

It was Mrs. Averly. She did have shapely legs. All of them.

The rest of the photos were more of the same. Most had two or three people in various positions and stages of undress. One even had a large German shepherd. I recognized most of people--not the dog. They were some of the city's most prestigious fathers and mothers. By the time I flipped to the last picture, I was flushed--and a little embarrassed, like I'd been caught sneaking a peek into someone's bedroom. I was also envious.

The rich fucked each other differently, too.

I clumsily rearranged the photos and began to slip them back inside the envelope. Suddenly, something dropped and hit my foot. I looked down and spotted a smaller envelope that I must have overlooked. I crouched down with the whole mess, trying to keep everything off the floor. I tore the seal on the small envelope and pulled out another photo. It was a sepia snapshot, about three inches by four inches. It was a picture of two men standing in front of a brewery truck. The shorter and younger man on the right carried a folded newspaper under his arm. He had some familiar features--eyes and mouth that I'd seen before--but I couldn't place him. The other man was older. He also looked vaguely familiar, but I didn't immediately recognize him, either. It struck me as odd to find an innocent snapshot like this amidst such a gallery of French postcard material.

While the station was brightly lit, my thirty-five-year-old eyes had begun to weaken. I couldn't make out the printing on the side of the brewery truck or the printing on the folded newspaper. Both could tell interesting stories, especially if Tony Coraloni had been killed for the picture. Maybe.

My detective brain was sorting out my options. I had a choice to make. Which picture, or pictures caused Tony's death? Were the sex photos embarrassing enough to draw gunfire? Maybe. They would be easy enough to follow up on. Hell, everybody depicted was a celebrity of sorts. I could just confront them with the pictorial evidence, watch them squirm and stammer their embarrassment, then politely inquire as to whether their kinky habits included killing blackmailers. Simple.

However, my instinct told me to follow the most curious piece of the puzzle, the one that didn't appear to fit into the puzzle at all. That would be the sepia snapshot. Could this be a link to the conspiracy Tony whispered about in the bar yesterday? It was the one clue I understood the least, and Sherlock Holmes mysteries taught us all to look into the least obvious.

I made my decision. I returned the large photos to the envelope and tucked the snapshot into my inside coat pocket. I would try to eliminate the darkest mystery first.

Back at the office, Rose appeared tired and red-eyed, like she'd not slept well. I quickly brought her up to date and told her I was worried about her safety.

"Go to the newspaper morgue," I said. "I want you to look up everything you can find about the Averly's brewery business. Skip the society stuff--I know more than I need to about that."

"You just want to keep me out of the office, don't you?" she pouted.

"True. It occurs to me that you may be in the line of fire. But I also do need to know more about what's brewing at the Averly's business."

"Funny man."

"When you're finished, don't bother coming back here. Go spend the night at my place. It'll be safer, and anyway, Uncle Bill needs some help. He can't walk."

"So what else is new?"

"I mean he really can't walk at all. Some goon tickled the bottom of his feet. That's what comes of overdue bills. Just watch out for each other. If I spend all my time worrying about you two, I'll end up making a mistake. That could be very unhealthy."

She started to protest, but I raised my hand with my end-of-discussion-and-I'm-the-boss look. She put on a pretty sulk and murmured, "at least it's nice to know you care."

"I just hate funerals, baby," I said.

Rose grabbed her hat. "Oh, I almost forgot, you've got to finish up Kelly's case. The canine caper? He's getting a lot of pressure all of a sudden. Political. It seems the wife of Councilman Morris has now lost her dog and she's frantic."

The whole silly affair reminded me of the photo of the dog, resting with the others in the manila envelope on my desk. I wasn't planning on showing them to Rose. I didn't want her to lose all her innocence before she met Mr. Right.

"Turn over all the material you gathered on our favorite dog food chomper to Kelly," I said. "I'm sorry, I completely forgot all about that crackpot. Probably cost Mrs. Morris her little pet. I think if

Kelly pays our ex-con a visit, he'll find the remains of all the missing mutts.

"My hero," Rose swooned, threw me a kiss and left.

I walked in and out of my office, slapping the envelope of photos in my hand like I was back out in center field with a stitched horsehide to play with. I spied the letter with the Red Sox logo hanging on the wall. It was framed in dusty, sooty, oversized wood. I laid it flat on my desk, pried off the back and slipped in the brown envelope. I rehung it and stepped back to look. The frame stood out a fraction of an inch further from the wall, but otherwise fit in perfectly with the neglected decor.

I thought about when I first saw that Red Sox letter. It was November, 1930. The previous June I'd graduated from high school, and in July Uncle Bill got me a tryout with the team at Fenway Park. He knew someone who knew someone, talked me up real good, and they said, sure, why not give the kid a chance? The team had gone to hell since selling Babe Ruth to the Yankees in 1920, and in '27 had hit less home runs all together than the Babe had hit alone. They boasted such famed names as Robby Reeves, Phil Todt, Bill Regan, and Ed Morris. Meanwhile, the Yankees were playing with the likes of Ruth, Gehrig, Lazzeri, Durocher, Bill Dickey, and Bob Muesel.

I'll never forget the anxiety in my gut. My eyes blurred and I actually wet my pants a little when they called my name to take batting practice against a retired major league hurler who helped out in the Sox bullpen during the season. I can still recollect the damp and heavy woolen pants on that ninety-degree day. I was about six feet tall, but the old pitcher looked like a giant anyway, standing on the mound sixty feet, six inches away. To this day, I have a gut feeling Uncle Bill greased the guy's palm to take it easy on me.

I could hear my uncle yelling encouragement from the stands. "Hit the hell out of it, kid," he hollered, sucking away at an orange spiked with vodka.

I knew I could hit, run, and throw better than most. I'd batted over five hundred every year in high school and over six hundred in the summer leagues.

The first pitch was slow and I swung too early. Almost fell down.

Boy, I felt embarrassed, but Uncle Bill was still hollering and I wasn't about to let him down.

The second pitch came straight across the letters and I swung under it, popping it high in the air.

Then I relaxed.

My sense of timing was there, and I started to pay attention to it, like instinct.

The third pitch turned out to be a nickel curve that hung out over the plate, right in my wheel house. I swung from the heels and felt the sting in my hands. The old pitcher looked back over his head as the ball flew out over second base, kept climbing, climbing, climbing, and landed some dozen rows into the center field bleachers.

"Great hit, kid. Great hit. Just like the Babe," I could hear Uncle Bill's voice. "That's my boy--taught him everything I know. Wait'll you see his arm. Like a rifle."

I hit a few more shots into the stands, went to the outfield and shagged some flies, and ran around the bases a few times. Then I showed off my rifle arm, throwing long balls in from center field for more than fifteen minutes, every base, every one dead-on accurate.

Finally, the tryout was finished. The manager, Bill Carrigan, patted my ass and said the team would get in touch with me about a trip south in the spring. Needless to say, I dribbled a little more in my woolen baseball pants. My dream was coming true at age nineteen, and Uncle Bill's dream was coming true through his nephew.

But, it never happened. A few months later, I twisted my knee real bad playing in the Boston Park League. The doc went in with the knife and said it would never be the same again. Said I shouldn't run and I certainly shouldn't play baseball.

When I received the official letter in November from the Red Sox inviting me to spring training, I wanted to cry--that old lump feeling in my throat.

I didn't cry.

Uncle Bill cried.

I got the letter framed, and it ended up on the wall of my dingy office next to all the other frames of my lackluster life, especially the one that held my 4-F notice from the Army.

On boring afternoons, after a few luncheon scotch without rocks, those two frames looked down at me like two doors, forever locked to paths I'd never get to walk. Thinking about the past usually put me to sleep, and today was no exception. My beat-up sofa over the years had taken on my form, and easily engulfed me in its frayed pillows.

I dreamed I was chasing a naked woman with the head of a German Shepherd wearing a monocle. I woke up in the dark, uncertain where I was until I heard the diesel trains in the railroad yards across the street.

After a cold water shave and an alcohol gargle, I felt myself again. My watch said midnight. Hell, I'd slept over eight hours. Maybe shooting someone in the gut takes more out of a person than I realized. I closed up shop and headed for the Merry-Go-Round. The restaurant was closed. I could see Doloras through the glass door sitting at a table with another woman. I knocked several times before getting Doloras' attention. She hurried to the door and opened it. "I was beginning to get worried," she said. "Find anything?"

"Just this," I said, handing her the snapshot and followed her back to the table.

"Lauren, this is Jonathan Dark," she said. "The detective I've been telling you about. He's okay."

Most of the lighting had been turned down in the closed restaurant, but the Gaslight lamp on the table revealed a pretty, petite black-haired beauty of not more than twenty years. Her wavy hair hung well over her shoulders and when she arose from her chair and extended her small hand, my heart leapt right into my mouth--a feeling not experienced since puppy love days in high school.

"How do you do?" I forced out the words while taking her dainty hand in mine.

"How do I do what?" she answered in a low, sultry voice.

That's all I needed. Another smart-ass. Her fingers were thin and soft. I shook several times.

"You can let go now, Mr. Dark," Doloras said. "She is lovely, though, isn't she?"

I was in no condition to speak. But if I could, I would have had to admit that Lauren was probably the loveliest thing I'd laid eyes on in years. I gave her back her hand and sat down beside Doloras. I forced myself to breathe. "Check the picture. Recognize anyone?" I asked.

Doloras removed a pair of spectacles from her purse and studied the photo under the light. "Richard Averly," she said. "He's the one on the right holding the newspaper. The one on the left looks familiar too but, I can't place him. Evil looking mug, though--don't you think?"

Maybe the time had come for me to invest in a pair of reading glasses, but my male pride still stopped me. It was easier to put it off and meanwhile pretend I could see one hundred percent. Who the hell would hire a blind detective? Back in my schooldays, we called the kids with glasses 'four eyes'. They played tennis, had skinny legs, and wore white shorts. I didn't want that label in my line of work.

"Let's get out of here," Doloras said. "I know a great after-hours joint in the North End. They even let Lauren and I dance together without the usual wisecracks."

I looked at Lauren. Her eyes were brownish, eyebrows soft and thick. Her lips were slightly full and glistening. She wore a semi-tight sweater revealing an ample bustline, but not too large. Her waist was thin. I began mentally undressing her as they rose to leave. My heart was pounding too fast and my chest hurt. A young girl, barely out of high school was doing this to me, a tough detective with a mind and body of steel. What the hell good is a steel mind?

"Let me make a call to Detective Kelly first," I said.

Doloras pointed to a phone in the back of the bar and I called Kelly at home.

"Forget the dead dogs case," he said. "You've got bigger fish to fry. Your own ass. You're wanted for questioning by the Province-town police," he informed me. "You're the number one suspect in a murder investigation, my friend."

"Bullshit. It was self-defense. But how do they even know I'm involved? You didn't tell them, did you?"

"You know better than that, Johnny. Your name and description were lifted from the impressions left on a pad of paper next to the phone. I thought you said you checked the body and the room."

"Dammit, I was moving pretty fast, looking for something else. How's Mrs. Averly?"

"Playing the part of the grieving widow. I almost believe her. Her society friends are rallying around her."

"Well, watch out for anyone smiling. Tony may have been blackmailing one or more of them. Have they identified the other guy?"

"Small problem, Johnny. The police only found one body in the room. Coraloni. That's the murder they're talking about."

"What? The Provincetown police think I killed Tony Coraloni? The husband of my client? The guy I was supposed to find?"

"That's the way they see it. Only it's not just them. They put out an all-points-bulletin and your description. Showed up on the wire a few hours ago, so every cop in the state is watching for you. They have your name and your description."

"This is crazy, Red. You've gotta believe me--this monocle man followed me all the way to the Cape and killed Tony, then came after me. It was a fucking war in that room. What did Mrs. Averly tell you?"

"She admits she hired you, but she can't say what happened when you found Tony. She wasn't there. The Provincetown bartender remembers you and gave a great description. Sorry, friend, you've been placed at the scene of the crime.

"Do me a favor. Have them check that carpet again. There were two bodies, and the blood splatter patterns will show that."

"Okay, I'll push them to look a little further." Kelly's tone shifted, becoming official. "Where are you calling from?"

My detective warning-light started flashing yellow, then red. "Does it matter?"

"I think you better come in so we can talk this over. I can meet you at the precinct in a half hour."

"Red, I can't. That'll give them just what they want--to take me out of action."

"Who's they?"

"Whoever took the dead body of the killer. Jeeze, I suspected they might be nearby. They must've been right on top of us the whole time in order to move in and out so quickly. They're pros with a clean up team. Regular hoodlums don't do that. These guys know who I am, but I don't know anything about them."

"So you think this is some kind of conspiracy? Interesting theory. Let's talk about it more at the station."

"Tony mentioned something about a conspiracy just before he was shot. I'm thinking maybe he was right. These guys moved too fast and too quietly to be just some Provincetown hoods who kill queers. Who do you know with that kind of talent?"

"Maybe the military? FBI? The mob? I don't know--that stuff is out of my league. Was Coraloni really a fairy?"

"Just between us girls? He was as queer as a three-dollar bill. But this isn't about that. Something else is going on, and I've got to find out what it is before someone else gets hurt."

"I'm asking you to come in, Johnny. This is the first and last time it'll be a request."

"You know I can't. All due respect to your brethren in blue, but I'll get killed waiting for Provincetown's finest to sort this out. Give me some slack and I'll keep you informed. This ain't no simple case, Kelly. I wish it was."

"Then this conversation never took place."

"Agreed. By the way, the dog case is solved. Call Rose at Bill's. She'll fill you in."

I dialed up Uncle Bill. He was fine. Rose was asleep. I told him to tell her to stay out of the office. "The police will probably bug our phones, and watch out for strangers."

"Johnny. This is me. I have some experience in these matters."

"Well, Rose doesn't. Kelly will be calling Rose any minute. Just keep the phone open for him or me. Load that old pistol and keep it beside your chair, just in case. I'm counting on you to monitor the news." Uncle Bill doted on the light of his RCA console radio. He knew every character on every soap opera, hummed every popular record, including 'Chicory Chick', and he followed the capers of all the radio detectives, wondering why my business was so boring. Until now.

The after-hours joint wasn't really a joint. It was probably one of the nicest restaurants in the city. It had no food or liquor license and was raided monthly just on general principles. I had been there a few times with Red Kelly and found it to be frequented by the mayor, the governor, and the police chief, along with the heads of different mob families. No one bothered anyone else and everyone had a good time--no questions asked. The jukebox in the corner played 'Don't Sit Under The Apple Tree With Anyone Else But Me'.

Doloras found us a table in a dark corner. I ordered a scotch on the rocks, Doloras a wine, and Lauren a Coke. All three were served in Coke bottles with straws. I recognized a few hoods, but also a few upstanding business leaders of the community. I couldn't help thinking about how they looked with their clothes off.

Doloras and Lauren excused themselves and got up to dance. Doloras was fortyish and on the big side--at least six inches taller than Lauren. They danced close and a couple of times kissed on the lips. No one seemed to notice or care but me. Like a fool, I was jealous. My heart still lodged in my throat every time I looked at Lauren. I began to vaguely understand what Mrs. Averly must have gone through to fall in love with Tony--an admitted, practicing homosexual. Poor Mrs. Averly. Poor me. Did I have a crush on a dike?

When they returned to the table, I handed the picture to Lauren's young eyes. "Can you read the side of the truck?" I said.

She pushed the snapshot under the candle, which was the only light on the table. "Averly Brewery. You can see that. Underneath it says..." she hesitated and squinted her eyes. "I think it says South Boston. Yes. S O U T H B O S T O N."

"Then we know the picture was taken here rather than at the Averly Brewery in Berlin," I said. "Whatever that proves."

"How about if we knew when the picture was taken?" Doloras asked. "Maybe that would mean something."

"How the hell can we tell that?" I asked.

"The newspaper?" Lauren piped in with a wide smile revealing perfect sparkling teeth.

"What can you read?" I asked her.

She again placed the snapshot under the candle. "Not much. Too small. It's the Boston Post. I recognize the masthead. But I can't read the headlines or dates."

"Lou Mills," I said.

"What's a Lou Mills?" Lauren asked.

More smart-ass remarks. "Not what," I said. "Who. Lou Mills is a photographer. Works for the Post. He's an old buddy of mine. Used to play some semi-pro baseball back when I thought I was going to be a star for the Red Sox."

Lauren flashed a soft smile. "I'm impressed," she said. "I love baseball. My favorite player is Ted Williams."

Williams was a tall, lanky kid who had burned up the American League for a few seasons before going into the armed services in 1943. He'd be back next season, along with a lot of other stars for the Red Sox, fueling a new round of dreams of a Red Sox pennant in 1946, including Uncle Bill's. He couldn't wait. I knew better. They hadn't won a pennant since selling Babe Ruth.

Of course, I was immediately jealous of Williams. "He's too skinny," I said. "Probably won't regain his old form. Three years away from the game is a long time."

"Shut up about baseball and tell me about your friend at the Post," Doloras said.

I lit a Chesterfield and offered one to Lauren.

"I don't smoke, but thanks anyway," she said and I thought I detected her eyelashes fluttering, which got me right in the groin.

"Don't drink. Don't smoke. One of those perfect persons," I remarked and blew a small ring through a larger one, showing off.

"Stop flirting," Doloras spoke harshly. "It won't get you to first base with Lauren. Tell me about this Mills person."

Did I detect a note of jealousy in Doloras' voice? Did Lauren have the same powerful effect on her as she had on me? "He works nights," I said. " Let's go over and ask him to enlarge this picture. Then maybe we'll be able to see when it was taken."

We finished our drinks, paid the bill, and hopped a cab across town to the Post Building. It was past midnight. The morning edition was being put to bed. Lou Mills would be working in the basement. I decided it was time for me to renew my subscription.

Chapter 6
GHOSTS
Boston Post **headline, Friday AM edition,**
December 10, 1945:
HUMORIST ROBERT BENCHLEY DIES
AT 56--APPEARED IN ROAD TO UTOPIA
WITH BOB HOPE AND BING CROSBY

I n the middle of the night, the Victorian architecture of the Boston Post Building made me think of a dignified, but cranky, society matron. She's an old building, and therefore deserving of respect, but ill-tempered because the world around her had changed too quickly in ways that were not altogether agreeable. It stood four stories high, every window brightly lit, making it the cheeriest place on the darkened block. I felt drawn to the warmth of the lights, like a delinquent high schooler approaching home after curfew, anxious at seeing the kitchen lights on, but vaguely comforted by the knowledge that someone loved me enough to wait up with cookies and warm milk, never mind the mild scolding. Of course, I missed out on all that. Uncle Bill believed in teaching me responsibility. If I never came home at all--that was my loss. So, he either went to sleep early or stayed out after me.

Photographer Lou Mills toiled in the basement six nights a week, isolated and insulated inside his darkroom beneath the brightly lit floors above. He insisted he liked working nights because, "That's when everything happens--murders, rapes, suicides." The paper had to be printed by four each morning in order to get loaded into the delivery trucks by five and hit the newsstands by six. The *Post* was competing with six other dailies, so things had to be done right. Lou was the best--a perfectionist.

In the twenties, Lou Mills was a baseball pitching prospect who tossed the ball over 95 miles per hour. He was even compared with

The Big Train--Walter Johnson. However, when scouted, the report read: Great fastball, good control, excellent curve, good prospect except he wears glasses. And that was that. Whoever heard of a four-eyed pitcher in the 20s? Poor Lou. He never got over it, stayed mad at the world, and became a real cynical bastard. He pretended to hate everything and everybody. At least, I thought he pretended. He still pitched in the semipros with me in the Boston Park League. Even now, in his early forties, Lou Mills could be seen fireballing hitters twenty years his junior every Sunday during the spring and summer.

My watch read three o'clock when we entered the Post Building. The rumbling presses vibrated the narrow set of stairs that led us down to Lou. He was frantically putting notes on photos spread out across his desk. Without looking at us, he held up one finger. He suddenly scooped the pictures into a messy stack, dropped them into a blue pouch, and pressed a buzzer on the wall.

He glanced up from his desk over thick bifocals. His thin face fit his thin head and thinner body. Lou stood over six feet, all skin, bones, and no fat. "Wanted by the police for murder, eh Dark?" he mumbled. "Don't think you can hide here."

The acrid smell of developing chemicals puckered the noses of Lauren and Doloras. I'd visited many times before and was used to it.

"If you turn me in, I'll tell everyone you throw a spitball," I said. And he did throw a spitball--a good, wet one that not only couldn't be hit, but couldn't be handled by any catcher. I counted my blessings that he and I played on the same team.

"What's up, Dark? I got no time for fun right now." He impolitely ignored the girls like they weren't even there.

"What else? I need you to look at a picture. And I don't think you're as stupid or deaf or blind as everyone says. And even if you were, you're the only photog open at this hour."

"You mean, I'm the only one who'll talk to you."

"That, too."

A copy boy suddenly slammed through the door, snatched the blue pouch off his desk, and disappeared. "Seriously, Lou. This picture may explain why someone is trying to end my life sooner instead of later."

"Fuck you and fuck your life. Probably another unhappy client," Mills mumbled, looking up again and noticing the females. "If you ladies expect to get paid tonight, you'll have to keep walking the street. Johnny here's always broke, and I'm too busy unless you want to wait till four."

Doloras whispered to me. "I thought this skinny mug was your friend."

"His bark is worse than his bite," I said. "He loves people, just hates himself." I dropped the snapshot on the table under Lou's pointed nose. "Can you make this big and clear enough so we can read the print on the newspaper under that guy's arm?"

Lou held the picture a few inches from his face and squinted at it. "We can work with this. I'll need to make an interneg, a picture of the picture, so we can blow it up." He pulled his lanky body out of his chair and said, "Follow me, ladies and gentlemen."

We walked behind him into a big darkroom. "Shut up and watch," he said.

He mounted the small photo on a copy stand, then hit it with lights from both sides. He took a few shots with the camera mounted above the copy stand, then removed the film for processing, finally relaxing for a moment.

I made the introductions.

Lou stammered an apology that Doloras just waved aside. He explained what he was doing as he went, and the girls seemed genuinely interested. I think he was lonely, too, maybe glad for an appreciative audience. I'd seen it all before, but I admit he put on a good show. Tall and shadowy as he was, working underground in the middle of the night, he could have been a medieval conjurer of the black arts.

The darkroom was small, and we were all bunched together to watch Lou work. I stood a few inches behind Lauren, not quite touching her, feeling her heat. I could smell soap, and smoke, and wildflowers in her hair. I found my thoughts wandering. It was in high school that I discovered girls could remedy my habitual hard-ons. After a date, I'd linger on their front porches, kissing passion-ately and rubbing against them frantically until--pop--oops--what a mess! Wet and sticky undershorts, but worth all the uncomfortable-ness walking home. Standing in the dim light of the darkroom behind

Lauren's behind, I fought the compelling urge to draw her to me, inhale her scent, kiss her neck and ears, and turn my hands loose to find their way to cup her breasts.

Instead, I forced myself to move away, seeking a distraction. I looked for whatever other photos I could see. I found a stack of proofs in a wire basket labeled "TODAY" and began to flip through them. Smashed car, smiling politician, and a burning building. I hesitated and stared at an obvious crime scene, dark pools of blood clearly visible. I rubbed my eyes, trying to focus. There was something about the picture...

"Hey, Lou--what's this?" He joined me, took the picture, and turned it over.

"Dead dogs. A dozen, maybe more. Found them in a basement."

"You got an address?"

"Says here..."

The address sounded familiar. I fished the scrap of paper from Rose out of my shirt pocket. Sure enough--the dogs were found in the alley of our crazy dog cannibal. More proof. "Can I send copies of these to Red Kelly?"

Lou didn't even look up. "Consider it done. I'll have them hand-delivered after work."

A timer dinged and we rejoined the girls. Lou flipped on a hazy red light, poured out some fluid from a tray into a sink, then refilled it with something real acid smelling. He turned away from us and fiddled with some kind of camera-looking contraption that hung from the ceiling. "Watch the table," he said.

We watched. He turned on the contraption. The picture appeared on the white-topped table. He turned a few dials and the picture became clearer. He turned a few more dials and the picture began to get bigger.

"You." He motioned to Lauren. "You look like you might have the best eyesight in this group of old coots. Tell me when you can read the print on the paper."

Lauren stood beside the table and stared. He slowly turned the dials. The picture got bigger and bigger. The bigger it got, the blurrier it became. But then Lou turned another dial and it became clearer and clearer. "November something," she said. "The rest of the date's in the fold."

"Could be any year," I said.

"We ain't beat yet," Lou said. "Read the headline on the paper. Then I can check our files for the year."

"The big headline's in the fold," she said.

"Keep looking. There's always a major sub-story," Lou said.

Lauren kept staring. Lou kept dialing. Even I could see the headline of the small sub-story come into focus.

"TOKYO ROSE ARRESTED. TO STAND TRIAL FOR TREASON," Lauren read.

"That'll do," Lou said. He flipped off the enlarger light, plunging us into red glare again. I saw him withdraw a large sheet of paper from a dark box beneath the table, then place the paper on the table. He snapped the camera on again, and we all stood still as a small clock somewhere ticked. I thought about Lauren some more. When a bell dinged, Lou snapped off the enlarger. He took the paper from the table and slid it into the foul-smelling fluid. He then repeated the exercise so we would have two more copies. Over the next few minutes we stared into the pan of fluid as though we were trying to read the future in tea leaves. All at once, an image appeared on one of the sheets of paper. He removed it from the pan, squeegeed it on a shiny plate, and locked it between two hot metal plates to dry. He did this two more times.

While the pictures were drying, Lou called someone upstairs and asked when that particular story about Tokyo Rose had appeared on the front page. He waited for awhile, then repeated: "November 19th of this year. That's almost a month ago. Yeah, thanks." He hung up and turned to us. "Satisfied?"

"We'll see," I said. "If I find what I'm looking for, I'm not even sure I'll recognize it."

"Didn't you use that excuse a lot last season, too?" Lou grinned. He loved a mystery as much as anyone. He suddenly lowered his voice and became somber. "You'll be in today's paper, Johnny, wanted for murder. I got a telephone call, told me to dig your photo from my files. I found a few and sent up the worst likeness."

"Thanks again, Lou. I'm wanted for something I didn't do. I'm hoping this picture will help clear me. Two people are already dead because of it."

"Let's see what we've got."

I followed Lou to a table where he began studying the photos. They were big now, at least twenty inches high and wide.

Lou asked, "Who are these mugs? Anyone I should know?" He squinted a bit more, adjusting his glasses. "The older guy on the left looks awfully familiar. What do you think?"

"We think so, too," I said. "But none of us can place him. The other guy is Richard Averly, owner of the Averly Breweries."

Lou continued to study, moving his glasses up and down his thin nose. He then reached for a black waxy marker and put a beard on the face of the unknown figure. He threw a glance back at us. We looked at each other.

Nothing.

Lou wiped off the beard with a rag and replaced it with a little square mustache.

He quickly gave us an appraising stare. We looked at the picture and each other, all gasping at the same time.

Lou quickly scribbled a black shock of hair drooping over the figure's right eye, then looked back at us again, this time displaying a broad smile.

"Adolf Hitler?" we all said in unison.

"Change the shock of hair to cover his left eye," Lauren said. "Every picture I've seen has it that way."

Lou followed her advice.

"Adolf fucking Hitler," Lou said. "I've printed his likeness thousands of times over the last ten years. This guy's a dead ringer."

"Maybe not," I said, studying the looming portrait."

"But he's been dead since April. Killed himself in a Berlin bunker, along with his wife and dog, just before the Russians took the city," he said in a surprised tone.

Lou pushed the picture aside and went back to his work. Doloras grabbed the photo and studied it closer. "If that really is Hitler, that might explain why Tony got killed. It would prove Hitler is not only alive six months after he's supposedly dead, but that he was in South Boston with Richard Averly on or after November 19th."

"Holy shit," I whistled. "Is this possible?"

"I read it in my own paper, you guys," Lou said, addressing us with a doubting frown. "Hitler's body--or someone's body--was burned beyond recognition in the Berlin bunker, so there was never a positive identification. The Russians claimed to have identified his teeth. Teeth are like fingerprints, you know. Some people think Hilter staged a clever ruse and escaped. And it worked, too. If anyone seriously thinks Hitler's still alive today, we'd have the greatest manhunt ever for history's worst war criminal. Hitler would have to hide under some rock."

"Or in plain sight like Averly's Brewery," I said.

"That's right," Lauren chimed in. "If no one's looking for him, he could live a normal life!"

Lou grunted in disgust. "What's a normal life for a monster like him?"

"This whole idea's absurd," Doloras said. "Maybe those two guys in the photograph are getting ready for a costume party."

"Halloween falls in late October," I said. "Not November."

Lauren nodded. Lou nodded. I didn't nod. "Tony started to tell me about some conspiracy that stretched from Boston to Berlin to Washington. I had no idea what he was referring too. His dying words were 'the key' and the key led me to this picture. No. I don't think he was killed because of a costume party. If this is Hitler, it would explain why Tony was hunted down like a dog and executed. A secret like this is as big as an atomic bomb. It might also explain Richard Averly's strange behavior. I hear he's become even more unstable. For my money, I think there's better than even odds that this is Hitler."

We were interrupted by a buzzer above our heads, and it made us all jump.

"That's just the press room," Lou said. "There must be some problem in makeup with one of the pictures. So, see you guys later-- much later, I hope, after you get this wild goose-stepping chase out of your system." Lou smiled charmingly, aimed at Doloras.

I reached out and touched Lou's shoulder. I knew Lou's weakness. He had never been recognized as a great baseball pitcher-- and he was. He had never been recognized as a great newspaper photographer--and he was. This could be the opportunity of a lifetime for Lou to get some recognition--the fleeting recognition he deserved.

"Wait a minute Lou," I said. "Have you ever heard the line that opportunity is fleeting and sometimes it comes along well disguised?" I wasn't sure I hadn't just made that up, but it sure fit this situation.

Lou turned around. "So what?" His thinly slit eyes opened up just enough to display interest.

I was thinking fast. "Let's just say that this is a picture of Hitler. I mean, Richard Averly did have a brewery located in Berlin and he did reopen it after his father was killed in an accident, so it's possible he knew Hitler personally. Hitler certainly would have appreciated the hard currency from the brewery, but he couldn't very well advertise the fact that he was being supported by selling beer to the Americans."

Lauren jumped in. "So say Averly and the Fuehrer knew each other. They would be used to sharing secrets."

"Right," I said. "Now let's say Hitler needs an escape plan. He knows the war is going badly, but he can't talk to anyone about his doubts. Again, his salvation comes in the person of his new best friend, Richard Averly. And let's just say that Hitler was in South Boston in November. And let's just say that Tony figured all of this out. After all, he was pretty involved at the brewery. Maybe he even ran into Adolf in the men's room or heard him being whispered about in the board room. He certainly saw the sales figures for the German brewery."

"Make your point, Johnny. As fascinating as this is, I'm fighting a deadline."

"Tony needed proof, and he somehow managed to get his hands on this picture. And he was killed because they knew that he knew."

Lou shrugged his stooped shoulders. "So what? The government's probably got a whole department set up for nutty ideas. Call them with this one, okay?"

"Think, Lou. I'm wanted for murder, so I can't exactly get my point across. They're going to say I made this whole yarn up. Hell, I'm even having a hard time believing it."

"So, what are you going to do?"

I turned to Lauren and Doloras. "If we can authenticate the photo and prove it's Hitler, you can print it in the Post and sell it to *Life* Magazine and all that stuff that you guys do with great exclusive photos."

Lou's usually inexpressive face lit up like he had just won ten stale cigarettes on poker night. The buzzer from the press room sounded again, but he ignored it.

"Johnny," Doloras said, "how do we authenticate the photo with Tony dead? And once we start nosing around, what's to keep the same people who killed Tony from killing us?"

"We don't have a choice. We have to try." This came from Lauren. "If Hitler's alive, this monster can't be allowed to walk around freely." Her voice was hard. She somehow was no longer an innocent young girl, and her strength and determination were contagious. "This is something we must do because it's the right thing to do."

I agreed, and at that moment, I knew for certain I was in love with her.

"Count me in," Lou said. "Though I have my doubts. I'm like you, Dark. I never served my country. I'm a confirmed coward." Lou knew about my trick knee, but liked to tease me anyway.

"We need a plan. How trustworthy is your boss?" I asked, on a hunch.

"He loves scoops," Lou answered. "The wilder the better. Seven papers in this city, all reporting on the same shit every day. He'd give a lot for something that would beef up our circulation."

"A picture of Hitler alive and well would certainly beef up circulation," I said. "Guaranteed."

Lou peered again at the picture. Held it up to the light. Turned it sideways, upside down, rightside up, then returned it to the table in front of us. "We're guessing. Without confirmation from either the guy who took the picture--most likely Tony Coraloni--or one of the mugs in the picture, my publisher would never use it."

"We'll take our own picture," I said. "We'll find Hitler and snap his photo."

I looked at the girls for support. Now it was their turn to shrug their shoulders.

"We'll what?" Lou asked, in a shrill voice.

"We'll take our own picture of Hitler. Show this to your boss, tell him what we're doing--just in case we don't come back--and ask him for a couple of days off to do some investigating. With pay, of course. I have a feeling that wherever we find Richard Averly, we'll find Adolf Hitler."

Lou looked at me.

He looked at Doloras.

He looked at Lauren.

Then he looked back at the picture that he had so neatly planted a mustache on. "You're right. My boss would pay good money for an international scoop like this."

"And if it turns out not to be Hitler?" Doloras piped up.

"Then we never print it," Lou finished. "Nothing ventured, nothing gained."

Doloras said, "If we could prove it was really Hitler, Lou would be a hero and probably get a raise and a Pulitzer Prize, and Johnny would get off the hook and we could all share in some kind of reward--right?"

"I'd kind of figured you two would stay out of the action. You know, stay safe?" I said tentatively, suspecting where this was going to end up.

Doloras laughed heartily. "What do you think about that, Lauren?"

I looked over at the attractive twenty year-old. Her pretty smile sparkled. A lump remained stuck in my throat. My heart ached.

"I think Mr. Dark wants to keep us womenfolk home because we're just amateurs," Lauren said.

"She's right," I said. "What we need is a professional private detective to look into this."

Everyone stared at me.

No one smiled.

I was joking, but the whole affair wasn't the least bit funny, and we all knew it.

"I'm all through here in about ten minutes," Lou quickly said. "Where are you staying, Johnny? I know you can't go home or to your office. The cops would pick you up in a skinny minute. And tomorrow your picture will be plastered all over the papers. You better get some sunglasses."

"And how about a mustache?" I said, kiddingly.

Lou walked over to me, studied my face and quickly painted the same type of mustache on my upper lip as he'd done to Hitler's picture. "It worked for Groucho Marx so it can work for you. All you need is the cigar and two funny brothers."

The girls chuckled.

I'd planned to stay at Rose's, but then remembered I'd sent her to my house. "I got nowhere to stay, I guess. How about your pad?"

"As good as done," he said. "Tomorrow we'll turn this information into a gold mine. Okay, gang?"

We all nodded.

My thoughts were racing ahead. Lou had become the next important piece in this puzzle. His camera could save us all. Or kill us.

Chapter 7
THE SWAN BOATS
Boston Post headline,
Saturday, December 11, 1945
FIRST DAY AT NUREMBERG TRIALS SPENT
READING ATROCITIES IN DEATH CAMPS
Sub Headline: LOCAL PRIVATE DETECTI-
VE SOUGHT IN PROVINCETOWN KILLING

My watch read nine-thirty. My skin read I should have worn an extra sweater. A brisk breeze whipped across the Boston Common reminding city dwellers just how filthy cities can become if not scoured daily. Candy wrappers, dirt, squirrel shit--you name it and it swirled into tiny tornadoes along the sidewalk that lead from the main street into the Public Gardens located next to the Common. I leaned against a large maple tree and waited, watching commuters scurrying to work, shoppers scurrying to Newbury Street and bums scurrying to stay one step ahead of the cops. A derelict wearing several layers of his wardrobe, most likely all of it, approached me with a soiled outstretched hand. I flipped him a dime just to get rid of him and not be noticed. He flashed a toothless smile and I wondered how he chewed steak. Silly thought. This guy hadn't seen a steak in years. Neither had a lot of people during the recent war.

The swan boats were running--probably for the Christmas season. I hadn't had a ride since my mother took me thirty years ago. It was one of the few fond memories I had of her.

I spied an almost floor length, obvious expensive fur coat enter the Gardens. The lady wearing it fit Helen Averly's description as closely as I could recall--tall and strikingly pretty. I ducked behind the tree and watched. Was she being followed? Not obviously. But

I didn't think I was being tailed to Provincetown and that misjudgment cost Tony Coraloni his life. I wasn't about to make the same mistake. I hoped.

Mrs. Averly sat on a bench near the ticket booth for the swan boats. A few people were beginning to stand in line. I figured the excursions started at about ten.

I waited.

I could see her keep glancing at her watch, cross and uncross her shapely legs that kept being revealed with her nervous movements. I wasn't presenting myself until I was sure it was safe. I still wore my Groucho mustache and a cheap pair of plastic sunglasses I'd purchased at Woolworth's. It would be a good test to approach her, walk past and see if she recognized me.

I did.

She didn't.

Good.

I turned around and whispered. "Mrs. Averly, it's me. Johnny Dark. Buy two tickets and I'll meet you in the back of the first boat."

Her head spun around in my direction. At first she acted as though she didn't know who I was. She removed a pair of eyeglasses from her purse, placed them over her nose and stared again. "Johnny?" she said too loud.

"Shh," I said, placing my gloved finger gently over her lips. "Buy the tickets."

She stood in the short line for several minutes. The window opened at ten sharp. Mrs. Averly bought the tickets and boarded the swan boat, taking a seat in the far back. I looked both ways and joined her. "Sorry to scare you with the disguise," I said. "As you know, the cops are looking for me and I can't very well get to the bottom of this if I'm rotting in some jail."

She removed a velvet glove and placed a painted fingernail along my top lip. "It's paint," she said, surprised. "It looks real."

I pushed my hat back on my head. "The rest of me's real," I said. "No thanks to the shooter in Provincetown."

"What actually happened?" Her voice was barely audible: "I want to know."

I placed an arm around her shoulder as the driver began to paddle the boat out into the small pond. The boat was about half full--several children with a young woman who appeared to be a teacher, probably from some local school--an older couple huddled close for warmth--two middle-aged women and a single man, snap brim hat pulled down and collar up. He looked too suspicious to be suspicious, so I ignored him.

In a low slow tone I related pretty much everything that I'd encountered since our first meeting. I omitted Doloras and Lauren, feeling they were irrelevant at this juncture. When I was finished I showed her the snapshot of her brother and Adolf Hitler--or who we surmised was Adolf Hitler. Through a gaggle of tears she identified Richard Averly, but couldn't swear the other man was Hitler or anyone she'd ever seen.

"I've got to talk to your brother," I insisted. "He's our only lead. I think he can unravel what happened to your husband and maybe explain this snapshot. Maybe the whole affair is a hoax. I certainly don't think Hitler's still alive and hanging around the brewery in Boston, Massachusetts. Do you?"

Mrs. Averly didn't answer. She appeared either frozen by the bitter weather or in shock.

"Mrs. Averly?" I shook her arm. "Mrs. Averly I have to talk to your brother."

"He's disappeared," she finally mumbled. "Disappeared right after Tony disappeared."

"Something else you didn't tell me," I sarcastically said. "Disappeared to where?"

She shrugged her shoulders. "I called the brewery. Sometimes he travels for weeks on end. We do have a plant in Berlin, you know. He could be there. He could be in some other foreign country planning to build a new brewery. I just don't know. I told you that even though I'm a fifty percent stockholder, he never consults me about anything."

"How about if he were hiding? Where might he go? Any favorite spots? That's how I found your husband, you know. A favorite haunt."

The swan boat had docked. We disembarked. The suspicious man walked off in the opposite direction. Mrs. Averly and I headed for the Ritz Hotel, across the street. It featured a warm first-floor bar with fireplace. Just the spot to warm my cold ass. I felt silly with my fake mustache, but realized it might be keeping me on the loose.

We passed a newsstand and I grabbed a Post. Tony Coraloni's picture jumped off the front page. My likeness was the old picture pulled out of the files by Lou Mills. It could have been me--at least twenty pounds lighter with no sunglasses and no mustache. I finally made the newspaper.

We selected a corner table with a view of the street and the Public Gardens. I politely took Mrs. Averly's heavy coat and draped it over a chair. Her turtleneck woolen dress appeared painted on. I'd forgotten just how perfectly put together she was. A short tuxedoed waiter approached our table. "Mrs. Averly," I said. "I'm so sorry to read about your poor husband. I hope they capture the culprit."

"Yes. Yes," Mrs. Averly said. I hoped she wouldn't announce that I was the other picture on the front page. I was at her mercy. Maybe I'd been set up. "Bring us something hot and strong, please." she said, waving him away with a flip of her gloved hand. I hid my face behind the large leather menu.

"Thanks for not giving me away," I whispered.

She reached across the table and grasped my hand. "I know you didn't kill Tony and I know you're only trying to help. You say favorite haunts? Richard loves to ski. He has a place in the Swiss Alps and he also has a place at Mount Mansfield in Vermont. It's a ski resort called Stowe. I know they're open already because I sometimes see his mail and last week they notified him that they received two feet of snow."

"I've heard of Stowe," I said. "Can't say I'm much of a skier. Think I tried it once as a kid. Fell a lot."

"I telephoned several times--but got no answer," she said. "Of course, that doesn't mean he's not there. If he's hiding, he's not about to answer the phone."

"How do I find it?" I asked.

"It's the only chalet on the slope. Two entrances. One is an old logging road. The other, you take the tow to the summit and ski about two miles to the house. Take your pick, depending on the weather. In the middle of the winter, the road is usually closed. With two feet of snow it wouldn't surprise me if the road was closed now. Anyone there will be hard to find."

"And if he's in Switzerland?"

"I called there, too. The caretaker hasn't seen or heard from him since last winter. Of course, he may be lying--but I doubt it. I go over every year, tip big, and he likes me. He also liked Tony and was quite broken up when I informed him of my husband's death."

The waiter brought something steaming hot in two mugs. I decided to be a snob and pretend I knew what it was, took a sip and burnt my lips. Mrs. Averly laughed. "Hot Toddy with Rum," she said. "Like it? I bet you've never had it before."

She was right. "Don't be too smart, my lady friend. It does warm my gut, though." I sipped again. She used a glass straw. La de da.

"Am I hired again?" I asked, reaching out to shake her still gloved hand and staring into her deep blue eyes. "I don't think anyone will be looking for me at Stowe."

Mrs. Averly shed a tear. "I'd do anything to get Tony back, but I know that's impossible. I guess the only consolation I'll ever have is if I help you find his killer. Do you have any more paintings for sale?"

Chapter 8
GONE SKIING

Boston Post headline, PM EDITION,
Saturday, December 11, 1945:
RUSSIAN LEADER MOLOTOF INSISTS
A-BOMB CANNOT BE KEPT SECRET
Sub headline:
LOCAL POLICE ARREST DOGNAPPER

L ou Mills had some vacation time coming and he loved to ski. His boss had been totally impressed about the picture and the prospect of an international scoop. He gave Lou expenses and told him not to come back until he had the story.

I admitted that my skiing ability left something to be desired, but Lou insisted that since I was a good athlete and kept myself in adequate shape, even with the bad knee, he'd have me crisscrossing down the slopes in no time.

"I want to help too," Doloras said as we all sat in the Merry-Go-Round bar late Saturday night. I explained about my visit with Mrs. Averly and we decided a trip to Stowe to find Richard Averly and his Nazi friend would be the only way to prove the authenticity of our suspicions.

"If he's anywhere, he's at Stowe," Lou said. "It'll be the best picture I ever took. Guys like me wait a lifetime for a break like this. Nothing could keep me away."

Manhattan number three slid down Lou's throat creating a brave photographer rather than the confirmed coward I knew him to be. Lou was one of those lugs who would have shot himself in the toe during basic training to keep from fighting in the war. He never got called to active duty and I never asked him why, especially since I also never served.

"Why didn't you get drafted?" Lauren asked later that evening, sipping on a Coke. The question shocked me, not knowing what it might lead to, so I gave Lauren a light kick under the table.

Lou didn't mind; or, the Manhattans didn't seem to mind. "Too tall. They didn't take guys over six feet six and I stood on tiptoes during my physical." Lou stood up straight, stumbled, but demonstrated what he meant. "I'm really six five and one half."

"He was a great basketball player too," I added.

"And a good baseball player, good skier and good photographer," Lou burped.

"What can I do to help?" Doloras asked. "I feel left out. Don't forget, Tony was my friend."

I thought about the case for a few minutes. What we knew, what we didn't know, and what we surmised. I said: "How about checking out the Averly Brewery in South Boston. According to Mrs. Averly, we know that Richard Averly won't be around; so, you won't have to worry about any interference from him. Try and find out if beer is the only thing they import and export. But be careful. Also stay in touch with Red Kelly. Tell him just enough to keep him on his toes. Don't tell him about Stowe and Hitler and all that stuff, but press him to look for the monocle man's body. I told Red I thought it must be buried somewhere around the hotel in the sand dunes. Just a guess on my part. But, if he finds it, that could go a long way in getting me off the hook for the murder I never committed."

Foggy smoke clung to the ceiling as the piano player rendered a medley of the day's latest hits including one that moved me to peer into Lauren's eyes. 'Dream When You're Feeling Blue. Dream, That's The Thing To Do - Things Never Are As Bad As They Seem. So, Dream, Dream, Dream'.

Doloras and Lauren were holding hands under the table, which made me feel kind of creepy. Lauren's eyes never caught mine, so the words of the love song were wasted.

My mind started to daydream. I liked Doloras and I liked Lauren too. Maybe a man at thirty-five (like Rose's favorite soap opera, The Romance Of Helen Trent) could learn new lessons on life. Whatever Doloras and Lauren did in private was their business as long as it didn't hurt anyone else. Who were they hurting? Lou certainly didn't give a damn.

The pianist started some boogie woogie which woke me from my semi-trance. Doloras checked her watch and bid us farewell for awhile. Her waitressing duties called. "I want you guys to take Lauren with you," she shockingly announced.

Lou and I exchanged blank stares. "Why?" I asked. "We don't need baby-sitting."

Doloras put her arm around Lauren. "Because I'm worried about bringing her into all this mess and I'd feel safer if she's with you guys. Around here she may end up like Tony. We don't know who killed him, we don't really know why, and we don't know who's watching us."

At that remark I looked around the half-filled room. Dark corners concealed dark tables with dark figures. Any one of them could be looking at us. I spied no monocles. But, Doloras was right. We still didn't know if Mrs. Averly could be trusted or if our trip to Stowe would end up like my trip to Provincetown, which turned out to be a trap all the way.

"Okay," I said. "If it's okay with Lou."

After three Manhattans, anything and everything was okay with Lou. So we agreed to agree. On Sunday morning, Lou and I and Lauren would head for Stowe in Lou's station wagon. We'd rent two rooms, take ski lessons from Lou and just meld into the crowd. Lou and I would attempt to get close enough to Richard Averly's chalet to snap pictures. Lou had special lenses that would take pictures up to a half-mile or so away. At least that's what the camera directions advertised.

Doloras would visit the South Boston Averly Brewery, snoop around and report to Red Kelly if she found anything out of the ordinary. Even though Kelly didn't know it, he was an important part of our team, especially since he was the only cop not seriously looking to arrest me.

If the real Adolf Hitler was in fact in this country, why was he here? Did the FBI know about it? and about a thousand other unanswered questions ran through my muddled mind along with the words from the song--Dream. 'Things Never Are As Bad As They Seem'. I hoped the song was right.

Chapter 9
STOWE
Boston Post headline,
Sunday, December 12, 1945, Morning edition:
BRITISH JET PLANE HITS RECORD SPEED
OF 606 MILES PER HOUR

We picked Lauren up at Doloras' apartment. It was a hair past eight as the sun rose over the Commonwealth Avenue apartment buildings and cast eerie shadows over the street and grassy parkway splitting the two sides of the road. Doloras allowed me to kiss her goodbye on the cheek. I was obviously gaining her confidence and friendship.

Lou asked me to drive since he had a terrible hangover. Lauren had bought some cute pink winter outfit that seemed to fit like a glove showing off her small, but well-rounded figure. Doloras had purchased some furry boots that resembled rabbits. Lauren, on the other hand, had a furry hat to match, in which she had tucked her hair. I had never seen her hair up and liked it just as much. Maybe love made people blind. Didn't someone once say that? Love is blind. Or did I just make it up?

I stopped at a pay phone, figuring the police couldn't trace the call as fast. I dialed Uncle Bill to inform him that things were okay. It rang a few times before Bill answered. He always slept late.

"I'm sure our line is being bugged so I can't talk," I told him. "Don't worry about me. I'll keep in touch." I hated to hang up so abruptly, but had no other choice. Bill was about the only person that really mattered in my life since my parents died so many years ago and now his days were numbered. Arthritis placed him in a wheel chair and old age did a number on his eyesight and hearing. I hoped I'd have an exciting story for him the next time I saw him. It would help lift his spirits, to say nothing about my spirits.

Lou had brought all the ski stuff, borrowing some from a friend for me. Stowe was about six hours from Boston and I had trouble keeping my eyes on the winding roads as I kept peeking at Lauren. The lump still lodged itself in my chest. We talked about everything light and unimportant. Movies, radio, sports, but not Doloras or murder. I asked Lauren if she had seen the movie *Laura*. She had. We discussed how pretty Gene Tierney was and I told her that Mrs. Averly resembled the star. I tipped my felt hat back on my head and asked her if she thought I resembled Dana Andrews. She said no, but maybe some other movie star that she couldn't recall. That puffed my ego.

I may have had a better chance if she thought I resembled Gene Tierney.

I said something stupid like if I made a movie I'd cast her as the lead. She said she'd heard that line and reached over and tickled my ribs. Her touch sent a tingle up and down my spine. What the hell did that signify?

I enjoyed the banter. A little bit about this and a little bit about that. She was better informed than I imagined. We even discussed about who the Red Sox could expect back from the war. Ted Williams, Johnny Pesky, Bobby Doerr, Tex Hughson: all the stars that made them a contender before Hitler tried to overrun Europe. I told her about my two chances at being a major leaguer and she acted impressed, tickling my ribs even harder.

I didn't usually talk much with dates. Picked them up, a quick dinner and then whatever I could get. Kelly and I had the same philosophy. Stay single and irresponsible. We dated a girl once and usually gave a false name. If you dwell on it, Kelly and I were jerks. Our dating habits were nothing to be proud of, but I avoided responsibility like the plague. I always blamed my father's stroke on the responsibility he accepted which included a wife and family, a mortgage and stressful job. His untimely death at forty-five never really left my system.

"Last summer my uncle encouraged me to try out again for the Red Sox," I told Lauren. "He insisted that if a one armed lug like Pete Gray could make the St. Louis Browns, why couldn't I make the Red Sox with my gimpy leg? 'Teams are hard up for players,' he said and he was right. The Washington Senators carried a guy named Bert Shepard who had lost a leg in the war."

"What happened?" she asked, leaning close to me.

I never minded telling the beginning of the story--I just hated the finish. "I reported to the tryout with my spikes and glove. Over a hundred hopefuls showed up--all sizes, shapes, colors and ages."

Lauren moved closer so our bottoms touched. I could hear Lou snoring in the back seat. "The Red Sox manager Joe Cronin ran the tryout. I think he'd shared a few beers with Bill over the years. As I fidgeted in the batter's box waiting for the first pitch I recalled fifteen years earlier standing at the same plate gazing out at the same big outfield. Since that time they had added a gigantic green fence in left field covered with advertisements--BURMA SHAVE SHAVES CLOSER, USE LIFEBOY TO BE SURE, GET WILDROOT CREAM OIL CHARLIE. If all the fans followed the advice on the ads, they'd be the cleanest crowd in the American League."

Lauren giggled and poked my ribs. At least she liked my sense of humor.

"The batting practice pitcher was some old timer, probably in his fifties and maybe a former player. I could hear Uncle Bill hollering from the grandstand: 'Hit the shit outta it, kid. You can do it, kid. Show 'em what I taught ya.'" I wasn't nervous enough. The pitcher threw a couple of easy ones that I fouled off. Then he reared back and grooved a semi-fast one. I lifted my front foot, put all my weight into the swing and slugged it over the ugly sixty foot wall. I could hear Uncle Bill going crazy. 'You're better than all these bums put together, kid.' I'm not sure that endeared me to the other players or coaches who began to take notice as I hit another and then another over the high wall."

Lauren hugged my right arm. "My hero."

"The story's not over yet," I reminded her. "The manager approached the batting cage and asked me what position I played. I told him center field and he sent me out there to catch some fungos."

"What are fungos, big boy," Lauren teased into my ear. It tickled and also brought a tingle to my spine.

"A long thin bat for hitting fly balls to the outfield," I said. "He hit me a few long ones and I snatched them real easy and showed off my rifle arm, throwing the ball all the way into the catcher's mitt on no bounces. Cronin waved me in and told me what a great arm I had. I recall he spit a wad of tobacco and missed my shoe by inches. I could still hear Uncle Bill cheering. I told Mr. Cronin that I played every weekend in the Boston Park League and kept in pretty good shape." 'Let's see you circle the bases, rookie,' he said. 'I'll time you with this stopwatch. Then grab a shower. I think we can use you.'"

"I felt my heart jump into my mouth," I said. "Joe Cronin, the manager of the Boston Red Sox said he could use me. It was my dream come true. Uncle Bill had been right. If one-armed Pete Gray could make it, so could Bill's nephew."

"What happened next? What happened next?" Lauren asked, excited like my tale would have a happy ending.

"Well, I had no choice but to attempt to run three hundred and sixty feet, the distance from home plate, around the bases and home again. A few of the regular players stood beside Cronin to watch. I remember the shortstop Eddie Lake giving me encouragement. 'Show him your stuff, rook,' he said."

"I have his autograph," Lauren said. "He came into the Merry-Go-Round with a bunch of the players. He's cute."

I felt a twinge of jealousy and tried to ignore the remark. "Cronin said 'on your mark, get set, go' and I took off as fast as my one good leg would carry me. I rounded first base with no mishap, feeling no pain, headed for second and crossed that bag forgetting all about my wrecked knee. I took a big swing around third and set my sights for the plate--ninety feet away--ninety feet away from a Red Sox contract. I could hear Uncle Bill in the stands lending reassurance. I could see cute Eddie Lake waving me on. Joe Cronin stood behind the batter's box holding a clipboard with a big grin on his face. From the over one hundred misfits, he'd discovered at least one diamond in the rough."

Lauren began bouncing on her seat like a little kid. She loved my story.

"I suddenly heard a crack, then felt a sharp pain in my damaged knee, up through the groin area, up my spine and into my head. Down I went on my face just like a soon-to-be-destroyed crippled horse at Suffolk Downs."

"That was it?" Lauren's mouth dropped open. "Couldn't you just have been a hitter?"

"Sorry," I said. "You have to be able to do a little running in the Major Leagues. Not like the Park League where I trot and get away with it."

Lauren hugged my arm. "Sorry, Johnny. That's the saddest story I've ever heard. You came so close. How many people come within ninety feet from their dreams?"

I'd never thought of it that way, but now I felt even worse about the whole thing. As we got to within an hour of our destination, I was reminded of Shangri-la. The hills became mountains covered with white. The ugly trees became either evergreens or dressed in ice. A wonderful winter wonderland.

Stowe was a small, quaint Vermont town built around its skiing industry--Mount Mansfield. It was the first ski mountain in the country to introduce a chair lift, which, of course, made it easier and more comfortable to travel up the slopes.

We checked into two second floor rooms at the famous Stowe Inn, a big, old wooden firetrap, the rocking chairs lining the front porch facing the mountain across the street. With binoculars, we could visually follow the tow to the summit. And to the left of the summit, about two miles away, stood a magnificent appearing chalet. We could have been looking into the Swiss Alps.

After we got settled, Lou and I in our room and Lauren in hers next door, we met in the bar for a drink. An oversized stone fireplace blazed in the middle of the room, throwing off enough heat to convince us we didn't need the three colorful sweaters we had purchased in the gift shop upon our arrival.

I ordered a scotch on the rocks, Lou a Manhattan, and Lauren a Coke. The bartender was closer to Lauren's age and immediately began flirting. I got a kick out of the whole event because I knew he wouldn't get to first base with her, and why.

I whispered in her ear. "Play him along and pump him for information."

"What do we want to know," she whispered back, slipping out of her new sweater, revealing a tight T-shirt, two pointy erect nipples and obviously no bra. I began choking on my heart again and felt a tightness in my groin. I took two deep breaths and wished for a quick cold shower.

"Ask him if they have Boston papers. I'd guess here in the boonies they don't keep up with much going on in the outside world, which is okay with me. I don't particularly want anyone seeing my face flashing in the newspapers and I'd like to wash off this silly mustache and take off these shades. Ask him about the chalet near the summit. How they get to it. Ask him how much ski lessons cost. Ask him his name. Just sound a little interested. Blow in his ear and he'll tell you anything. I would."

She flashed me a cutesy smile. "Okay boss. I'd tell you any-thing." She squeezed my hand and turned her attention to the bartender.

Lou and I concentrated on our drinks and perusing the rest of the room. Lou had procured a map of the mountain showing all the trails and tows. "How about I'll give you two guys a lesson in the morning on the Bunny slope. In the afternoon you and I can go to the summit and Lauren can shop. Dames like that stuff."

"Sounds good to me," I said.

The bartender walked to the far end of the bar to serve three attractive young women who had just entered the room. Normally, I would have thought them date prospects and suggested to Lou that we attempt to pick them up. But now I only had eyes for Lauren. She poked my back to get my attention away from Lou. "I see you eyeing those chicks," she said.

"No interest," I said.

"Something queer about you?" she asked, chuckling. "You can tell me. I'll understand."

I knew she was teasing, but maybe also testing. Uncle Bill told me about that. You tease someone, pretending not to be serious, in order to test them. If they fail the test, you can pretend you weren't interested in the first place. Was Lauren jealous? I doubted it, but hoped so.

"I'll explain later," I said. "What did you learn from Don Juan?"

Lauren moved her barstool closer, so her legs were touching mine. In a low tone she said, "The Boston papers are delivered two days late every afternoon along with the New York Times. Richard Averly owns the chalet and was seen in town a little over a week ago. He owns a horse and sleigh which travels over an old logging road to the chalet. The bartender's name is Joe and he says he's in love with me and wants me to give birth to his children. His telephone number is..."

I placed my hand softly over her mouth. "I don't care about that stuff and neither do you."

Lauren laughed out loud. I was glad she was having fun at my expense. Testing and teasing. I forced a laugh. "Good job, Lauren. You make a swell flatfoot. It's good Doloras didn't hear him flirting with you. She'd probably punch him in the belly."

"Lower," Lauren said. "But you're right. She's very protective of me. Has been for the past few years. I don't know what I'd do without her."

We ate nice roast beef dinners. Topped it off with heavy desserts of pie and ice cream. Lou drank his usual three Manhattans, got drunk and excused himself at around nine o'clock for bed. "See you for breakfast at eight and lessons at nine," he babbled, leaving Lauren and me sitting in front of the big fireplace.

"How about an after-dinner drink?" I asked Lauren. "It's early. I'm not tired and we can talk. I enjoyed talking to you today in the car."

"I've never had a drink of alcohol," she said. "Doloras warned me that if someone ever starts, sometimes it's difficult to stop. I don't smoke either."

On that reminder, I lit a Chesterfield and blew two smoke rings, a smaller one through a bigger one.

"That's great," Lauren said. "What else can you do clever like that?"

The question aroused me so I decided to attempt to behave myself. If she'd been some pickup, I would have had a flippant comeback and blown a few more great rings.

I waved to the waiter and ordered two Tia Marias on the rocks. "Put cream in one of them," I said. "It makes it taste like a frappe."

I signed the bill, added a tip, and motioned to Lauren to follow me. "Don't worry," I said, "I'm more harmless than I look. Doloras is my friend and I'd like to also think you and I are friends."

She followed me to her room. I asked for the key, unlocked the door and we both entered. It was small, with a single bed, small table with wooden chair, an overstuffed easy chair, bureau, wash basin and mirror. Her second story window overlooked the mountain across the street. I placed the drinks on the table and lit a cigarette. Also across the street stood another hotel, of sorts, or rooming house. I thought I noticed a flicker of light in a second story window directly across from us. A curtain moved open, then closed quickly. Probably my imagination. No one could know where we were this soon. I closed our curtain, just in case.

Lauren took her drink over to the bed, kicked off her high heals and sat down facing me. I relaxed in the overstuffed chair.

"Like it?" I asked as she sipped the sweet drink.

"You were right. It tastes just like a sweet chocolate frappe. I certainly can't taste any liquor in it."

Both drinks were mostly ice and were gone after a few gulps. "Want another?" I asked. "I can call room service. And how about something to eat?" My watch said a bit before ten-thirty.

"My stomach and neck are beginning to feel warm," she said. "Does that mean I'm getting drunk?"

"Most people don't get drunk on one drink," I answered. "Besides, there's very little alcohol content in Tia Maria," I lied. The bottle label read 75%. "I'll order some shrimp cocktail. It's here on the room service menu."

"Okay with me," she said. "Are you sure a person can't get bombed on just one little drink? Maybe it was something I ate."

She was only wearing the T-shirt and shouldn't have been hot.

"I'll protect you," I said.

"Mind if I change?" she asked.

"Go ahead. Got something flimsier than a T-shirt?" I was feeling flippant and enjoyed the relaxed atmosphere.

"Close your eyes," she demanded. "No peeking."

I heard the bureau open and some rustling of clothes.

"Open," she said. "Like?"

She had changed into a bright red, frilly, long sleeved silk shirt, coming to just below her bottom--the top two buttons open. She fanned herself with the menu.

"Nice," I groaned and meant it. "Pretty classy like Scarlet in *Gone With The Wind*."

She curtsied and laughed. Lauren wore no panties. I didn't know about Scarlet.

I dialed room service and ordered two more drinks. Doubles along with twelve shrimp and crackers. That would hold us.

Lauren's eyelids were heavy, her eyes a bit glassy and staring across the room at me.

"Tired?" I asked.

"Just tranquil," she answered. "You're the first man I've ever been relaxed with that I can recall since..."

I quickly debated with myself on picking up on the direction of the conversation. Then I decided, for some unknown reason, that I needed to get to know her better.

"Since what?" I asked.

She dropped her head, hiding her expression from me.

"Nothing," she replied. "Nothing important."

I knew she had a story. Maybe an uncomfortable one. I was probably pushing too fast and didn't want to break any progress the liquor might be providing.

We finished our drinks in silence.

A small radio sat on a table by the window. I flipped it on and dialed till I found some soft music. Evelyn Knight warbled 'A Little Bird Told Me That You Love Me And I Believe That It's True'. The announcer said it was number two on the Hit Parade. I tried to catch Lauren's eye, but she was glaring into the melting ice cubes. I pulled the curtain back just an inch or so to see if I could detect any activity from the window across the street.

Nothing.

I didn't need another monocle man.

Our semi-dark room carried a faint odor of sweet Tia Maria along with the slight sniff of perfume Lauren wore. She continued to gaze into her glass.

I gazed at her.

The spell was broken by a soft knock on the door. I let the waiter in with his tray, signed the bill and thanked him. I detected a ludicrous grin on his face as he left. If he only knew that Lauren was a lesbian.

"These drinks are bigger," Lauren noticed. "Are you trying to get me loaded?"

"Moi?" I said. "Don't drink it if you don't want it. But try this shrimp with the hot sauce. I guarantee it's delicious and it'll help absorb the alcohol."

I had pulled my chair up to the table and started devouring the shrimp.

Lauren joined me, took a few sips from her double Tia and gobbled a few shrimp. "Right again," she said. "These are scrumptious."

She concentrated on finishing the food as I attempted not to concentrate on peering down her opened blouse. A third button had come undone by itself, revealing the round and mounded tops of two inviting erect purple nipples, quite a bit larger than I'd imagined.

"Now I really do feel hot," she announced. She rose from her chair and stumbled to my side. "Touch my forehead."

I obliged. It was hot. Her face was flushed. "Go lie down," I ordered. "No more alcohol for you. You're too young."

"But, I like it," she argued, slurring her words and laying back down on the bed. "I feel great. I promise to behave."

"Remember what Doloras warned you about drinking?" I reminded her. My true mission for loosening Lauren up was to find out about her life, not seduce her. I decided it was time to coax her a little and began asking her questions about her childhood.

"I was born right near Boston," I said. "What about you?"

"Order me another frappe and I'll tell you," she was grinning ear to ear.

"Can I trust you?" I was testing and teasing.

"You're old enough to be my father," she slurred. The words hurt, but I knew it wasn't by design.

"I'm only thirty-five," I said. "Babe Ruth was still hitting homers when he was over forty."

Lauren pretended to count on her fingers. "That's only fifteen years difference," she mumbled. "I guess I should be afraid of you. And, has anyone ever told you how handsome you are? In a rough sort of way, of course."

I dialed room service again. It was last call. "Repeat the last order," I said. "Leave out the shrimp and crackers."

"I was born in Quincy," she said. "Right near the beach, Squantum, next to the air base."

I knew the area across Dorchester Bay from Boston. As a teenager, I'd taken dates swimming there.

"It's none of my business," I said, "but tell me about you and Doloras. I mean how you met and stuff like that."

Lauren had the bad habit of chewing her cuticles until they bled, but apparently only when she was nervous. Now she began chewing frantically and noticed her open blouse. She gave me a jovial smile and fastened two of the three undone buttons.

Foiled again.

"You don't have to tell me anything," I assured her. "I'm only interested because I like you and I like Doloras. I don't care about any of the private...well, you know. Your personal life is your own business and I don't judge people. Especially nice people like you and Doloras."

Her smile widened, showing how white her teeth were. Had I ever noticed a dame's teeth? Maybe, I never cared before. About teeth, anyway.

"Doloras is nice to me," she said. "She's sort of a mother/father-/protector figure all rolled into one. I love her."

The waiter brought our drinks, this time flashing a more ludicrous smile seeing Lauren on the bed in her short silk outfit. In his mind, I was making good progress. I wrote my name on the check and added a healthy tip. He glanced at it and whispered, "Good luck, pal. She's a knockout."

The waiter couldn't have been over twenty and before he left the room he flipped the radio dial. "Not many stations around these parts," he said. "My buddy's an all-night announcer on this one. Just plays romantic music for lovers, if you know what I mean." He found the station and Perry Como was singing 'A You're Adorable'. As the waiter left the room he sent me a condescending smile.

Lauren cocked her ears to the melodious sounds as Perry sang 'B You're So Beautiful And C You're A Cutie Full Of Charm'. She turned her attention back to me and said, "I'm only twenty, but I matured real young. When I was eleven, I had the body of a woman. Like I have now." She puffed up her chest. The lump in my throat grew along with the ache in my heart. Perry sang 'V You're So Very Sweet' and I was thinking that all the alphabet words fit Lauren to a T.

She continued her story. "It's not good to grow up too soon. At least it wasn't good for me."

I noticed tears beginning to flow. I felt guilty and joined her on the bed, taking her hand in mine and wiping her tears with the sheet. "You don't have to tell me any of this intimate stuff," I said. "It's really none of my damn business."

She placed her head against my shoulder. "I don't mind telling you." She was really slurring now. The alcohol had finally taken its toll. "You're my new friend, Johnny, and I want you to understand. You shared your baseball failure story with me."

I reached for my handkerchief. It apparently was the same one Mrs. Averly had used earlier in the week. Lauren blew her nose. "Thanks," she said. "What kind of perfume do you use?"

I smelled the hanky. "It's...it's Mrs. Averly," I confessed. "Just business. She shed a few tears when I informed her about the death of her husband."

"What a nice man you are, Johnny," Lauren said. "I'm beginning to feel woozy. Is that from the alcohol?"

Lauren leaned back, her black wavy hair flowing against the white pillow. To me, she resembled a vision. A Madonnic vision.

"No more booze for you," I said, feeling her warm forehead.

"But I like it," she reached for her half-empty glass.

I pushed it out of reach. "Doloras told me to look out for you. She'd be real upset if she knew I introduced you to alcohol."

"Okay, Johnny. Do you think I'll throw up?"

I quickly moved away. "I hope not. Let me get a towel, just in case."

"No, no. I'm just kidding. I feel fine. Relaxed. Loose. Like nothing matters."

"Lay back," I said. "You're in good hands."

Lauren lay back onto the pillow again and continued her tale. "When I was eleven, my parents went away for a weekend, leaving me with my uncle. He chased me for two days and nights. I was naive. 'Just touch it,' he pleaded. 'And I'll leave you alone.' I kept resisting until he got rough and finally raped me. He weighed at least two hundred pounds. And you can see my size. I only weigh a little over a hundred now. I was about eighty pounds then. He kept saying that if I didn't do what he wanted, he'd tell my parents that I was a tramp and was the one who had chased him." The tears were flowing freely and Lauren chomped desperately at her cuticles making some of them bleed. I gently took her hands in mine. "It's not easy for a girl to mature early," she sobbed. "I felt guilty all the time. You know? I guess you can't know. The boys called me names and the girls avoided me. I was the first girl in my class to have breasts, and the first girl in my class to have my period."

I felt my face blush. Did I want to hear these confidential details? I knew this immature child wouldn't be spilling her guts like this to me if she wasn't drunk. But, I guess I was glad to hear it. It helped me understand how someone could turn against men. She certainly had enough reason. I cradled her in my arms and rocked her back and forth.

"He was real rough," she went on. "It hurt and he kept pushing it in. I bled all over the place and cried and even screamed. But, no one was around to hear me or save me and he didn't even care."

Lauren blew her nose again. She wasn't looking at me when telling the story but just over my shoulder into some past infinite distance. Suddenly, she pulled away and riveted right into my eyes with hers and continued. "An hour later he did it again. This time I didn't even put up a struggle and I barely remember any of it. I know it hurt and I bled some more. After that, I locked myself in the basement. He yelled at me to come out and said he'd break the door down if I didn't. But, I just sat there, huddled in a corner near the furnace. It seemed like hours and hours until my parents finally came home and I didn't dare tell them what had happened. To this day, I never have."

"You told Doloras?"

"And now I've told you. No one else ever. I couldn't. I didn't want to remember. But somehow I feel better since telling you. Does that mean anything?"

Doctor Edge would tack some deep significance to it. I gently took her hands in mine and pulled her close. "I have a friend who's a psychiatrist. He told me lots of stuff about Sigmund Freud. You know, the father of psychology. Freud taught that the more a person talks, the better a person feels. I guess it works. Something like the Roman Catholic confessional on Saturday. You confess to the priest all your sins and he sees to it that God forgives you. Doctor Edge says it's really you forgiving yourself after telling the stories out loud. But, what difference does it make if it works? At least that's what I think."

"I'm not Catholic," Lauren said. "But it seems to make sense to me."

The radio was now playing 'Doin' What Comes Naturally' by Dinah Shore and it got me thinking that with Lauren, I couldn't ever do what comes naturally. "Ever date guys after that horrible experience with your uncle?" I asked, giving her back her hands.

She'd stopped crying. "Tried to in high school. But they all seemed to be the same. Groping. Trying to feel me up all the time. Rough. Wise guys. You know the type. Doloras says all men are the same. All they want is to get...well, you know. You're a guy."

Lauren was pickled and it was my fault. I walked across the room and flipped off the overhead light. I lit a butt, blew a few perfect rings and snuffed it out on the floor. Then I returned to Lauren's bed, sat down beside her and cradled her head in my lap, rocking back and forth until she slept. "I would never be rough," I whispered. "And I'll never allow anyone else to be."

She was so little and innocent. So soft and fragile. I kissed her hair lightly.

I must have sat like that for an hour, my heart breaking inside my chest.

Lauren my love--a love I would never have.

Chapter 10
THE SKIING LESSON
Boston Post, sports page headline,
Monday, December 13, 1945:
MAJOR LEAGUE BASEBALL RELEASES
OFFICIAL STATS: STIRNWEISS BATTING
LEADER WITH .309;
CAVARRETTA LEADS N.L. WITH .355

We ate our breakfast amidst the smells of sizzling bacon, something foreign to all our noses during the war. Lou ordered a raw egg in a glass of tomato juice and two aspirin. When Lauren found out it was a remedy for hangovers, she ordered the same.

Lauren's eyes were puffy. I surmised it was mostly from crying the night before, not from lack of sleep. She had barely stirred until seven in the morning, never lifting her head out of my lap.

I slept fitfully, not moving for fear of waking her.

Lou never asked any questions of why my bed hadn't been slept in. Either he had a rare attack of being a gentleman or he just didn't care. I assumed the latter.

He and I wore white, baggy waterproof snow pants and a heavy parka with hood. Lauren looked more stylish, wearing pink colorful ski clothes designed for the purpose of attracting attention rather than for convenience. When I asked Lou why he'd selected all white for us, he proved to be a better detective than I'd ever given him credit for. "If you and I think we might sneak up on that chalet, we better blend into the snow, don't you think?" he asked.

The glare and moving curtain in the window across the street I'd detected the night before still bothered me. But, I decided not to tell Lou or Lauren, figuring the less upset we all became, the better.

Besides, tough private eyes should carry all burdens. At least, that's what Uncle Bill would say.

Lou decided to order a Bloody Mary to top off his breakfast. I talked Lauren out of it explaining that it was the 'tail of the dog that bit you the night before', and that it might lead to puffier eyes. Apparently, the way to a woman's mind is through her vanity, and the way to a man's heart is not through his stomach, but through his fly. I wondered if I'd made that up.

Lou perused a Boston Post newspaper.

"Two days ago?" I asked. "My picture in it?"

"May first 1945," he said. "I borrowed it from the newspaper library and brought it with me so I could read about Hitler. Supposedly he committed suicide on April 30th."

I lit a Chesterfield and sipped my coffee. Lauren pulled her chair closer to Lou's in order to see the paper.

"There's his picture," she pointed. "Looks just like the guy in our picture."

"Read the article Lou," I said. "Read it aloud."

Lou adjusted glasses on the end of his thin nose. "Berlin, Germany, May 1, 1945. On April 29th, Adolf Hitler, 55, desperate and bitter, smelling Germany's demise, summoned a municipal official and ordered him to conduct his marriage to longtime companion Eva Braun. Hitler appointed Admiral Doenitz his successor--allegedly angering Hermann Goering who had earlier sent a telegram asking for the job. On the 30th, after a good lunch, Hitler and his new wife went into one of the private rooms in the bunker. One shot was heard. Joseph Goebbels and Martin Bormann went to the room and found that Hitler had shot himself through the mouth. Eva had taken poison and was also dead along with Hitler's favorite dog, Blondi. During his reign, Hitler had vanquished nine nations, repulsed Europe's greatest power, devised an economic and social fabric based on the deadly subjugation of millions and hypnotically imposed his will on millions more. Over 65 million Germans glorified this demagogue as the savior of Deutschland. In the end, he forced them into the abyss of a nightmarish hell."

Lou looked up from his paper and stared at us. "What do you think of this guy? He may be up on top of that mountain across the street."

I blew a small smoke ring in Lauren's direction. She put up one finger and pretended to catch it.

"Ringer," I said. "Any more Lou?" I asked.

Lou turned his attention back to the seven-month-old newspaper and read to us. "Always aware of the importance of due ceremony, Hitler had left detailed instructions for the disposal of the bodies and they were carried out precisely. All three bodies were taken up to the garden of the Chancellery, soaked in petrol and burned. Goebbels kept the deaths a secret for a day and then announced them on the radio on May 1st, saying that Hitler had died heroically at the head of his troops. The man that millions would salute as 'Mein Fuehrer' was born in Braunau, Austria in 1889. His father worked as a customs official, and it's been reported, violently beat him. Young Adolf grew up to worship the works of Beethoven and Wagner and gained employment in Vienna painting postcards. In Vienna, he embraced attitudes typical of some middle-class Austrians: intense anti-Semitism and fear of Marxism."

I waved to the waiter for more coffee and he refilled all our cups.

"Sounds like he had a tough upbringing," Lauren said. "Maybe the things that happen in our youth mold our futures in ways we can do nothing about."

She might have been right about Hitler, but I hoped she was wrong about herself. On the other hand, Mrs. Averly had tried for over two years to remold Tony Coraloni and failed.

Lou continued reading: "At the outbreak of World War One, Hitler was lifted from obscure artist to determined soldier. He recorded in his book, *Mein Kampf*, that the war elated him. After the German defeat in WWI, Hitler joined the ultra-nationalistic German Workers' Party, later called the *National Socialist German Workers* or Nazi Party. Using his zealous oratory, he convinced some rich industrialists to back his drive to redeem Germany's humiliation at Versailles. Hitler also formed the Storm Troopers and tried to oust the government at Munich. When this failed, he was jailed where he wrote *Mein Kampf* and plotted his path to absolute power."

I was learning more from this reading than I'd ever known about Hitler before. I'd always thought him a madman with a lust for power and a hate for Jews. I certainly had never read *Mein Kampf* and had no plans to. Lauren winked at me so I winked back, not having any idea what it meant. Her wink or mine.

Lou droned on. "Following his release from jail, the Nazis and their leader grew in popularity and on January 30, 1933, Hitler was appointed Chancellor of Germany. With his new authority, the little man with a little mustache crushed all opposition, instituting a totalitarian regime. His paramount and most dangerous ideological principle was that Germany must develop a pure Aryan race. This crazed notion, and his demonic drive to dominate Europe, ignited an inferno of horror for millions of Jews and other innocent people who died tragically in his death camps. Reportedly in 1941, Hitler ordered the head of his SS, Heinrich Himmler, to get rid of all Jews, gypsies and Slavs. He called it *The Final Solution*. Hitler's military victories created in him an overconfidence which eventually derailed Nazi momentum. In the final days of the war, Hitler ordered all males between 16 and 60 to be drafted and then was quoted as saying 'All my Generals sold me out'."

Lou looked up. "Is that it?" I asked.

"One more paragraph," Lou said. "Maybe the most important. Informed sources report that Hitler, suffering from Parkinson's disease causing trembling hands, Eva Braun, 32, and their German shepherd dog, Blondi, were all dropped in a hole and burned beyond recognition."

I lit another cigarette. "Convenient," I said. "Burned beyond recognition." I addressed Lou. "Ever wonder who informed sources are?"

Lou shrugged.

"Listen to this," he said and finished his reading. "That Hitler wrought the greatest act of genocide the world had known is indisputable. That he was a genius of political maneuver is almost above discussion. He was at one time the greatest leader, the greatest achiever and the greatest evil of the twentieth century. Few, if any centuries have seen a man who can be compared with him in all those characteristics. It may yet prove that Adolf Hitler was the greatest paradox of history."

"What's a paradox?" Lauren asked before I got a chance.

"It's a puzzle--a contradiction," Lou said.

I guess we learn by asking. It was a bright, sunny Monday morning. Temperature ten degrees. Wind ten miles per hour. These were important facts for skiers. Sometimes the wind chill factor could approach ten or twenty below and that caused frostbite. The slopes weren't crowded on weekdays--but watch out weekends and holidays. The sport of skiing was beginning to catch on and Stowe was an innovator--the first mountain in the country to offer a chair lift, a single seat designed to carry skiers upwards. This season they'd added a few double seats.

I couldn't wait.

Lou took us to a two hundred yard easy slope called The Bunny Hill. He spent several minutes teaching us to just stand up and move forward and sideways without falling. Lou was right about my athletic prowess. I caught on fast. Unfortunately he was wrong about my knee. Every twist aggravated it a little bit more. I kept repeating the words: "Tough detective, tough detective."

"How's your knee holding up?" Lou once asked.

"Great," I lied.

Lou then spent another ten to fifteen minutes showing us how to hold onto and ride a rope tow. It wasn't as easy as it looked. Almost too heavy for Lauren. Beginners would fall off and other beginners would ski over them.

When we'd finally mastered the rope tow and reached the top of the Bunny Hill, Lou demonstrated snow plowing, which was placing the front of your skis in a V shape and digging in the sides. A good snow plower could navigate any trail without danger. "If in doubt," Lou warned, "fall down on your butt."

We did that a lot.

By lunch time, both Lauren and I were sore but could maneuver down the Bunny Hill without misfortune. Lou had taught us how to turn and stop. Lou did one show-off run and I could see that his skiing ability was as good as his baseball pitching. It seemed Lou excelled at everything he attempted. Not a paradox. I labeled guys like him one hundred and fifty percent people. He was great at baseball, skiing, photography and even a great drinker. He told me once, "Anything worth spending the time doing, is worth doing 150 percent." Funny thing, Uncle Bill had the same motto, secretly drank out of oranges and blew much better smoke rings that I did.

"Lunch is on me," Lou announced. "You guys are great students. Lunch is your graduation gift."

Lauren went to her room to change and wash up. Lou and I went to ours. I unwrapped an ace bandage which had tightly held my knee in place. Parts of my leg tingled where I'd cut off the blood circulation.

Lou noticed. "Sure your knee's okay?" he asked. "Looks pretty gimpy to me."

"A hot tub will fix it up," I said. "Maybe I shouldn't have the bandage so tight."

I called Uncle Bill's apartment. Detective Red Kelly was there with Rose.

"How'd you find Rose?" I asked.

"What kind of a fool do you think I am?" he asked.

"How many different kinds are there?" I flippantly answered. I couldn't help following up on his straight line with a line I'd learned from Curley Howard of the Three Stooges. Their movies were always shown at the Old Howard, between strippers and comics.

Red chuckled at my cleverness. "Good news for you, buddy," he said. "You're off the hook. We found the monocle man's body."

"Was I right? I asked. "Was it near the hotel buried in the sand?"

"You were right about that too. Less than fifty yards from the restaurant. But, of course, no one knows anything."

Red Kelly had been a good buddy since he joined the force ten years ago. For some reason we just hit it off. Maybe because his life's ambition was to put in his twenty-five years on the force, retire with his pension, and hang out a *Private Investigator* shingle like mine. He hated being called Red, but he had the reddest hair I'd ever seen on a man. And at thirty plus, he still had a few freckles that all redheads have as youngsters. Other than that, he was of average build, with a soft but handsome and trusting face. In addition, he remained single and irresponsible like me. Another Curley Howard line became our motto: "Are you happy or are you married?" Many times on his night off we'd attend the Old Howard burlesque theater which would leave us horny; then we'd roam the Scollay Square bars, flirt with the waitresses and sometimes link up with one of the strippers. Who could knock free entertainment?

Red's father had been a cop (with mine) and so had his grandfather. Red was clean, he liked me and helped me secure jobs that the department couldn't or wouldn't handle. Some were guarding conceited minor dignitaries or celebrities who insisted they were more important than they were. I occasionally was handed a woman who was being harassed by an old boyfriend or an ex-husband. These never amounted to anything too dangerous, but paid the freight. The best case he dropped on me was finding a missing kidnapped Siamese cat for a rich, old Beacon Hill dowager. I solved the case, and the gratuity was more than the money I earned in a month of Sundays.

"Can you tell me where you are?" he asked.

"Not yet, buddy. Too many lives are in danger until we know what we're dealing with. I trust you. You know that. But the fewer people who know where we are right now, the better. I'm afraid we're onto something real big and real scary."

"Maybe so, buddy," he said. "Now I got some bad news for you. Maybe you already saw it in the papers. It's on the front page of this morning's Post."

"The papers are late here. We wait two days," I heard myself say by mistake and if Red really wanted to narrow down my where-abouts, that little tidbit of information would help.

"Rose says you know a girl named Doloras Raines. She waitress-es at The-Merry-Go-Round in the Copley Plaza?"

"Yeah, I know her," I admitted. "Good kid. Good friend. As a matter of fact, she's involved in the case I'm working on right now. Why? What happened?"

I noted a long silence on the other end of the line which didn't suggest any good news. "She was in an auto accident," Kelly said.

"Is she okay?" I held my breath.

"Dead," he said. "Drowned in the South Boston River."

I immediately thought of Lauren.

Poor Lauren.

Then my mind flashed to the last time I'd seen Doloras. Poor Doloras. Loyal to the end to her friend Tony. Doloras was a special breed of human. Not many people risk their lives for a friend or what they believe in. Most people just sit on the fence and watch the world go by, waiting for that knock on the door from the grim reaper. 'Where have you been? What took you so damn long?'

"What time?" I asked.

"They found her at dawn. The coroner says she drowned at about midnight. She was loaded with alcohol. Bad accident."

"Was her car coming from South Boston or going?" I asked.

"Does it make a difference?" Kelly asked.

"All the difference in the world," I answered. "She was doing something for me in connection with the case I'm working on. If she was coming back from South Boston, I strongly suggest it was no accident."

There was silence on the phone for several seconds. Then Kelly said, "By the angle of the hole in the guardrail on the bridge and where the car landed, she was coming back from South Boston. So what does that mean? If there's any chance that she was murdered, I want to know about it."

"Do me a favor, Red, autopsy her body. I bet a week's pay you'll find no alcohol in her system. Then I want you to do me another favor. This one won't be easy, but necessary. Call Mrs. Helen Averly." I read him the number from my small black address book. "Tell her what happened to Doloras. Then ask her for permission to exhume her father's body. He's the guy who started the Averly Breweries. Supposedly he was in the same type of accident two years ago. I strongly believe you'll find no alcohol anywhere in his system either."

"What if she refuses?" Kelly asked.

"Then go to the DA with the information about Doloras and Tony Coraloni. Tell him you suspect they're connected. He'll cooperate. Maybe. But I think Mrs. Averly will agree. She hired me to first find her husband. Which I did. Then she hired me to find her brother. Which I think I have. All this connects. It's vitally important to find out if Mr. Averly was murdered the same way as Doloras."

"Where can I reach you?" Kelly tried to trick me.

"I'll call you tomorrow at your office. Maybe I'll have more information from this end."

Kelly clicked off. I told Lou what had transpired.

"Sorry about Doloras," Lou said. "I was beginning to get the hots for her."

"She was a lesbian," I assured Lou. "But a hell of a nice person."

"Lauren's a lesbian too," Lou said. "Doesn't seem to stop you from falling in love."

Lou was too damn observant. "Can't always tell one's heart how to behave," I said.

"Well, I couldn't tell mine either," he said. "So there." He gave me the finger. "I thought we made a good foursome and I had some real interesting fantasies for when we all got back together."

"Guess that won't happen now," I said with my head bowed.

"Guess not," Lou agreed. "But it can't stop us from our mission. We gotta get a picture. Maybe that's the only way we'll stop all this killing."

"Or speed it up," I said, wishing I'd kept the pessimistic thought to myself. Uncle Bill always warned me that your worst fears can be realized, so block them out of your mind.

Chapter 11
LAUREN AND JOHNNY
Boston Post headline,
Monday, December 13, 1945:
HIDDEN CITIES WHERE ATOM BOMBS
MANUFACTURED REVEALED--CALLED
THE MANHATTAN PROJECT, THE CITIES
ARE OAK RIDGE, TENN; HANFORD,
WASH; AND LOS ALAMOS, NEW MEXICO

We met Lauren in the hotel dining room for a six o'clock dinner. Lou had wanted to get an early start the next morning, and suggested we get a good night's sleep. We all ate heartily, Lou keeping his drinking to one Manhattan. After dinner, he excused himself on the guise that he had something to do. I knew that he didn't particularly want to be around when I told Lauren about Doloras. Come to think of it, I didn't relish being around either.

Lauren and I moved into the large parlor-room featuring the big stone fireplace which was blazing and emitting great waves of heat. I removed my sweater and she removed hers. Her hair was up and tied tightly in a bun. I liked it down and flowing. I couldn't help stare at her erect nipples which were so apparent under her skimpy black T-shirt. I wanted to ask her if the heat made them erect, but realized that a conversation like that should take place in a bedroom and not a crowded parlor and also by people that maybe knew each other a little better than Lauren and I did. The ache in my chest had never waned since I'd first set eyes on her, and I had no idea how she would take the news of Doloras's death.

We ordered after-dinner drinks. She wanted the same as she had the night before. "It relaxes me," she said. And I did want her relaxed. We talked about *nothing* stuff, the news of the day, sports, movies, songs, radio shows.

"Do you think the survivors in those cities where they dropped the atom bomb will feel any aftereffects?" she asked me while scanning a Boston Post laying on a coffee table. For a moment I'd forgotten that the story about Doloras might be in it. I grabbed the paper away.

"Let me see that paper on the bomb," I said real quickly. 'Informed sources say that over sixty thousand died after the blast in Hiroshima', I read. "Of course that was a bomb being dropped. I don't know how much effect just being around the bomb will have. Maybe none." I didn't know the first thing about radiation. Who did, other than the Japanese?

"I wonder how the guy felt who actually pressed the button that dropped the bomb?" she asked.

All I knew is that I felt nothing when I shot my first person--the monocleman. But, of course, it was in the heat of him trying to kill me. That may be a difference. "Maybe you feel nothing when you can't see the whites of their eyes," I answered even though I'd seen my victim face to face. "I'm sure dropping bombs on unseen people isn't like shooting someone point blank."

"How do you think the scientist feels who invented a bomb of that magnitude--that can kill so many instantly?"

"Oppenheimer I think his name is," I said, feeling intellectual. "War is war, I guess. Didn't someone once say that all's fair in love and war?" I was glad we were talking about news of the day stuff, but I knew that eventually we'd have to get to Doloras, which most likely wasn't written up in the paper we were reading. Two days old. I could wait. But I knew it wouldn't go away.

"Listen to this," Lauren said, pointing to a column on the bottom of the front page, now moving beside me so she could see the paper. "The Nuremburg war crime trials have opened in the Palace of Justice in Nuremburg, Germany. On trial, among others, are Germany's most monstrous criminals, Herman Goering, Rudolph Hess, Albert Speer and Joachim von Ribbentrop. The chief American prosecutor is Supreme Court Associate Justice Robert H. Jackson."

"Hitler is among the missing," I said.

After three drinks Lauren seemed quite relaxed. She wasn't even biting her cuticles. I paid the tab and requested room service bring nightcaps to her room. She invited me in and we sat in the same seats we'd occupied the night before--she on the bed and myself in the stuffed chair, which I moved around a bit to catch a view of the second floor window across the street.

"That was nice of you to stay with me last night," she said and slurred her words. The erection of her nipples had subsided, which helped me concentrate more on the important business at hand.

The waiter brought our drinks along with shrimp and crackers. It was the same young waiter carrying the same ludicrous grin which I would have enjoyed punching. I signed the check and gave him a wide smirk, then joined Lauren on the bed. We both sipped for a few minutes without talking. It was almost like she was reading the ominous vibes from my mind or my body.

She finally broke the silence. "You got something on your mind, Johnny?"

I said nothing. She undid the bun and her hair fell half way down her back. She fluffed it up and I felt sexually aroused.

"Doloras is dead," I said just like that. No preface. No whisper. No touching her hand. Just a cold, matter of fact, "Doloras is dead."

Her eyes went blank. The corners of her mouth dropped. I waited for verbal reaction. None came. Then she flailed out with her fists, hitting me as hard as she could. In the face, on the chest, shoulders and arms. She kept punching until her arms were too tired to punch any more.

"Oh, Johnny. I've drawn blood." She took a Kleenex from the bedside table and began wiping my lip and nose. "Oh, Johnny. What have I done to you?" Her eyes were still blank like in a trance.

I took her small hand in mine. "It's okay," I lied. "It doesn't hurt. I'm going to run you a hot tub. It'll relax you, then maybe you can sleep."

I quickly left the room, walked down the hall to the bathroom, which was fortunately empty, and ran a steaming hot bath. When I returned, Lauren had undressed and put on her white terri cloth bathrobe. She had her soap and hairbrush. Her eyes were still blank like a zombie.

"Ready?" I asked.

"Wait for me here," she said in a low monotone.

While she was gone I finished the shrimp and occasionally peaked out the window.

No glare tonight.

No curtain movement. At least, not yet.

When Lauren returned, her hair was done up in a towel like a turban. The fresh smell of soap radiated her body. She handed me the hairbrush and lay stomach-down on the bed. "Would you brush my hair, please," she asked in a monotone. "Doloras used to brush my hair after my bath. You're my only friend now, Johnny. You know that?"

Suddenly I felt a tear forming in my eye. When was the last time I had cried? At my father's funeral? At my mother's funeral? Maybe at both. I tried not to cry at either because I knew that big boys didn't cry. But, as I remember, I couldn't hold back. Now was the same. I couldn't hold back. Something about Lauren trusting me to brush her hair or saying that I was her only friend and the fact that she hadn't cried yet or all the above or none of the above. If I ever got back to my regular Wednesday night poker game, I'd have to ask my psychiatrist friend. He'd know. He knew all these things.

"Are you going to brush?" she asked in a whisper, still in a monotone. I think she was suffering from mild shock.

I removed the towel from her hair and began stroking.

"Long, firm, but soft strokes," she directed.

I obeyed. Long, firm, but soft strokes. Her hair got softer and drier. She moaned. I thought I heard her mutter Doloras's name a few times. Then I thought I could hear faint sobs.

"Are you okay?" I asked, leaning close to her face. I could see the tear stains on the pillow.

"I'm okay if you stay with me," she said. "With Doloras gone, you're all I have. She took care of me and she was so gentle. Gentle like you're being right now. Can you be gentle Johnny?"

I put down the brush and began rubbing her shoulders. My father had been a cop. My mother had been a masseuse, so I'd learned things from both. Mom had taught me pressure points of the body like acupuncture. She could put me and my father to sleep by using those points. She could also remove pain, headaches, backaches--now

I was wondering if I could help remove Lauren's heartache. My mother never showed me that point.

"That feels good," she purred. "Where'd you learn that stuff. It feels professional."

"My mother," I said. "She taught me how to rub."

On a whim, I glanced out the window.

It was there.

The glare.

So I turned out the light. I could have pulled down the shade, but then I would have broken the spell I was casting on Lauren's back, and I knew if I continued, she would soon be asleep.

It was a half-moon which lit the room just enough for me to see Lauren's prettiness, but not enough for anyone to see into the room from across the street, no matter what kind of viewing device they were using.

Lauren wriggled out of her robe, but remained on her stomach. "This make it easier?" she asked.

"Yes," I gasped looking at her back, her round but firm buttocks, down her shapely legs to her little feet. "Much easier to find the pressure points."

I moved my fingers deftly up and down her spine. She moaned.

I kept staring at her bottom, her legs slightly spread so I could detect a soft mound of dark fuzz between where her legs came together. Then I placed my fingers gently in a place that my mother had never told me about. Lauren's first reaction was to tighten up, but she quickly relaxed again and spread her legs a little wider. I continued rubbing ever so gently. The more I rubbed, the more she moaned.

Rub, moan.

Rub, moan.

She rose herself up on her knees just a few inches, giving my hand more leeway to maneuver. I rubbed with longer strokes. She was wet. And the wetness was hot.

Suddenly, she jerked her body--once--twice, then collapsed on my hand.

"Okay?" I whispered.

"Okay now," she whispered back. "With Doloras gone I hope you'll take care of me. I have no one I can trust in the whole world--

except you. Doloras liked you Johnny, so you must be all right. And I like you too, Johnny. You're gentle like Doloras. She always told me that men were all alike. But she was wrong about you, Johnny. You're different. I can tell. You care about people. You care about me. You care..."

Lauren was mumbling. She was totally relaxed. Totally spent. Soon she was deep in sleep. I rolled over on my back and soon followed her into the land of dreams. Things never are as bad as they seem, so dream, dream, dream.

Chapter 12
THE CHALET
Boston Post headline,
Tuesday, December 14, 1945:
PRESIDENT TRUMAN HAS REQUESTED NATIONAL HEALTH INSURANCE

U ncle Bill sighed relief upon hearing my voice. "I'm running out of fresh groceries," he said. "Want me to start eating out of cans?"

"Send Rose shopping," I said, then told him some of what had occurred during the past few days, leaving out the Hitler part. "She'll shop for you. Tell her to stay out of the office till I get back. I don't like the people I'm dealing with in this case. And I'll make it up to you guys at Jake Wirth's for a nice dinner."

I dialed Red Kelly. They'd autopsied Doloras's body and I was right. No alcohol. Then he went to see Mrs. Averly using my name as a reference. At first she hesitated. Then, after hearing about Doloras and the possibility that the same people who killed Doloras may have killed her husband and her father, she changed her tune. No one had ever even told her that alcohol had been involved in her father's accident. Her brother had taken care of all the funeral arrangements.

Kelly showed her the official accident report and it was just as Tony had reported to me. Mrs. Averly swore her father never touched alcohol, so assented to the exhumation, which would be held this afternoon.

I still hadn't told Kelly about my suspicions about Hitler, thinking he'd declare me nuts. Everyone in the world knew that Adolf Hitler, his wife Eva Braun and his German shepard dog had died in a Berlin bunker. No Americans had ever seen the bodies or remains, but everyone still believed.

Lou was chipper and ready to go. He had had a good night's sleep, downed eggs, bacon, toast and coffee. My sleep was as fitful as it had been the night before, but at least Lauren's head wasn't on my lap all night.

I enjoyed a large bowl of oatmeal, toast and orange juice. Lauren sat in silence, never looking up from her plate of scrambled eggs. Once I reached over to touch her hand. She quickly pulled away. "Please don't take my attitude personally," she said to both of us. "Time. It'll take me some time to get used to not ever seeing Doloras again. We were special friends. She was my only friend."

I wondered if Lauren had forgotten about the past night. What she had said to me and what I'd done. Then she began sobbing, got up from the table and excused herself. "I'll be okay later. Good luck today, guys. Sorry I can't be of more help."

Then she left the room.

"Hit her pretty hard, didn't it?" Lou said. "Sorry for her and sorry for you. I know how much you care. But, time. She's right about that. Time heals all wounds."

Lou borrowed one pair of snowshoes from the hotel. When we left, I checked the second story window across the street and thought I saw the curtain move. But, then maybe I was just imagining it. I felt kind of jumpy, anyway. Lack of sleep. Lauren. Doloras. The exhumation. Uncle Bill and Rose together without me for protection. I was overly anxious.

We rode up the mountain on the first chair-lift. A sparse crowd on a midweek day. The temperature seemed to cooperate. Twenty degrees. Wind five miles per hour with a bright sunshine.

Do our worst fears really come true? I couldn't help look back each time the chair-lift reached the next high tower--some of them over sixty feet above the terrain.

"Don't be such a 'fraidy cat'", Lou teased. "What can happen? Stowe's the first mountain in the country to use chair-lifts. They're all brand new."

I shivered as we reached one tower at least seventy feet high, slowed down and stopped. "That's what I'm worried about, Lou. We're guinea pigs for this operation. What happens if this thing slips backwards?"

Lou grinned and poked me in the arm. "They have safety brakes for that eventuality, silly man. Don't worry so much."

I felt my heart jump into my throat as the chair began to slide back towards the little house from where we began--about two thousand yards straight down. "When do they apply those safety brakes you told me about, Lou?"

We were early enough in the day so only about every other chair was occupied. Maybe thirty to fifty people. I noticed some of the skiers on the lower chairs closer to the ground had already jumped off--maybe six to ten feet above the snow. Lou and I were still over fifty feet high. I knew I couldn't fly and I wasn't ready to break a leg just yet. "Tell me when to evacuate, pal," I called through the wind-whipped cold air hitting our bodies.

For the first time Lou's face appeared concerned as he squinted and tightened his body. "See the next tower?" he pointed as we approached at an increasing high speed. The metal towers were high and the dips between, quite a bit lower. "After that one, it looks like we'll only be about twenty feet above the snow at the lowest dip. If the brakes haven't kicked in by then, we'll bail. Okay?"

As we speeded up, out of control, anything seemed better than the thought of crashing into that house at thirty or forty miles an hour.

We slowed down as we reached the top of the tower, then sped up again like a roller coaster. "Get ready to drop your skis," Lou yelled--"and your poles. You don't want to get skewered."

I was ready, but scared shitless.

Just as we approached the lowest dip in the cable, maybe twenty feet above the trail, the chair-lift came to an abrupt halt. "Told ya," Lou forced a smile. "Great safety brakes."

We sat for about two minutes, freezing our tails off, before the chair-lift began its ascent back to the summit.

God, I hated skiing.

I agreed that Lou would go ahead and I would stay at the summit to make sure no one followed. He would get as close to the chalet as possible--then snap pictures through his telescopic lens, hoping to get something worthwhile. Mainly, Mr. Hitler.

"If I'm not back by three-thirty, that means we're fucked," Lou smiled. "But I'll be back long before that," he assured me.

He strapped on his skis and was gone over the first hill toward the chalet. I stood and watched for several minutes, then spied a binocular contraption affixed to a tripod and inviting the insertion of a nickel. It was aimed at New York state, I don't know how many miles away. I pushed and pulled and twisted. It budged, then slid around just enough to catch the corner of the chalet. I put in a nickel and immediately saw Lou climbing a small hill with his snowshoes. If I had enough nickels I could probably follow his progress almost to within a half mile of the chalet. I checked my watch. Ten o'clock. I decided to ski down the easy trail marked by green. Blue was harder and black the most difficult. I'd stay away from those. I'd get lots of nickels and ride back up the lift. I wouldn't be gone more than an hour, depending on the lift lines. What could happen in an hour?

I hooked a ride with a snow grooming machine on the way back to the top. I think I'd had my fill of shaky new chair-lifts. My watch read exactly eleven-thirty. Someone was using the binoculars.

Then someone else.

Then me.

I pushed in the nickel and turned the contraption toward the chalet.

Nothing.

I watched for at least a half hour, feeding the thing furiously with nickels.

Still nothing.

I walked over to the spot where Lou had put on his skis and left me that morning.

Something seemed out of place. I spotted Lou's parallel ski tracks. But, right beside them were another set of tracks, not there earlier. We had been the first people to the top of the mountain so they couldn't have been there before. Someone had followed Lou's tracks and I didn't need many guesses. The person behind the moving curtain?

There were several people milling around the deck. One older gentleman was sitting with his back against the building wall, sunning himself.

"Excuse me," I said, touching his side with my ski pole. "How long have you been up here?"

He opened his eyes, squinted into the sun over my shoulder and grunted. "Who wants to know?"

"My name's Jonathan Dark," I answered. "A friend of mine went off toward that chalet over there early in the day. I wonder if you saw anyone else go in that direction?"

The older gentleman seemed to be checking me out. Was I okay? Finally he must have decided I was harmless. "A ski patrol guy. Tall, blond with a heavy accent. Hans, I think his name is. He hung around for awhile, then took off over there." He pointed toward the chalet. "Funny. He carried snowshoes and a long leather case. Looked like a fishing pole, maybe. I didn't know there were any ponds up here."

"Thanks," I said. "Sorry to interrupt your sunning."

I felt inside the back of my parka. Shit. I'd left my pistol in the room. Great detective. Movie star Dana Andrews wouldn't forget his weapon. On the other hand, he had the advantage of reading the script. I hadn't.

Gunless, I began to follow the double tracks, praying I wouldn't be too late. I didn't think our ski patroller was going on a fishing expedition. More than likely his leather case concealed a rifle. Damn. I had no snowshoes either. Plus, I was a lousy skier with a bum knee.

Before I arrived at the first steep incline, I had fallen at least a dozen times. I could see where the snowshoes had taken over for the skis.

Four indentations.

Two men.

I removed my skis and walked in the snowshoe tracks, which had been matted down somewhat. Sometimes, I sank down almost to my knees, which hampered my forward progress.

At the top of the next hill, I put on my skis and pushed as fast as possible. This time I must have travelled about a thousand yards and only fell three or four times. I was improving.

The next hill was higher and harder. The snow was deeper. But, I made it.

From the peak I could see the chalet. I must have trekked at least a mile. But, I still couldn't see any sign of life. Neither Lou nor Hans was in sight.

I clamped on my skis and off I went. Faster and fewer falls. The next incline appeared almost impossible. Over most of it I moved on my hands and knees. When I arrived at the top, I noticed that the snowshoe tracks changed direction. There was a flat terrain for about five hundred yards. Lou had gone one way, Hans another. I figured that the shortest distance between two points was straight ahead. Did I make up that philosophy? I deduced that Lou had gone straight. Hans must have decided he was getting too close to his prey and maybe circled around. I put on my skis and pushed forward again. Not up and not down, just straight. I made pretty good time.

Between the bright sun glaring off the white snow, my total exhaustion and the violent pain in my knee, I began to feel frustrated and useless. I couldn't travel another hundred yards, possessed an empty holster, and maybe was lost.

Suddenly I saw the epitome of the devil. Hans, dressed all in black, standing with his side to me behind a three-foot wall of snow, aiming something that glittered in the sunlight. Apparently he'd built a snow fort, hid in it to observe something--most likely Lou. I estimated him at about two hundred fifty to three hundred feet away. I could yell, then maybe attract his attention and get shot. Or, I could try something else. I didn't have much time. I removed my mittens and tried to form a snowball, but the day was cold and the snow fluffy.

One chance.

Wet the snow.

With what?

I racked my tired and cold brain.

Yes.

Piss.

I lowered my pants and pissed as fast as I could. My dick almost froze, but luckily, the liquid didn't. Must've been the previous night's alcohol. I quickly rolled up a yellow snowball, reared back, aimed and fired, recollecting my many throws from center field in the Boston Park League, nailing surprised runners at home plate.

Bullseye.

The snowball hit its target somewhere on the face.

The crack of a rifle split the wintery silence, hopefully alerting Lou from wherever he was hiding.

I squatted down in the snow and waited.

Nothing happened.

I peeked toward Hans' hiding place.

No sign of him. No sign of Lou.

I decided to backtrack and follow the other trail, hopefully to where Lou built his fort. My knee ached, my leg tingled and began to freeze. Maybe that would help to keep me going. Didn't they stand bad-legged race horses in ice before races?.

It must've taken me a half hour to double back, find Lou's trail and follow it to a dead end. Or what appeared to be a dead end. Instead, it was the biggest snow fort I'd ever seen. Higher than Hans had built. At least five foot walls of snow. I crawled forward, and around, quietly as to not be shot by my own ally. There was Lou, sitting in a snow hole with his tripod and telescoped camera aimed at the chalet that was less than a half mile away.

He turned quickly, aiming a pistol at my head. "What are you doing here?" he asked, looking back at his apparatus.

"A mysterious ski patroller's been following you all morning," I said. "I think you're lucky to still be alive. Didn't you hear the gunshot a little while ago?"

"Maybe we're both lucky to still be alive," Lou said. "With the strong wind blowing away from the chalet I can't hear anything behind me. Then again, maybe my snow fort fooled him. Did you have any trouble seeing me?"

"If it wasn't for your tracks, I wouldn't have seen you at all," I answered. "But Hans saw you from another angle and would've blown you away if I hadn't hit him with an ice ball." I decided not to explain how I'd manufactured the snowball in the dry flakes.

The back and left side of Lou's fort boasted five feet walls. The front about two feet and the right side, three feet. Hans must've been off somewhere to the right to have been able to place a crouching Lou in his sights. Unless, of course, he was hunting deer, which never dawned on me. At least I was sure he wasn't fishing.

"See any sign of deer around?" I asked.

"Too high up," he said. "Deer eat bark and leaves. No trees up here."

That crossed the deer possibility off my list.

"Hans may have both of us in his sights right now," I said.

Lou moved the snow around, dug his hole deeper and peeked toward the right with his high-powered camera lens. "Can't see anything," he said. "Maybe your ice ball knocked him out."

Lou turned the lens back toward the chalet. "Look," he said. "I've been staring through this thing all day."

I looked and saw the chalet pretty clearly. In front of the building was a large deck. On the deck appeared to be some sort of a pool with steam rising from it. "What's that pool?" I asked.

"In Switzerland they call it a hot tub. Over one hundred degrees. Skiers sit in it naked after skiing and then jump into the cold snow. Hot. Cold. Does something for the system. Must be invigorating."

"Anyone use it today?" I asked.

"A few," he said. "I got some good pictures of them. I'm waiting for our pal Adolf to use it."

We both took turns watching for the next few minutes. Lou had brought some chocolate bars which kind of kept our stomachs from aching for food. I borrowed Lou's pistol and kept it in my hand, half expecting Hans to jump us at any moment.

"Look at that woman," Lou said, pushing my head in front of the tripod. "Look familiar?"

She did. But I didn't know why. She was about thirty, brownish hair, nice athletic figure. She removed a robe and climbed into the tub. A few minutes later she was followed by an older man, dark haired, not overweight, but definitely familiar.

I handed the tripod back to Lou. "Recognize that man?" I asked.

Lou frantically started clicking his camera. "Got to get a good clear picture of this. That's Eva Braun in there with Adolf. I read somewhere that she was an accomplished gymnast. That explains her hard build. Supposedly he promised to take her to Hollywood someday and get her in the movies. Not a bad-looking woman." He continued clicking. "Hey, here comes two more. A pretty chick with big tits and...yup...it's Richard Averly."

We had what we wanted. Proof that Hitler was still alive and his exact location. But, the information was no good if we couldn't get it off the mountain and I suspected that Hans had no intention of allowing that.

"I'm going to follow the other tracks again," I told Lou. "You pack up and get ready to leave. Give me a half-hour. If I don't come

back, get the hell out of here as fast as your little skis will carry
you."

Lou nodded.

I put on my skis, borrowed Lou's pistol and backtracked across
the flat terrain to the spot where the tracks had parted. I no longer
had any feeling in my leg. Was that a good sign? Then I began
following Hans's tracks. For awhile it was easy. Same flat terrain.
Then it went down a bit where I fell a few times. Then up. I
wondered if Hans might not have moved from his original spot.

A piss snowball couldn't have killed him.

No such luck.

I stopped and looked. I stared into the whiteness of snow, snow
and more snow. I had heard of the term--snow blindness. I could
have been staring at Hans at that moment and still not have seen
him. Hans could have been staring at me and have me in his rifle
sights.

Then I saw it.

Hans's fort.

Not as high walls as Lou's. But, definitely a good hiding place.
I would never have spotted him earlier if he hadn't stood up to take
aim at Lou and the sun glared off his rifle. He wasn't more than fifty
yards from my location. I dropped my skis and drew Lou's gun. The
next fifty yards would be travelled on my stomach. If Hans saw me
and decided to shoot, he'd have a small target. The top of my head.

I got to within five feet of his fort. No one had shot me yet. It
must have been my lucky day.

I crawled three more feet, then jumped up and sprung over the
top of the fort wall. Hans couldn't turn fast enough to stop my
momentum as I crashed into his back. We both fell to the snow
together. I flailed out with my mittened hand and caught him on the
side of his head. It stunned him for a moment, long enough for me
to right myself, sit up and aim Lou's gun at his gut. "Playing in the
snow, Hans?" I asked, waving the pistol.

"Vat you do here, svine?" he yelled. "I just do my job."

"Ski patrolling?" I asked in a flippant tone and noticed blood
seeping from his left eye.

"No. Follow you. I do vat I'm told and ask no questions. I'm
loyal."

"That's what those criminals are saying at Nuremburg," I said. "Good defense, but I don't think it'll work. Someone's gotta pay for those six million Jews who burned in your ovens."

"Jews. Jews. Too many Jews," Hans mumbled. "This whole thing is fault of Jews. Don't you see? If everyone just left Hitler alone, he vould have saved vorld for Aryans like you and me."

I held the gun firmly, aiming at Hans' midsection. From his vantage point, he could see Lou's fort just about a hundred yards away. I wondered why he hadn't made a second attempt on Lou's life. Or mine.

"What were you waiting for, Hans?" I asked. "You got a great bead on my partner over there."

"I aim vith this eye," he pointed to the bloody, closed one. "Something hit me few hours ago. I don't know vat it vas. An icy snow ball. A smelly one."

I looked around his fort. Skis. Snowshoes. A knapsack and a rifle with silencer. "What's the rifle for Hans?" I asked. "Hunting bear?"

He flashed me a 'fuck you' expression.

My watch said it was time to go back to Lou. "I've got to leave now, Hans," I said. "How can I trust you not to plug me in the back?"

Hans grinned, revealing a missing tooth. "Take rifle vith you," he said.

Little did he know that I'd only shot one person in my life and that was more instinct than planned. The monocled man.

I didn't know what I'd do if Hans ran.

I didn't know what I'd do if he grabbed for the gun.

I did know I had to protect Lou.

I picked up Hans's rifle and threw it about thirty feet away. Then I did the same to his knapsack. No sense in taking his skis or snowshoes because he could easily walk to the chalet. Then I bid him goodbye. "Don't follow or I'll shoot," I threatened, hoping he'd believe me.

I headed straight for Lou. Not the roundabout way I'd followed in Hans's tracks. After not more than twenty feet, a loud crack broke the snowy silence and I felt a sharp pain in my shoulder. I dropped and turned around at the same time to see Hans aiming a small pistol directly at me, flame spitting out of its barrel. A pellet whistled by my ear. I reached back, drew Lou's pistol and fired. Once, twice, three times. All the years practicing at the Berkeley Street target range with Red Kelly seemed to pay off because Hans grabbed at his stomach. I fired the final three shots just because I was pissed at him for shooting me or pissed at myself for being so stupid to turn my back. Then I watched Hans fall forward onto his face.

I felt nothing.

No remorse.

No thrill.

I'd just killed another human being and felt nothing. Did I have a lot of choices in the deadly matters? No.

Maybe I would've made a good infantryman in the US Army. I wondered what the guards felt in the Dachau prison eliminating prisoners in the horrible ovens? How many choices did they have? Weren't they just doing what they were ordered?

I turned towards Lou, who I found out later was watching through his telescope.

He met me halfway, bandaged my shoulder as best he could and we began our trek down the mountain. "Do you think anyone heard the shots?" I asked.

"I barely did," he answered. "Luckily the wind was blowing against you. No one on the chalet deck ever looked in our direction."

My shoulder ached worse than I let on. My knee had no feeling at all. I'd been a private eye for ten years and in one week had shot my first two people and been shot once. As William Bendix said every week on radio's popular *Life Of Riley* show, 'What A Revolting Development This Is'. The entire adventure was a new experience that I didn't relish.

"Only a flesh wound," Lou assured me. "I'm sure you'll get lots of sympathy from Lauren."

When we made the bottom of the hill, I immediately sought out the first aid room and asked Lou to check the building across the street and see who occupied the second floor center suite.

An overweight, but jolly nurse asked lots of questions about my wound, saying she was excellent and bored at setting broken bones, but out of practice at fixing bullet wounds. "Would you believe a hunting accident?" I said.

She poured peroxide into the wound and I yelled OUCH. "Hunting season's been over for a month," she replied. "You're mighty lucky the bullet was small and went clean through."

I felt I would have been luckier if the bullet had missed completely. "How about I was cleaning my gun?" I said.

She gave me a warm smile and said, "That sounds a little more plausible. I don't have to report gun-cleaning accidents."

I dropped my drawers and showed her my mangled knee.

"Old injury?" she said, probing lightly with her fingers. "Appears to be out of joint." She squeezed and twisted quickly and tightly, immediately bringing the feeling back to my leg--enough feeling to make me scream out loud.

"There," she said. "Get your feeling back?"

I grunted with tears in my eyes. "I certainly have. What the hell did you do?"

"Osteopath stuff," she said. "Studied it in school. Not used much, but sometimes works wonders."

"Will I be able to walk ever again?" I asked, noticing the pain subsiding.

"Maybe better than ever," she smiled.

"Where were you when I tried out for the Red Sox?" I asked.

She flashed a quizzical look, then offered some pain-killing pills which I readily accepted.

Lou returned to pick me up and the nurse assured him I would live. "A good night's rest will do him a world of good." She handed me a wooden crutch. "You may need this for a day or two."

Lou helped me limp back to our hotel. "The room across the street is registered to a Hans Kaufman," he said.

"I guess we don't have to worry about Hans Kaufman spying on us anymore," I added.

Chapter 13
THE FBI
Boston Post headline,
Tuesday, December 14, 1945:
CHARLES DE GAULLE ELECTED
PRESIDENT OF FRANCE

T hey exhumed Mr. Averly's body," Red Kelly told me on the phone. "You were right again. No alcohol. His daughter totally lost it. Broke down and had to be sedated."

Poor Mrs. Averly, I thought. What could happen to her next?

I related the day's happenings to Kelly, leaving out the shooting of Hans Kaufman and the suspicions of who was on the rolls of film taken by Lou. I bit my tongue several times in lieu of revealing the perfect strike I threw at Hans Kaufman's eye that most likely saved Lou's life. I was sure it wouldn't show up in any of tomorrow's box scores.

"I got a pal with the FBI," Kelly said. "After finding out that Mr. Averly was murdered and that his brewery in Berlin reopened right afterwards, I decided to call him. Funny thing, though. He seemed to know all about the case. Almost more than I do. What do you make of that, Johnny?"

I didn't know and didn't want to pretend to know. But, I did know that Lou had pictures of Hitler, Eva Braun and Richard Averly frolicking in a hot tub. And, I knew that Tony had told me he had something Richard wanted, maybe enough to kill for. Obviously, Tony had either told or showed Richard the photo taken in South Boston and asked for the money he needed to cover his gambling debts. If he hadn't had that disagreement with his wife, the whole affair may never have happend.

"How much do you trust this FBI guy?" I asked.

"He and I served in the Marines together," Kelly said. "We risked our lives storming a beach-head side by side, making us like blood brothers, or some shit like that--I guess."

Since I'd never served, I didn't know what that shit meant, but did trust Kelly. If he said the FBI guy was okay, that would have to be good enough for me. For now.

"We've been watched the whole time we've been here," I told him. "Like someone knows our every move."

"Not by the Boston or Provincetown police," Kelly said. "You're not even wanted anymore. I told you that. But, Erv Locke would like to talk with you."

"What's an Erv Locke?" I asked.

"He's my FBI buddy," Kelly answered. "After I told him about your story he seemed quite anxious to talk to you. Are you in Vermont?"

Kelly surprised me with the question. He didn't know where I was. I hesitated. Had I slipped up that much in my phone conversations?

"Yeah. How do you know?" I asked.

"I told you that Erv seemed to know more than I did about your case. He mentioned Vermont. I think by mistake, so I didn't pick up on it. But, if you're in Vermont, maybe whatever you're into is federal."

"Lou's going back down to Boston tomorrow morning," I said. "I want you to meet him at the Post newspaper office. Bring the Feds if you want. Lou'll develop the pictures right while you guys are there. I can't think of a better witness than someone from the FBI. When you see what he's got, you'll shit."

"How long a drive from Vermont?" Kelly asked.

"He'll leave at eight. Give him six hours. He'll meet you guys in the newspaper darkroom at two in the afternoon."

"Now that I know where you are, can you give me some kind of number where I can reach you?" Kelly asked.

I obliged. I told him the name of the hotel and the telephone number.

Lauren and Lou were waiting for me in the dining room. Lauren seemed more with it and the two of them were briskly chatting away.

Lauren was wearing a dress, off both shoulders like a gypsy. I liked the look. I liked the soft milky whiteness of her shoulders. I believe I was biased. She kissed me on the cheek. "How's your shoulder?" She noticed me admiring hers and seemed genuinely concerned with mine.

"It hurts a little, but I'll survive. I got these great pain pills. They send me on a trip."

"And your leg?" I placed the crutch against an empty chair.

"Better than the shoulder," I answered.

She seemed to be studying my wrecked body. "Someone once told me that the best way to get rid of a pain is to get a worse one. In other words, if you have a headache, then get a toothache; you'll soon forget about the headache."

Lou and I glanced at each other. "Makes sense, "I said, shrugging at Lou.

"Makes sense to me too," Lou said. "If we cut his finger, he'll forget about his shoulder and knee."

The three of us laughed.

Lou had ordered me a scotch on the rocks. A double. Along with the pain pills, I now felt no pain, so no need to cut my finger. Lauren was sipping something fruity-looking and Lou was downing a Manhattan.

Our dinner was interrupted by a phone call from Kelly that I took in the phone booth located in the lobby. "What's up Red?" I asked. "Didn't we just talk?"

"Yeah. Yeah," he said. "I told Erv about the pictures. He suddenly got real concerned. Then told me that Richard Averly's a government agent and that the guy you took pictures of is a high ranking Nazi informant who is dealing with the prosecution in the Nuremberg trials. That guy, whoever he is, is in a special Government protection program. That's why they've got him sealed away on top of a remote mountain."

I didn't know how to respond. Was I in any position to argue with the FBI? I didn't think so, especially over two hundred miles away. As far as Kelly was concerned, the Nazi in the chalet was just a high-ranking official in the German hierarchy. Lou and I and Lauren knew differently. Doloras and Tony knew differently too, but they were now dead. "Does Erv know who the guy is?" I asked.

"Ask him yourself," Kelly said and put FBI Agent Erv Locke on the line.

"John Dark?" He had a brusque, officious voice and talked fast. All business. "Allow me to introduce myself. Ervine Locke, Boston branch of the Federal Bureau of Investigation. We've had our eye on you ever since you were hired by Mrs. Averly. Were you aware of that?"

"I was aware that I've been watched on and off for the past week. Yes," I said. "But I didn't know it was the FBI."

"Well, it has been us all the time. That Nazi informant is most important to the Nuremberg trials and to chief prosecutor Jackson's case. Up to this point, the information he's fed us has guaranteed at least nine hangings and several life sentences. Thanks to him, we know all the lies they're going to tell before they testify. When they lie, they're trapped. Our informant is a valuable cog in the wheel of justice. Do you want to fuck that up, Dark?"

"No, sir," I answered hurriedly. "Not in your life. I would never want to interfere with any government stuff. But I didn't know. All I know is that ever since I was hired on a simple case to find Mrs. Averly's husband, people have been dropping dead like flies. That usually doesn't happen to me. I never even fired my gun till this week."

"Time's come for you to drop out of the case," the agent said in a firm and almost threatening tone. "Then maybe no one else will get hurt."

Was he intimidating me? Or, was this just a friendly warning? I decided to be an asshole and ask a few questions. Hell, I was a taxpaying citizen and had my rights. "Do you know the identity of the informant?"

There was a moment of silence on the other end of the line. I could hear the inhaling of a cigarette which reminded me to light one of my own. So I did, filling the small booth with smoke and causing me to cough. As I slid open the door so I could breathe, Locke answered my question. "All I know is that he's a high-ranking official that Richard Averly helped smuggle out of Berlin. They don't tell us any more than we need to know. Satisfied?"

Locke's attitude was beginning to grate on my nerves. "Is it important who murdered Mr. Averly?" I asked. "Or doesn't that have anything to do with this case?"

Locke cleared his throat. "That's not in my jurisdiction. Ask Detective Kelly about that."

I decided to be an asshole again. "In other words, you guys do your job and don't give a shit who killed Averly or Mrs. Averly's husband."

Locke cleared his throat again. "I didn't say that, Dark. I just follow orders and Red will tell you I'm good at what I do."

I thought about his answer and decided to shove it up his ass. It was becoming all too familiar. "Isn't that the defense the Nuremberg defendants are using? All they did was what they were told?"

"Different," Locke stuttered. "Much different with our government."

Fortunately, he couldn't see the negative nod of my head. "Look Mr. Locke, or agent Locke, whatever you're called, I was hired to do a job and just did what I was told. First, I found Tony Coraloni, Mrs. Averly's husband. He was killed right in front of me by some guy wearing a monocle. Then I was hired again by Mrs. Averly to find her missing brother. I found him. Here. In a remote chalet on Mount Mansfield. So my job is done. Okay?"

I detected a deep breathing. "Red didn't tell me you found Richard Averly," Locke sounded frantic.

"What do you think I'm doing in Vermont?" I asked.

"Looking, not finding," he answered.

"Ask Red. He'll tell you I'm also good at what I do."

"Maybe too good for your own good," Locke mumbled so I could hardly hear.

"What was that?" I asked.

"Nothing. Nothing," he said. "Red did tell me you're a good detective on small matters."

I accepted the backhanded complimented without a wisecrack. "Put Kelly back on the phone, please," I said in my most pleasant voice. I was beginning to dislike my friend's marine buddy.

I waited for a few seconds.

"Johnny?" It was Kelly's voice.

"Locke is a pompous ass," I said. "You may trust him, but I don't. Something's fishy. I can smell it and feel it."

"He's okay," Kelly said. "He's just trying to protect their informant. It's his job, damnit."

"Just do this one favor for me, Red. Meet Lou tomorrow. Look at his pictures. Then call me. Bring pompous ass with you, if you want. Let him look at the pictures. I'm telling you, Red, there's a lot more to this whole thing than meets the eye. People don't die this mysteriously for no reason."

"Okay John," he said.

"Be careful," were my last two words before hanging up and I didn't know why I'd uttered them. Be careful of what? I didn't know. But the more I thought about it, the more I meant it. All of us had better start being careful.

We finished our dinner. I filled Lou in on the conversation with Kelly and Locke. He didn't seem concerned. As a matter of fact, he almost seemed relieved that the FBI was in on the case. "J. Edgar Hoover is one the most respected officials in Washington," he said. "A personal appointment by Franklin Delano Roosevelt. I think we can breathe easier now."

After Lou's third Manhattan, he bid us goodnight and was gone. Lauren and I sat in front of the fire for almost an hour without conversation. I didn't know what to say about Doloras or even if I should bring it up.

Finally Lauren broke the ice and told me about a poem she had learned in school called *Nature Boy*. It ended with these lines: 'The greatest thing you'll ever know is just to love and be loved in return'.

"You agree with that?" she looked over at me and asked.

The flickering flames from the fire were playing shadow games on Lauren's pretty face and shoulders. I had wanted to kiss her moist lips all evening. I had wanted to kiss her moist lips ever since I met her last week. "Agree with what?" I asked, not quite tuned into her thoughts.

"The poem, silly. The poem I just told you about *Nature Boy*."

"What are the words?" I asked. "My mind was wandering."

"The greatest thing you'll ever know is just to love and be loved in return," she said melodically.

I thought about it. "I guess," I answered. "I mean, I don't really know. It's only a poem and all poems are about love."

She dropped her head and I began to feel like an asshole because of my unfeeling answer. Lauren wasn't seeking an analytical interpretation. She was looking for something more emotional. Guys are analytical. Dames are emotional. Let's face it. The Lord made us differently. But, He also gave us the gray matter to reason and figure out when we screwed up.

"You're probably right," I said quickly, placing my hand on her bare shoulder. She didn't remove it. "Yes. The more I think of it, you're right. That is the greatest thing someone can learn. But not easily attainable."

Lauren broke out in tears. I'd said the wrong thing again. I should've stopped while I was ahead and not added the part of how hard it was to attain that feeling. Especially since she'd already found it with Doloras. Lauren had found love and had been loved in return.

I moved my chair beside hers and put my arms around her so she could cry into my bulky sweater. She did lots, and I could feel the wetness seeping onto my chest. "There, there," I said. "Let it all out. Big girls can cry all they want. It'll do you good. Think of it this way. Better to have had the relationship and lost it than to never have had it at all."

She looked up at me, her eyes red and swollen from the crying. "You think so?" she said in a whisper. "Maybe some people never have that experience. Maybe a person could go a whole lifetime and never experience what happens in the poem, *Nature Boy*."

"I never have," I said, telling the truth. "Not even close."

She kissed my chin. "Poor boy," she said. "Poor, poor Johnny. Maybe you can learn to love me."

Chapter 14
LOU DISAPPEARS
Boston Post headline,
Wednesday, December 15, 1945:
PRESIDENT TRUMAN NAMES GENERAL
GEORGE C. MARSHALL SPECIAL ENVOY
TO CHINA IN ATTEMPT TO MEDIATE
CIVIL WAR WITH COMMUNISTS

Private investigators develop instincts of impending doom. Something was telling me that Lauren and I should get the hell out of the hotel where we were staying. Erv Locke had admitted that the FBI had had their eyes on us since we arrived. He all but admitted that Hans worked for the FBI and Hans seemed to me like a loyal Nazi. I wasn't too mixed up. With Hans gone, I wondered who else had their eyes on us and how safe we were even staying in Stowe. It certainly was no longer a secret hiding place.

Lou and I had made up our minds of the importance of someone making sure the group from the chalet didn't fly the coop until he could release his pictures. I volunteered.

Lou's trip to Boston set up one of the greatest news stories in history with pictures to prove it. Once made public and the hoax uncovered, Lou would become a world renowned photographer. And, he deserved it. He'd risked his life for those pictures. And mine.

Before Lou left for Boston in his station wagon, he handed me an undeveloped roll of film. "I took two rolls," he explained. "Good photography dictates lots and lots of shots of the same thing. You can never know what you've got till the developing fluid rolls over the paper. Keep this in a safe place. I hope for my sake, you never have to develop it."

One main highway led into Stow and I'd noticed a cabin park just on the outskirts of town. A good lookout spot to check who leaves and who enters the area.

Lou left me his tripod and telescope, and from the cabins, I could catch a glimpse of the entrance to the old logging road leading to the chalet. I instructed the town's only cabby to drop Lauren and me at a bus stop located about a mile from the cabins. When the cab was out of view, we walked.

I always carried an authentic looking alias in my wallet. Mr. U. N. Owen, an insurance salesman from Springfield, Massachusetts. I picked up the name from an Agatha Christie murder mystery, *The Ten Little Indians*. Mr. U.N. Owen meant Mr. Unknown. I carried an authentic drivers license, a social security number and even a 4F draft card with Owen's name.

We checked into the Stowe cabin park under the name Mr. and Mrs. Owen. "Lucky it's Wednesday," the bald seventyish clerk said. "On weekends we're filled to the rafters."

I noticed a payphone on the wall of the office and a Sunday edition of the Boston Post. I gave him a nickel for the two day-old-paper and wondered if the exhumation of Mr. Averly had been covered by reporters who hung around morgues.

The cabins were small one-room affairs but contained a fireplace with gas logs, bathroom with shower stall, sink, ice box, two-burner plug-in, dining table, four chairs and a radio. Lauren turned on the radio, then lay down on the smallish bed while I set up my tripod to look out the back window at the logging road.

About a half-mile away was a gas station and grocery store. I picked up supplies for two days--cold cereal, milk, bread, margarine, Pepsi and some beer. I also picked out some magazines: *Life*, *Colliers*, and the *Saturday Evening Post*, for which Norman Rockwell had painted a ski mountain scene on its cover. It looked like Stowe. It could very well have been Stowe, since Rockwell was a native New Englander.

The grocery bags were heavy. The war had only been over a few months and people in the 'boonies' were still using food stamps--of which I had none. That meant no fresh meat, but canned meat, canned beans, and canned vegetables. But no steaks. I decided to attempt a small bribe. No harm in that. I flashed a hundred dollar bill at the proprietor, a middle-aged, heavy set man with thick hairy arms exposed by his rolled-up, food stained sleeves.

"What's that for, son?" he grunted. "Who've I gotta murder?"

"Lamb chops?" I said with a smile. "My stamps were stolen." I hoped he'd feel sorry for me.

He went behind the meat counter. I heard him chopping something. Then he emerged, more stains on his shirt and with something wrapped in white paper, placed it on the scale, which read four pounds. He took my hundred, rang it up in his register and handed me back ninety-five dollars. "The war's over friend," he said. "I got some nice goodies for people I like."

I flashed my friendliest smile, pushed a fiver into his hand, and tightly folded his fingers over it. "And I only tip people I really like," I said.

It was mid-December, vacation beginning for school kids, meaning heavy crowds and an early dropping sun. I'd planned to wait till five and call Lou.

Upon my arrival back at the cabins, I dialed the newspaper. No one had seen Lou since he'd left for vacation. Alarmed, I dialed Red Kelly. He'd been out on an important appointment since two o'clock. Now I was really alarmed.

At five-thirty I duplicated my calls.

Nothing.

At six I called again.

Again nothing.

At six-thirty I reached Kelly. "What the hell happened?" I asked.

"He never showed," Kelly said.

"What do you mean, never showed?" I asked. "He had to show. It meant his whole future to show." My voice rose enough to draw the attention of the proprietor and someone in the corner fiddling with a pinball machine. I calmed my voice down. "The only way Lou wouldn't show is if something unforeseen happened to him," I said.

Kelly didn't respond. Neither did I. We were both thinking, probably the same forbidding thoughts.

Finally I broke the silence. "What about Locke?" I asked. "How long did you guys wait?"

"Locke waited till three. Then took off. Said he had another appointment. To call him when Lou arrived."

My spine froze all the way to the back of my neck. No one had opened a door or window, so it was another kind of message. "You've got to get out of there," I yelled to Kelly. "Get your ass up here as fast as possible."

"Why?" he said. "What's going on that I don't know about? So what if Lou doesn't show up? His boss says he's still on paid vacation and you and I both know he likes his Manhattans."

I decided to tell Kelly the entire story, including Hitler, Eva Braun and who I thought to be an FBI agent--the Nazi Hans. I was forced to repeat myself several times since I cupped my mouth with my hand so no one would overhear.

When I'd finished, I could hear Kelly's breathing, heavier and uneven.

I tried to sum up. "So I figure when Mr. Averly closed the brewery in Berlin, that cramped Richard's plans. Richard decided to have his own father knocked off in order to get the plant open again. Richard, a double agent, arranged to smuggle Hitler and Eva out of Berlin in return for information on all those maniacal officers. If you need a stoolie, who better than the leader who gave all the orders? Somehow, I figure that Tony got hold of that picture taken in front of the Boston Brewery. He had it for a few months, but didn't know what to do with it. Then he suddenly needed dough and tried to blackmail Richard. That stupid act got himself killed."

"Sounds good so far," Kelly said. "Go on."

"I sent Doloras over to the South Boston Brewery to see what she could learn. And what did that get her?"

"She got murdered," Kelly said. "Just like the old man two years ago. Quite a coincidence."

"You agree they were murdered?" I said too loud. The proprietor turned my way and frowned. "Talking about a radio show," I called across the room to him, then cupped my hand again to converse with Kelly in private "Now Lou took the pictures that'll blow the lid off the whole operation, and what happens to him? Only you and I and

Locke knew he was coming to Boston. What time and where. What does that add up too?"

"I don't dare guess," Kelly said. "But I think you've convinced me. Maybe the guy you killed, Hans something--maybe he was FBI. Maybe not. I don't know. But I do know that Erv Locke knew a hell of a lot about Stowe and he was real concerned with you being there. Come to think of it, he waited till three o'clock, got a phone call and took off. Never called the paper or my office again. It seems as though either he wasn't interested or already knew what happened to Lou."

"Something's not right about this guy Locke," I said. "If Hans worked for Locke, maybe that guy with the monocle who shot Tony Coraloni was FBI, too. It seems that anyone who gets involved with Richard Averly's activities gets killed."

Silence dominated the other end of the telephone line.

"You still there, Kelly?" I finally said.

"I'm worried about Lou," he said.

"Join the club," I said. "Your life's in danger, too. So is mine and Lauren's. Let me ask you a question. Are you sure there's no message from Locke on your desk."

I heard some rustling of papers. "Not that I can see," Kelly said. "Let me ask around."

A few minutes passed, then I heard Kelly pick up the phone. "No call. Locke knew Lou wasn't coming. That's the only explanation."

"I agree," I said. "Make up some story to your chief and get up here on the double. I'll rent a cabin for you next to mine. The Stowe Cabins on Route 302 just before you get into the town. You can't miss it. It's the only road in and the only road out."

"You sure we're doing the right thing?" Kelly asked.

"You want to stay alive?" I asked. "Lou left something with me that may end up keeping all of us alive."

"What's that?" Kelly asked.

"Another roll of film," I said. "It could kill us or save us."

"I'll be there in six hours," Kelly said.

"Bring extra shells for your gun," I advised. "And extra shells for me too. I finally learned how to really use it. It's a 38."

Chapter 15
THE DRUNKEN PLAN
Boston Post sports page headline,
Wednesday, December 15, 1945:
RED SOX TRADE EDDIE LAKE
FOR SLUGGER RUDY YORK
PENNANT HOPES BOOSTED

As I walked back to the cabins from Stowe with a fifth of scotch disguised in a brown paper bag like the winos in Scollay Square, my fuzzy mind flew in various directions. Plus, I still ingested some of the remaining pain pills that the kind nurse had given me. The way I saw things, Mr. Averly, Tony, Doloras, and now maybe Lou were deceased because a fifty-five year old maniacal murderer had the whole world hoodwinked into believing that he'd committed suicide in a Berlin bunker. A division of our own FBI was using him for their own supposedly glorified purposes.

I'd purchased a few fifths at the liquor store before leaving downtown Stowe and was now guzzling one. It seemed that as long as Hitler was alive, me and everyone involved with me were in danger of losing their lives. I could only think of one way to end the carnage.

Hitler had to die for real.

He had to be assassinated.

It was a brilliant idea because no one would ever investigate his death. Hitler was already officially dead. He'd been allegedly plopped into a hole with his wife and dog and burned with gasoline. Emulsified. The perfect setup for the perfect murder. I mean-- assassination.

I continued drinking and thinking. I never had the opportunity to serve my country in wartime because of my knee. Now was my chance to be patriotic.

Old Mr. Averly had tried to be a patriot. Oops. That got him croaked. That wouldn't happen to me. I would be the assassin and remove the worst criminal the world had ever known. Adolf Hitler.

I wondered if Kelly would agree. I wondered if Kelly would ever make it to the Stowe Cabins. I wondered if Kelly would be the next victim. I wondered if I would black out soon. I wondered if the bottle had one last sip.

It did.

I drained it and threw the bottle as far as I could into the snowy woods.

I debated telling Lauren about my new plan. I debated telling Lauren about Lou. I debated telling Lauren that I was drunk as a skunk. I wondered when and where skunks got there booze.

"Did you talk to Lou?" she asked when I stumbled into the cabin. She was beginning to cook the lamb chops, the magnificent tasty aroma reaching my dulled nostrils. I had dipped my head into a snow bank and sobered up some. I think she pretended not to notice my condition.

"Yeah. I talked to him," I lied.

She turned and stared at me. "You okay? You sound funny."

"I'm fine," I lied again. "How about heating me up some black coffee. I'm just cold."

"Sure thing," she said, walking over close to me and most likely smelling my liquor breath. "You sure you're okay?"

"I will be after the coffee. I drank a little scotch and took some of those pain pills. I don't think they mixed well." I burped. "Excuse me."

"That's okay," she said with a wide smile. "Up till now you've been a perfect person. No one's perfect all the time. As a matter of fact, there's only ever been one perfect person. I studied about him in Sunday School. You know what they did to him."

I didn't realize that Lauren was also a philosopher.

"You've been a knight in shining armor," she said. "You have every right to blow off some steam."

I collapsed myself onto the overstuffed chair. "Thanks for that," I said. "I was beginning to feel guilty. I promise I'll be okay after coffee and a good supper in my stomach."

"About the past few days," she began as she opened a can of peas and carrots, "I haven't been as nice to you as you deserve."

I debated smoking or napping. I lit a Chesterfield. "Don't mention it. We've all been under a lot of strain. Especially you with your personal loss. I understand."

She cooked and I smoked, blowing smaller rings through bigger ones. She brought over a hot cup of coffee and held it to my lips. My watch read seven. Kelly would arrive by midnight. I'd rented the cabin next door, telling the clerk it was for my brother. He didn't seem to give a shit and he didn't seem to believe that Lauren was my wife, but didn't care about that either.

Maybe that was the way to be in life. Not to care about a lot of things. Especially things that didn't concern you. What's that serenity thing that alcoholics are supposed to adhere to? GOD GRANT ME THE SERENITY TO ACCEPT THE THINGS I CAN- NOT CHANGE, THE COURAGE TO CHANGE THE THINGS THAT SHOULD BE CHANGED, AND THE WISDOM TO KNOW THE DIFFERENCE.

"If everyone would mind their own fuckin' beeswax and only take care of stuff that concerns them, the world would be a safer place to live." I mumbled.

If Hitler'd stayed put in Germany instead of invading all his neighbors, I wouldn't have been stuck in the cabin worrying what tomorrow would bring for me and Lauren. Both our lives were in danger and I knew it. But, I decided not to worry Lauren's pretty head about it. I wanted her to think everything was hunky-dory. It always amazed me how alcohol would bring such insightful thoughts from the depths of one's brain to the forefront.

"My friend Red Kelly's coming tonight," I blurted out.

"He's the cop you keep calling on the phone?" she asked.

"A red-headed policeman who we can trust," I said. "You'll like him. Girls think he's cute."

"Not as cute as you, I bet," she turned and blew me a kiss with her fingers. Her dark brown hair was tied back and she wore little makeup. Her slacks were loose, but her sleeveless frilly blouse offered a frontal view of small cleavage which excited even my alcohol filled system.

Dinner was delicious and timely. My stomach needed substance to soak up the alcohol, or I might have become embarrassingly sick. Big boys don't throw up.

I'd also purchased two bottles of cheap red wine, the sweet kind, that we both drank with dinner.

I sipped. Lauren gulped, never having drunk wine before.

"Tastes like grape juice," she said. "Flows down real easy. I like it."

"Who taught you to cook so well?" I asked, meaning it.

"I took a course in high school," she said. "Is wine supposed to make your head feel hot?" she asked, placing my hand on her forehead.

I felt a warm perspiration. My head felt the same, but the small room was warm from the gas log.

"Wine is the nectar of the gods," I said with a smile. I immediately wondered where I'd heard that corny line or if I'd just made it up. Maybe a comic at the Old Howard burlesque theater had used it. "Wine is the lubricant of lovers," I continued. I had never talked like that to any past dates. The one-night-stands I mingled with didn't seem interested in romance or small sweet talk, or even any foreplay, for that matter. Wham, bam, thank you ma'am. That's the way it was and that's the way they liked it. I think. I never stayed around long enough to find out.

Lauren blushed.

After dinner I insisted on doing the dishes. Lauren showered, threw on her terri cloth bathrobe and lay on the small bed, thumbing through magazines. Occasionally, I looked out the window at the highway and saw nothing unusual. No one checked into the cabins, which was okay with me. The less the merrier.

I peered out the back window, over the field to the beginning of the logging road. I didn't expect to see anything and didn't.

Lauren played the radio softly. Perry Como sang the country's latest hit--TEMPTATION. Lauren sang along with him: "You came, I was alone, you were temptation."

"Like that song?" I asked. "I think I've been alone most of my life." The alcohol began wearing off, leaving me with a slight romantic urge. I blamed Perry Como.

"You're not alone anymore," Lauren said from the bed. "Now you're stuck with looking after me."

I felt a tightness in my chest. I'd never wanted to be responsible for anyone or anything. It's what killed my father. His death left my mother almost a vegetable. All I ever had was Uncle Bill, and he accepted life as it came. Never made waves. Lived for the moment and taught me to do the same.

Suddenly, meeting Lauren had changed my entire outlook on life. Suddenly, I wanted to be with someone. So much, it hurt. I wondered if that was what love was all about.

I dried the last dish. "I'm thirty-five years old," I heard myself babbling and didn't quite know why. "Probably old enough to be your father--almost."

Lauren peered her sparkling brown eyes over the top of *Life* Magazine. It was dated November 12th and beautiful Ingrid Bergman's face adorned the cover. I'm not saying Lauren's prettier, but in my eyes, just as cute and certainly more available.

"I don't care how old you are, silly," she said. "When you're sixty-five, I'll be fifty. What's in age anyway? We can only live one day at a time, no matter how old we are."

"Hmmm. I never thought of it that way," I said. "But you're right. We can only live minute to minute. Hour to hour. Day by day with no guarantees what tomorrow will bring. When I'm a hundred, you'll be eighty-five--an old hag."

Lauren laughed. I laughed and joined her on the bed. "Ticklish?" I asked.

"Of course not," she lied as I knew everyone lied about being ticklish. Even me. So, I gently tickled the bottom of her bare foot. And, of course, she tried hard to hold back--but finally giggled.

"Want to brush my hair?" she asked, holding out her brush.

She lay flat on the bed on her stomach. I sat beside her and brushed. Long, steady strokes. Her soft hair smelled clean and perfumed. I stopped when it seemed dry. Unlike two nights before, Lauren turned over onto her back, facing me with a slight, closed mouth smile.

"You promise to be gentle?" she purred, so I could barely hear. "Please be gentle."

She sat up and slid out of her robe, revealing all of her tender nakedness. I hadn't realized how skinny she was. But she offered firm, full-rounded breasts, large pink hard nipples and solid hips. I mentally decided that ten more pounds would just about make her the prefect model or movie star. My heart found itself in my throat again and I couldn't force out a word. Not that I would've known what to say under the rare circumstances. Rare for me. For the first time in thirty-five years I realized what it meant to be speechless.

I sat for a long time feasting my wanting eyes on her body, which glistened in the half moonlight seeping across the room. I mentally devoured every curve and crevice.

She reached up and unbuttoned my shirt. I helped, removed it and pulled my undershirt over my head, undid my belt, unbuttoned my fly and slipped out of my pants, then shoes and socks.

Lauren watched in silence, the slight, closed-mouth smile still framing her lips. I felt like Sally Rand at the Old Howard, but wasn't as slow and graceful.

I began by massaging the pressure points taught me by my mother. Lauren moaned just as she had during the first massage, two nights earlier. I started at her feet, then moved up her legs to her knees, skipped a few areas to her flat stomach, then both arms, neck and face. Her eyes were closed tightly at first, then more relaxed when I gently touched her lids, eyelashes and temples. I kissed her breasts with a slightly open and wet mouth, then lightly licked each nipple, playing no favoritism.

I moved my head down her chest towards her belly and further down. She moaned louder and her legs began to slowly spread apart. I recalled the poem she had recited to me about the greatest thing you'll ever know is just to love and be loved in return. I was loving Lauren like I had never loved anyone before.

Suddenly, she reached down and guided my head back up to her face. Once there, she pulled me close and kissed me hard with open lips. Again and again, her hot tongue searched every corner of the inside of my mouth. With a free hand she reached down and touched my exposed genitals.

Now Lauren was loving me in return.

I allowed her to guide me into her body as gently as she desired. I didn't push. I just lay still, partly inside and waited. She continued kissing and soon began pushing herself up and down, up and down, deeper and deeper. It seemed to go on for several minutes, but in reality closer to a few. At the deepest thrust, she jerked her entire body once--then again, and then collapsed on top of me, soaked with sweat--hers mixed with mine.

I never climaxed. And, for the first time in my entire sex life, it was okay. In my mind, there would be many more thrusts, many more moans and groans and jerks and orgasms would follow.

I thought I heard her mumble: "I love you."

Maybe.

Soon she slept.

I lay there with her fragile body on top of me awaiting midnight and the arrival of Red Kelly--my friend and ally. Red Kelly was the one person who might make heads and tails out of a baffling, life-threatening situation.

Chapter 16
THE INSURANCE POLICY
Boston Post headline entertainment section,
Thursday, December 16, 1945:
**RAY MILLAND NOMINATED FOR BEST
ACTOR IN *LOST WEEKEND AND
GENE TIERNEY FOR BEST ACTRESS IN
LEAVE HER TO HEAVEN***

I dozed on and off while Lauren slept deeply. As light as she was and as much as I adored her, she was still an uncomfortable burden lying on my chest. After about a half-hour or so, I gently pushed her to the edge of the bed and covered her over with a blanket. Not that I didn't enjoy viewing her nakedness, and not that it didn't keep my maleness aroused for the entire time, but I decided not to awaken her.

The radio played softly in the background. I enjoyed the thirty-minute mystery shows, especially Arch Obler's *Lights Out*. That usually began at midnight and was designed to scare the living hell out of its audience. I would never admit it (being a tough detective) but it scared me too.

Apparently, I was half asleep and half awake, when I heard a familiar radio voice saying 'Lights Out Everybody'. I sat bolt upright and reached around my back for my 38, which wasn't anywhere near my hand. What a prepared private eye I was.

It was midnight on the dot and time to look for Red Kelly's arrival. I threw on a pair of trousers, a sweater and shoes, then pulled a chair over to the front window and began smoking.

At one o'clock and after five butts and a small tobacco headache, I started with the negative thoughts. If Lou never made it to Boston and Doloras never made it back from South Boston, what made me think Kelly would ever make it to Vermont?

Lauren never moved.

The radio played soft music. Hoagy Carmichael tickled the piano keys with a song from Bogey and Bacall's new movie, *To Have and Have Not.* I wondered how Humphrey Bogart would handle my situation. He'd roll a few cigarettes, curl his lip, swig some whiskey, pull an ear lobe, and then read the script. That would tell him just what to do. The right thing every time. Hollywood style. Movies and real life. Never the same. Not even close. If only I had a script.

I dozed again.

At exactly two o'clock, I was awakened by a soft rap on the door. "Johnny. Johnny. It's Kelly. Let me in," I heard.

My heart dropped to my feet, a jubilant feeling of relief. Without hesitation I jumped up and unlocked the door.

Dumb detective move.

If it hadn't been Kelly, I would've been a dead duck, standing up and unarmed.

But, it was Kelly. My friend Kelly. I hugged him tight and pulled him in out of the frigid weather. He pushed me away. "You a homo now?" he asked in a fake lisp.

"Fuck you," I answered in a whisper, not wanting to wake Lauren. "I'm just glad to see your ugly red head and know you're alive and well. What took you so damn long?"

Kelly removed a heavy navy blue parka, woolen stocking cap and leather gloves, placed them on a chair near the fireplace and said: "Got something to warm a buddy's insides?"

I fetched him one of my fifths of scotch. He took a long swig. "Ahhh. That warms the cockles of my heart and stomach," he said in a silly Irish brogue. "I broke into Locke's FBI office and I'm afraid you're right. I found these documents." He handed me some folders with the big black letters NUREMBERG TRIALS written on the front.

"That particular folder contains correspondence from the chief prosecutor Jackson himself. I'm afraid your whole caper goes all the way to the top--or close to it."

I removed some papers from the folder. They were all stamped OFFICIAL. TOP SECRET. One read KEEP SENDING. INFORM-

ANT'S INFO. SO ACCURATE, TRIPPING UP GOERING'S LIES. GREAT WORK.

"We still don't know if they're aware who the informant is," I said. "But my gut from this note tells me they don't know--and probably don't care. The information they're revealing is so authentic and condemning, why the hell should they care where it's coming from?"

"You're right," Kelly said. He swigged again. "People are dying regardless. It's the old MEANS to the END philosophy. The END is to get these fucking Nazis found guilty and hanged or imprisoned for the rest of their lives. And, don't get me wrong, they certainly deserve it. But, since when does the MEANS justify the ENDS?"

"That's--since when does the ENDS justify the MEANS," I corrected him.

Kelly gave me a loud Bronx cheer.

"Shh. Don't wake Lauren." I pointed to her shapely silhouette on the bed. She'd rolled over onto her back. "She doesn't know a lot about this stuff. I decided not to worry her."

"Locke knows I'm in Stowe," Kelly said. "It won't be too hard for the FBI to find us here. Maybe a day or two. That equals that whatever you and I decide to do with what we know--we got about forty-eight hours--then we're dead. Or, at least you're dead. Locke and I have this Marine bond. I'm sure he won't betray me. We went through too much together."

Kelly sipped my scotch. He appeared to be pondering the problem. "I'd like to think that our days in the Marines meant something to him and maybe they do," he said. "But I can tell that you don't think so. Do you, Johnny?"

I didn't really want to burst his unrealistic vision. "Who knows? None of us will know anything until the time comes, will we?" I was convinced, after talking to Locke on the phone, that he wasn't the same happy-go-lucky guy he probably was when he hit beachheads with Red and the other gungho Marines.

"He may let you live for old times' sake," I said, "but he don't owe me nothin' or Lauren, and he owed nothin' to Lou."

"You're right," Kelly said. "Lou's probably dead, damnit. I liked Lou. Even though I think he sometimes cheated me at poker."

"Lou never cheated," I said. "He had a knack of remembering all the cards played. Ever play him in gin rummy? He kept track of every card and could beat you every time."

Kelly was beginning to get sloshed. "I didn't know poor Lou that well," he stammered.

I decided to relate all my earlier drunken thoughts. How I would do my duty to my country and assassinate Hitler. No one would investigate because Hitler was already officially dead. I figured it was a perfect crime. The perfect murder plot. How could I pass it up? It would also end the caper and the rest of us would be saved. No need to shut us up after Hitler was really dead.

Kelly kept drinking and nodded as though he was agreeing.

I talked.

He drank.

I talked.

He nodded.

"I don't really think I could do it," I said. "But it certainly seemed like a good idea when I was filled with alcohol."

"I'll do it, then," Kelly burped. "I'm a much better shot than you, anyway. Bang, bang, you're dead." He was slurring his words. "Got anymore booze?"

I handed him my final fifth, but not before twisting off the cap and swallowing a swig. "You mean to say you'd assassinate Hitler?" I asked, trying to sound serious. "And you agree we could get away with it? The perfect crime?"

Kelly had just driven six hours, drank almost an entire fifth of scotch and I wasn't sure he knew what he was saying.

He waved the bottle in the air. "Kill all Nazis. Revenge the Jews. Revenge Lou." He was loud, but Lauren never stirred.

My watch read almost three. "Let's turn in," I suggested. "We'll plan all this in the morning."

Kelly didn't say no, so I helped gather his things together and walked him over to his cabin next door. I had started his fireplace earlier, so it was already toasty warm. I helped him off with his shoes, which I'd done several times before over the years when he and I had returned from some big nights on the town. I also could recall a few nights that he'd poured me into bed.

I tucked him in and pulled the blanket up under his stubby chin. "Night, night," I whispered.

He answered with a loud snore.

The smell of scrambled eggs sifted into my nostrils when I awoke. My watch said nine. I first noticed Lauren's back leaning over the double burner, then the window told me it was snowing hard. Maybe the storm would give us more valuable time.

"Kelly showed up safely," I said.

"I know," she turned around and approached me with a plate of hot eggs and toast. "We've met, shared breakfast and he's gone to town."

"You mean I slept through all that?" I asked, sitting up and placing the plate on my lap.

Lauren sat down beside me on the edge of the bed. "Well, I slept through his arrival and your party, didn't I?"

"Did he tell you what we talked about?" I asked as I mashed the yellow into the white.

"He told me to ask you. I like him. He's got cute red hair and freckles."

"Don't mention his freckles to him," I said. "He doesn't like them. Thinks they're childish."

Lauren wore her white terry cloth robe. Her hair was pulled back with a ribbon. She wore no makeup, but, in my biased mind's eye, didn't need any. Her eyes remained locked on mine. "You going to tell me?" she asked. "I think I'm entitled. My best friend died for this cause. Or did you forget?"

I knew she was right. She was entitled, but I still didn't feel a frightened female was an asset to any case I was working on. "Kelly thinks we can safely be home within forty-eight hours," I lied. But maybe I wasn't lying. Maybe we would be safely home within forty-eight hours. I hoped so. Uncle Bill had preached that hoping and wishing never made a thing so. Only doing got things done. Wishing was for Dorothy from the *Wizard of Oz*.

"Okay," she said. "Whatever you say. I don't have a lot of choices. My life is in your hands now." As she talked, she stood up and untied her cloth belt, allowing the robe to fall open. I don't think I could ever remember being hornier than at that very moment. She lifted the plate off my lap and then pulled down the blanket. I was naked from the waste down and sported the biggest erection in history. Well, maybe not quite. The Empire State Building, built just nine years ago, climbed one hundred and one stories.

Her eyes widened. "Looks like you're ready for...for...I guess dessert," she chuckled.

I swallowed the last piece of egg and seemed to choke. It wasn't the egg. It was my whole insides revving up for what was about to take place. Lauren slowly climbed on top of the bed, then slid over beside me. She carried a bottle of some kind of cooking oil, which she opened and began pouring between my legs. It felt warm and slippery. When she finished, she began stroking me slowly and wetly up and down.

I watched.

She stroked.

"If I had one of these," she mumbled, "I'd do this all the time. This is fun. How long can you hold back?"

I was speechless and couldn't answer and didn't want to answer because I didn't know the answer. Suddenly, I felt the tickle, reached for her bare shoulders and pulled her over on top of me. She wiggled around, up and down and around and around. Soon, I had slid into her and we were both moving in unison. This time, it was my thrust and her thrust. My thrust and her thrust. Then I jerked forward. My back arched. She jerked. Once. Twice!

Her back arched.

"That was the best breakfast I ever had," I said, finally recovering my voice.

"Not fattening for me, I hope," she replied with a small laugh.

Kelly returned at ten o'clock with a few groceries, three bottles of wine and a Boston Post. "I called O'Brien, my chief," he said. "He told me that Locke was looking for me."

"What did you tell him?" I asked.

"Said I was home in bed with a head cold."

"Did your boss buy it?" I asked.

"He doesn't give a shit. But Locke will check it out, find I'm not home and put two and two together. Don't you think?"

Lauren, now dressed in her colorful ski sweater, slacks and the furry rabbit boots, took the bags from Kelly and began putting things away.

Kelly grabbed a bottle of orange juice and opened a new bottle of aspirin, picking out four and popping them into his mouth. "I've got a headache," he announced. "Maybe I'll cut my drinking down to two glasses a night rather than the whole bottle."

I laughed. Lauren frowned. "He's just kidding," I said. "You'll notice very little drinking till this thing's over and done with."

Kelly nodded.

Lauren jumped onto the bed with a copy of *Life* Magazine. "Want to tell me what you guys are up to?" she asked. "Maybe I can be a help."

Kelly and I exchanged concerned glances. We both shrugged at the same time. "She might as well know now," he said. "If Locke is on his way, her life is in just as much danger as ours."

Unfortunately, Kelly was right, and it interested me that he now put himself in the same dangerous category as the rest of us.

"We want to assassinate him," I boldly announced.

"Assassinate who?" Lauren asked, putting down her *Life* Magazine, the page coincidentally opened to a picture of Adolf Hitler standing beside Eva Braun under a heading: MARRIED ONE DAY-- DEAD THE NEXT.

Kelly and I both looked at the page, then at each other, our eyebrows lifted. "That's right. Him," Kelly said, pointing to the page. "We figure that the reason everyone's been knocked off is to protect the fact that he's hiding out on top of Mount Mansfield in Averly's chalet. If we assassinate him, no one has to protect him anymore and we'll finally be safe. Make sense?"

Lauren hesitated, pondered the bizarre situation for a moment, then nodded.

"And I believe we got some insurance," I added. "Lou left me a second roll of film. It proves that Hitler's alive and well and living in Richard Averly's plush chalet in Stowe, Vermont. Do you think Life Magazine would like to own those photos?"

Both Kelly and Lauren smiled at the same time at the same thought.

I went on. "We assassinate Hitler, contact Locke that we have the pictures and I think that'll end the whole affair."

"It's the only chance we got," Kelly said.

Lauren nodded, this time with more vigor.

I gazed out of the window. The snow had subsided a bit, but it was still too stormy to plan a ski trip to the summit.

"Tomorrow," I said. "Tomorrow we'll all go to the summit. Lauren will stay at the summit house and look through the binoculars while you and I go to the same spot where Lou took the pictures."

"We'll need a rifle," Kelly said. "I only have pistols."

I lit a Chesterfield. It was enjoyable to smoke fresh cigarettes for a change. I blew a ring. Lauren and Kelly watched it float toward the ceiling, change form, then disappear into nowhere, or wherever dying smoke rings disappear to. "I know where there is one," I said. "The one I took from Hans and threw into the snow. But, I wouldn't want to count on finding it. I'm sure it's buried along with everything else that was there that day, including Hans."

"Isn't this great hunting country?" Kelly asked. "I'll go into town and purchase a rifle. Shouldn't have too much of a problem after I show my badge." He flipped open his wallet, revealing his shiny and impressive police badge.

Lauren and I looked at each other, then back to Kelly, our favorite policeman friend. "Glad to have you on our side," I said. "Get one with a telescopic sight."

"What if they don't have one?" Lauren asked.

"Then I'll drown the Nazi bastard in his hot tub," I said, laughing quietly.

Chapter 17
THE PICTURES
Boston Post headline,
Thursday, December 16, 1945:
CARE TO SEND PACKAGES OF GOODS
TO AID NEEDY EUROPEANS

Kelly returned at about three in the afternoon wearing a large smile and a head full of snow. "You won't have to hunt through the deep snow for Hans' rifle," he said.

Lauren and I had been entertaining ourselves playing Cribbage at a penny a point. She was ahead almost fifty dollars. "Where'd you come up with a rifle?" I asked.

"I was right. There are two sports shops in town. Sell skis, skates and guns. No problem. No questions asked, especially after I showed him my badge and told the proprietor not to ask any."

"Do they keep a record of who buys guns?" I asked.

Kelly said, "Sure. But so what? We'll be long gone by tomorrow night."

Lauren and I shared glances, then we both looked out the window at the piling snow. "Not if it keeps snowing," I said.

Kelly removed his parka and placed his wet shoes in front of the gas fireplace. "If it keeps snowing, no one leaves the chalet and no one comes into town."

He was right. As long as we were snowed in, we were safe. At least it would seem that way and felt good to think that way.

"Locke has to know we're in Stowe," I said. "Maybe Hans wasn't the only agent they had planted here."

Kelly poured a half glass of scotch and began sipping. "Maybe Hans wasn't even his agent. Maybe a lot of things. Maybe we should get our insurance policy in place."

I shared glances with Lauren again. The cabin was warm, so she wore a skimpy T-shirt and loose slacks. Her hair was up in a bob. I liked it down and loose. Every time I caught her eye, I could feel the lump in my chest. I pointed to my hair and motioned for her to let hers down. She got the message and removed the elastic from the bob. Her soft, black hair dropped around her shoulders. Nothing sexy about it, but in my eyes, every time she moved her hand or her mouth or her legs or her body--it turned me on. I felt it in the crotch area. And, that damn lump in my chest. Did I like being in love? Did it have to mean responsibility--something I'd successfully avoided for over thirty-five years?

Kelly, an ex-marine, and I could storm the chalet, kill Hitler and everyone else in it. I didn't care about that. But Lauren. What would happen to her? The FBI could storm these cabins and kill Kelly and me. I didn't even care about that.

But what about Lauren? I did care about her. I don't think I welcomed the responsibility.

"Let's get our insurance in place," I agreed.

I trudged through the snow over to the office. "Anyone check in today?" I asked.

"Nope. Not yet," the manager answered. "But I did get a phone reservation for tonight. Strange call too."

I didn't like the word strange. "Why strange?" I asked.

"Well, this officious deep voice asked me a lot of questions about the camp. Which is not unusual. I mean, people want to know how clean it is, how we heat it, how far from the mountain, about the views, and all that stuff. I mean, those questions are expected. But after this guy asked those questions, he wanted to know all about the guests, how long they'd been here, what they looked like. A real nosy fella."

I suddenly felt a new lump in my chest, but it wasn't love. "What did you tell him?" I asked.

"I told him everything I could. I mean, why not? Besides, I want business, so I always answer all the questions people ask. Funny though." He scratched his balding head.

"Why funny?" I asked.

"He didn't make the reservation until I described you three. As soon as I told him about what you looked like and what your brother looked like. I saw your brother go out this morning, red hair and all. And what your wife looked like, he immediately made the reservation for the two cabins."

"Two cabins?" I asked.

"Two cabins. Four guests," he said.

"Give a name?" I asked.

"Sure," he answered. "In the log book on the desk."

I looked.

There it was.

Mr. Key and party of three.

Key.

Locke.

Smart-ass.

It was Locke all right. No doubt about it.

"Got a phone book I can look at?" I asked.

He handed me a small yellow book from behind the counter. "What's it you lookin' for?" he asked.

"Local newspaper," I said. "Got any around here?"

"Sure do," he answered. "Mr. Parsons got a little weekly paper right over in Littleton. Only two towns away. Comes out every Friday. Nice little paper. Tells us all the gossip, what's goin' on at the churches and town meetings. What do you want him for?"

I found the number. "Got a hot story for him," I lied.

I placed a nickel in the pay phone slot and dialed. A gruff male voice answered. It was Parsons. I talked quietly so the proprietor couldn't eavesdrop and told Parsons I was a Detective Kelly from the Boston Police Department and would like him to develop a roll of pictures, post haste. He agreed. Even sounded excited and gave me directions to his office.

The snow wasn't letting up, but Littleton was only ten miles away and time was running out on the whole caper, especially if Locke and his three accomplices made it through the storm to Stowe by some time tomorrow. The weather forecasted snow through the day and night, letting up in the morning. That would mean the earliest Locke's crowd would show up would be in the afternoon. Kelly agreed it was important we get the pictures developed and then hidden in a safe place. We decided to take Lauren with us to

Parsons' newspaper office. It seemed wise that we all stick together. Safety in numbers.

It took us close to an hour to drive ten miles. We witnessed several accidents and a few cars skidding off the road. We all agreed that Locke would never get through. We had at least twenty-four hours lead time.

Parsons turned out to be a pleasant old country gentleman. Bushy white hair, stooped shoulders, sweater that buttoned in front and a pipe hanging out of the side of his mouth.

"How didja know I hadda darkroom?" he asked after letting us into his office.

"Detectives figure those things out," I said.

Kelly produced his wallet with badge. Parsons looked impressed. "Not much ever happens in these parts that warrants police from outta town," he said. "Hadda murder in 1936. Found a man bludgeoned to death in his hunting cabin. They arrested his companion and almost hung the poor bastard. Then they found out that the marks on the body were made by bear claws. Never caught the bear." Parsons chuckled.

"Here's the film. Let's get started," I said.

We followed the old man into his darkroom. He turned on the red light. "Don't open the door now--any of you. It could overexpose the whole roll. You wouldn't want that to happen."

He was right.

He went through the mixing of chemicals and then began making the prints. "This film is dated," he said. "Everyone should use this kind of film so they can tell what date the film was used."

I thought of Lou using dated film. Smart. The three of us leaned over Parsons' shoulder as the pictures developed under the acrid liquid. He was making them all five by seven in size.

"Looks like Mr. Averly's chalet," he remarked holding the first picture out in front of him and under the red light. "I'll hang this one up to dry and let's see the others," he said.

The next seven pictures were of the chalet, a few far off mountain scenes and one of me approaching Lou's fort. Nothing of the hot tub or Hitler.

"Not much of a scoop in these pictures," Parsons remarked as he put the last print under the developing liquid.

We all stared. I held Lauren's hand and squeezed. She squeezed back. Slowly the print came into focus. There it was. Just as I remembered. The hot tub with four figures. "I didn't know Averly had a hot tub up there," Parsons said.

The picture became clearer and the faces in more focus. I recognized Richard Averly from the original picture of Tony's. Then I recognized Adolf without his mustache and I recognized Eva from a picture in *Life* Magazine. The other slut, I didn't know or care to know. I hoped Parsons wouldn't recognize anyone other than Richard.

"Who are Averly's playmates?" he asked as he took the picture out of the chemicals and rinsed it in a clean water tray. "The dark-haired man looks familiar. Does he live around here?" He didn't wait for an answer. "That's Sally Swinton in the buff." He pointed to the young naked companion of Richard's. "Sally's got a tough reputation around here. I thought she worked full-time as a waitress. Maybe she waits part-time on Averly at the chalet," he chuckled an old man's chuckle. "I don't recognize the well-formed dark-haired girl. But the older man. He somehow looks like I've seen him before."

"No one you know," I tried to assure him.

"Someone I've been looking for," Kelly said. "A fugitive from justice. We'll give you the story when we arrest him. But don't let the cat out of the bag. If he hears we know he's at the chalet, he'll skedaddle and you won't have any story."

Parsons smiled and nodded. "You can count on me," he said. "I'd love to have a good story. Something juicy. Maybe even better than the bear story of 1936."

I winked at Lauren. "I assure you it'll be much better than your bear story," I said.

We requested four prints of the hot tub scene. Eight by tens. Big enough to easily identify all three figures.

I handed Parsons a hundred dollar bill on the way out. He tried to refuse, but I insisted. It was well worth it to us. The cheapest insurance policy we could possibly buy.

On the ride back to the cabins I asked Kelly how we could use the pictures for insurance.

"Mail them to important people," he said.

"How about the President of the United States," Lauren suggested.

"He'd never get it," Kelly said. "One of his aides would intercept it and think it a fraud."

"How about J. Edgar Hoover," I said. "We'll send him a note with it saying that upon our untimely deaths our lawyer turns the picture over to *Life* Magazine and *The New York Times*."

"And how about one to Locke saying the same thing. We know he'll get it," I said.

"And I'll send one to my chief," Kelly said. "Not to be opened until my death."

Sounds good to me," I said. "What do you think?" I asked Lauren.

She was cuddled under my arm as Kelly wended his way through the blizzard. "How about each one of us have one picture and send it to whoever we think will do the most good. Whatever will keep us alive."

Kelly and I nodded. "I'm sending mine to my boss," Kelly said.

On the way back through Stowe we stopped at a ski shop and purchased white outfits for Lauren and Kelly. I still had mine from Lou. We also rented three pair of skis and boots to be used the next day. We even bought two-day tow tickets so we'd be ready when we had to be ready--hopefully the next morning. We stopped at the post office and I kept one copy of the eight by ten photo and mailed the other to my office address with my own name on it. Lauren had to get *Life*'s address from the magazine and Kelly wanted to call his chief first.

Back at the cabin we made final plans. No new cars were in the parking lot, which allowed us to sigh relief. Even though we were all convinced that it was impossible for Locke and his goons to make it up to Stowe through the snow storm.

"When the tow opens in the morning, we'll be there waiting," I said. "Upon our arrival at the summit, Lauren will stay behind and make sure we're not followed."

I placed my arm around Lauren's shoulders. "You'll have to dress extra warmly," I said. "You may be standing around for several hours."

She displayed a modest grin and buried her head into my heavy sweatered chest.

"Then Kelly and I will try and find the area where Lou built his fort." I continued. "That was an excellent spot to view the chalet and to pick off anyone who walks across the deck."

Kelly nodded. It must have sounded good to him.

"Then Kelly and I'll come back to the summit and we'll all ski down. Hopefully the death of Hitler will end anyone wanting to silence us. Especially with all our insurance mailed."

Lauren had purchased two manila envelopes from the cabin office and copied the address off the publisher's block in *Life* Magazine. She licked the stamp, affixed it, scribbled an explanation letter and sealed the envelope. "I'll mail it tomorrow morning on the way to the ski area," she said.

Kelly put together the same kind of package and called his chief, telling him to watch out for the envelope that he would send in the morning mail. The police department had a private attorney and the chief agreed to give the picture to him when or if Kelly met with an untimely accident.

"So, our insurance is solid," Kelly said. "We'll mail the envelopes tomorrow morning and then rest easier."

Lauren and I nodded.

As we ate our supper, consisting of a special hot vegetable soup conjured up by Lauren, I remembered one loose end. We'd left the negatives with Parsons. That was a mistake. Maybe even a mistake for Parsons, since it made him a potential victim.

The snow was swirling heavier than any time during the day. I promised myself that I would rise early and drive to Littleton to retrieve the negatives before our ski trip in the morning. My guilty conscience didn't need any more dead witnesses, and if anything happened to old Parsons, I'd definitely feel responsible.

Chapter 18
PREPARATION FOR FINALE
Boston Post headline, late edition, Thursday, December 16, 1945:
OLD BLOOD AND GUTS GENERAL GEORGE PATTON KILLED IN AUTO ACCIDENT-- WANTED TO CONTINUE FIGHTING--DRIVING RUSSIANS OUT OF BERLIN

A static radio announced that the snow would let up by late morning. 'Clearing and cold, temperatures climbing to twenty by midday. Wind five to ten miles per hour'.

I put an arm around Lauren as she dried the supper dishes. "You won't freeze tomorrow at the summit," I said. "And if Locke is listening to the same type forecast, he won't attempt to drive here till morning, getting him here no earlier than mid-afternoon. Hopefully, we'll be finished, long gone and safe."

Kelly drank an after-dinner scotch and played cards by himself. A solitaire game called clock. He finished second every time. Lauren packaged three box lunches for the next day and then we sat together going over our plans, one more time.

"Are we all agreed that this is what we gotta do?" I asked, already knowing the answer.

Both Kelly and Lauren nodded in unison.

"I mean, who are we to interfere with the United States government and prosecutor Jackson?" I said. "If we can't trust them to do the right thing..."

"The end result is right," Kelly interrupted. "But, the means is wrong. Dead wrong, and you know it and I know it and I'm sure they even know it. But, it makes things a lot easier and smoother for them to have a grade A informant."

Lauren butted in. "Do the police use informants?"

Kelly looked at me as though he needed permission to reveal some secret information. I winked.

Kelly pulled his chair closer to the table and whispered. "We cops use informants all the time. And, we all have our favorites. Some of them get real cushy deals by squealing on someone else. I don't always like the mugs I deal with, but without a stool pigeon's information, sometimes we'd be lost. We encourage them and often help them hide out if they're endangered by the information they give us."

"So that's what our government's doing with Hitler," Lauren said. "They might not like him, but he's helping them get a job done."

Kelly nodded. "The Nuremberg prosecution must've gone totally ape-shit when they discovered a stooly the magnitude of Adolf Hitler. They actually had an informant who'd given the orders. How can any of the defendants at Nuremberg get away with lying?"

"They can't," I said. "As long as Hitler feeds the information. But, the higher-ups might not even know the information's coming from Hitler--just a high-ranking official."

Kelly looked at Lauren and me. "What would you two have done under the same circumstances if you wanted to nail the twenty obviously guilty defendants? Especially after viewing the pictures of the thousands of dead bodies at the concentration camps."

I scratched my head. "The same, I guess."

"What about you, Lauren?" Kelly asked.

"I don't think about it," she said. "I think about Doloras. Innocent Doloras. She didn't deserve to die. That was wrong. It's hard to believe that our own government sanctioned her death as the means to an end. I don't like to think about it."

Lauren wasn't wrong. Uncle Bill preached the same philosophy. What you don't think about can't hurt you. I think if Tony, Mr. Averly and Doloras hadn't been murdered for the cause, I'd be the first in favor of going away and not dwelling on it. I couldn't help thinking about my father constantly concerned with his causes, many of which he could do nothing about. He took on everyone else's stresses and died for it.

We listened to the radio and eventually played some penny poker just to pass the time and keep our minds off the uncomfortable, but inevitable events of the next day.

From time to time I noticed Kelly staring at Lauren and me. I finally asked, "What the hell are you staring at Kelly? You're making me nervous. Have I got spinach in my teeth or something?"

Kelly grinned. "I've never seen you show so much attention to a dame," he admitted. "You gonna let this young lady tame you?-- settle you down?"

Lauren reached across the table and grasped my hand. "He's free to do what he wants," she said in a soft tone. "I don't have any ropes on him or anyone else."

I held her hand and directed my attention to Kelly. "You've known me a long time Kelly," I said. "You and I've been through a lot of shit together."

Kelly shook his head and fingered his cards.

"Lauren and I like each other. We got something in common right away when we met. I can't explain it. Don't even understand it. But it's there. A feeling. A good feeling for both of us." I looked back at Lauren. She was nodding. "So what can I tell you, Kelly, except you're right. I've never wanted to show so much attention to any skirt."

I kissed Lauren on the cheek.

Kelly looked up, smiled and shrugged. "Don't make no difference to me," he said. "Just as long as she allows you out Wednesday nights for poker."

We all laughed together.

At eleven Kelly excused himself. "I'm going to take a look around, then turn in. If I see any strange cars in the parking lot, I'll check back here. But, I don't expect any in this storm."

Lauren and I locked the door and climbed under the blankets, naked. "We should try and get some sleep," I said, half meaning it.

"Yeah, yeah. Sure thing," she purred, moving her hands across my lips, over my chin, down my chest and into my groin area.

We did sleep, off and on.

Chapter 19
PARSON'S OFF THE HOOK
Boston Post **headline,**
Friday, December 17, 1945:
FINAL REPORTS ON AUGUST 6TH BOMB:
OVER 70,00 KILLED IN HIROSHIMA,
HUMANS EVAPORATED, SAND TURNED
TO GLASS, STRUCTURES DESTROYED
WITHIN TWO MILES OF BLAST.
BOMB NAMED *LITTLE BOY*

By sun-up the snowfall had ceased and the clouds were breaking up. My watch said six and I wanted to get the negatives from Parsons. The first tow began at eight-thirty and we'd agreed to be on it. I lightly crept out of bed, dressed, sipped a glass of orange juice and wrote a note. "Dear Lauren. I've gone to Littleton to retrieve the negatives we forgot yesterday. Be back by eight. You guys be ready. Next week's Christmas. Let's hope we have something to celebrate. Love you. Johnny."

I read over the note. It was the first time I'd used the words 'love' with Lauren and had only heard her say it once the other night when I wasn't really sure she had said it at all. But, I guessed two people don't really have to say it to mean it. Didn't someone once say that action speaks louder than words?

I was confident that she loved me and I knew that I loved her. I also knew that I was ready to take on the responsibility of another soul and I would tell Lauren the first chance I got. Maybe over a Christmas present.

I glanced down at her Madonna-like face. She was flat on her back, head to one side buried half in the pillow. Her loose silken dark hair spread out, covering most of the pillow. Her lips were partly open and wet--glistening from the sun beginning to seep through the partly-drawn shades. The blanket didn't quite cover her bare shoulders, so I pulled it up under her chin, gently ran my hand through her hair and leaned down to kiss her forehead. She stirred just a little, but never woke. I must have stood over her for at least three minutes, memorizing every square inch of her pretty face. I'd actually give up being a private eye for her and get a real job. Doing what, I didn't know. But something would come along. Somehow, this little fragile broad had tamed the big tough Jonathan Dark.

About time.

I departed, locking the door behind me.

The roads had been pretty well cleared by the plows and the driving to Littleton was easy. It reminded me that the driving from Boston would also become easy.

I found Parsons up and already working on his next edition. He asked to keep a copy of the picture with Richard and his friends. I said no, but I would send him one after Kelly made his arrest. He gave me the negatives, offered me hot coffee, which I declined, bid me good morning and I headed back to the Stowe cabins. The roads were now clear and the morning sun helped to expose some of the black pavement.

I made good time.

As I approached the cabins, I felt a strange chill riding up my spine toward my neck. The car window was tightly closed and the heater was blasting. Something didn't seem right. I couldn't immediately figure it out.

Maybe nothing.

Maybe something.

I reached back and felt my gun in its holster. Smoke curled out of Kelly's cabin chimney. Smoke curled out of several other cabins. That's what wasn't right. Smoke was curling out of two cabins that had been vacant the night before. I hadn't checked in the morning when I left. I also noticed a truck behind one of the cabins that hadn't been there last night. A heavy truck with big wheels. Obviously a vehicle with better ability to maneuver through the snow than a light car.

I drove past the cabins, up the road about a hundred yards and pulled into a gas station. My white suit was in the trunk along with boots. I put them on, along with a woolen stocking cap and ski goggles. My own uncle wouldn't recognize me. I circled around behind the cabins. I peeked inside the window of the first, a two-room, one bedroom jobby. The embers in the fireplace were still sizzling, but dying down. Two suitcases sat on the floor in the corner. The lone table featured a bottle of scotch, four half-filled tumblers and a box of donuts. Otherwise, the cabin seemed empty.

The cabin next door presented pretty much the same scenario. Dying fire, two suitcases, but no food or drink. It also appeared empty.

I walked over to Kelly's cabin and peered into his back window. Empty.

Next door, no smoke flowed out of my cabin chimney. I snuck up to the back window and glimpsed inside.

My entire six foot frame froze--not from the cold weather.

Kelly and Lauren were plainly visible.

I turned my head and vomited into the snow. It was orange. Orange juice. The only thing I'd ingested that morning.

I looked all around the property and didn't see anyone stirring. My mind spinning and eyes blurry, I carefully entered my cabin, gun drawn.

Kelly lay on the bed, fully dressed in his white ski outfit, his throat slashed from ear to ear, reddish blackish blood still oozed out of his neck soaking into the white sheets and into his red hair. His face was black and blue and swollen as though he'd taken a bad beating.

I wondered if he'd talked, and if so, what he'd talked about. Beside the bed, on the floor, lay his addressed manila envelope, ripped into many pieces. His insurance. Our insurance.

So much for Marines being blood brothers.

Five feet away, sprawled on the floor, I leaned over Lauren and lifted her head into my arms. She was wearing her white terry cloth robe, open in the front, revealing her nakedness. I could see by the bruises on her thighs and stomach that she'd been brutally raped. Blood was still oozing out of her private parts. This had to be the worst way Lauren could ever had died and must have brought back cruel memories of her uncle from years ago. Memories, I thought I was helping her forget. She had warned me that Doloras said all men were alike.

Was she right?

Are all men alike?

Why couldn't Locke and his goons have just killed her? Why did they have to rape her?

I had no answers.

Lauren had a single small hole in the middle of her forehead. They'd probably made her watch them torture and question Kelly, then, assuming Kelly kept his mouth shut, questioned her, raped her and shot her. Beside her body lay pieces of another manila envelope. Lauren's insurance. Never mailed. Never used.

I walked into the bathroom and threw up again. This time nothing came up.

I gazed into the mirror over the sink. It didn't reflect the young, bright-eyed and bushy tailed thirty-five year old Johnny Dark I was used to primping with in the morning. But, an older man with deep circles under his puffy eyes and a gray skin color resembling death itself. I must have aged fifteen years in the past five minutes. I was surprised my hair hadn't turned white.

I filled the sink with cold water and soaked my face for at least five minutes, then walked back into the room and covered the bodies. Before I covered Lauren, I noticed a piece of paper half falling out of her bathrobe pocket. It was my love note. Maybe they hadn't seen it. Then again, maybe they were waiting for me at the chair-lift.

The way I figured it, the plans hadn't changed, except I was now the sharpshooter and I'd have no lookout at the summit.

I opened the icebox and removed a fifth of scotch. It always tasted better chilled. I took a long swig until I felt it reach and warm my stomach. The three box-lunches still sat where we'd stored them the night before. I removed two. One would be my breakfast.

I pulled the top of the blanket away from Lauren's face, stared at her for a long minute, then kissed her closed eyes.

She was cold.

I kissed her closed lips.

They were cold.

Then I covered her again. I wanted to say lots of stuff, but I knew she couldn't hear and it was much too late to say I was sorry. Or, don't worry, I'll protect you. Or, I love you. Or, will you marry me? Or anything else. It was all too late for us. For her. For me. And Kelly. Too late for him. My friend Kelly. My best friend. Lou was also my friend. Too late for Lou.

I felt numb all over. Was this what it was like to be in shock? What the fuck had happened to my life in the past few weeks?

I didn't have the answers.

Only one.

I had a job to do. The three of us had agreed to do a certain task. Now I'd carry it out to its finish, even if only for them.

Chapter 20
ASSASSINATION
Boston Post headline,
Friday, December 17, 1945:
88 GERMAN SCIENTISTS HOLDING
NAZI SECRETS ARRIVE IN U.S.A.

Another set of heavy tire tracks carved themselves in the snow behind the second cabin, leading me to believe that Locke had come in two trucks and they were all off somewhere in the other. Probably looking for me.

My watch ticked eight-thirty.

I drove to the mountain parking lot. Seeing no trucks, I parked as close to the tow as possible. Being a Friday after a big storm, only a few skiers had showed up for the day's activities. The weekend would bring hoards of school Christmas vacationers.

I placed the rifle and lunch in a white ski bag so it appeared I was carrying a second pair of skis. I threw a pair of snowshoes over my shoulder. I already had my ticket, so I was ready to go. I had discarded my crutches but not my limp.

I rode to the summit in a new double-chair with a pimply teenage girl who had already started her vacation. I wondered if Lauren had pimples when she was a teenager.

I had.

"You on vacation?" she asked, just to make conversation.

"Sort of," I answered without much enthusiasm. I still felt numb about what I'd found back at the cabins and I couldn't help wonder if the chair-lift might slide backwards again. I guess I'd never forget that scary episode.

"We get two weeks vacation this year, mistuh," she said in a Boston accent. "I love to ski and I love these new tows. Beats those rope things." She babbled. I half listened. "Where do you live?" she asked.

"Boston," I said.

"Haven't seen you here before. First time?"

I nodded.

She looked at me, laden down with equipment. "Whadaya got in the ski bag, mistah?" she asked. "Looks like a gun."

I knew she was kidding, but it startled me anyway. Fortunately for her, she followed the remark with a giggle, so I knew she was teasing. I wasn't quite shocked enough to expect a pimply teenage spy. Yet.

"A new pair of skis," I fibbed. "I'm gonna try them out on the upper trails." That sounded reasonable to me and apparently to her because she shut up for the rest of the trip.

"Good skiing," she waved when we exited the lift.

I walked around the deck twice, just checking for strange faces. No one other than skiers, and only a few of them.

The wind was light and the sun was warming up.

I clamped on my skis, threw the shoes over my shoulder, and along with the ski bag, off I went, very slowly, snowplowing so as not to fall--too often.

I reached the first incline without mishap. I removed the skis and strapped on the snowshoes.

From the crest of each hill I caught a glimpse of the chalet getting closer and closer.

It took me over an hour before I reached the spot where I thought Lou had built his fort. The heavy snowfall had covered up any signs, and as I looked around, I realized the heavy snowfall had also covered Hans' body.

Several times since the shooting I'd thought of burying it, but felt assured mother nature would oblige.

She had.

During my tiring trek, I attempted to invade Locke's head and figure what he'd do next, assuming neither Kelly or Lauren had told him anything. He would obviously talk to the cabins proprietor, who only knew that we'd called Parsons on the phone and paid him a visit. They would then probably travel to Littleton and question Parsons. The newspaper owner would tell his whole story--no reason not to--hopefully to convince them that he didn't recognize who was in the picture, tell them of me picking up the negatives and that would end the search. I prayed they wouldn't kill the innocent old man. A short prayer because I didn't know any long ones.

I decided to build the same type fort that Lou and Hans had built. With my white attire, it would be almost impossible to see me.

My watch read eleven-thirty. Unlike the freezing cold day I had pissed in the snow to make a snowball, the warming sun dampened the new snow just enough to aid in rolling snowballs large enough to construct a big and solid fort. I was actually having fun. I hadn't built a snow fort since grade school.

I set up Lou's tripod and placed the rifle with telescopic sight on top. Then I peered at the chalet.

No movement.

What if they never came outside?

Negative thought.

Uncle Bill taught me that man can scientifically only have one thought in his head at one time, so to always replace a negative thought with a positive one. So I did. I imagined all my enemies together in the hot tub and me placing them in my sights and picking them off one by one.

Positive thinking.

My stomach told me to eat. I opened the lunch that Lauren's delicate hands had prepared for us. The lump returned to my chest. I felt a cold tear roll down my cheek.

I guess big boys do cry.

At first, I loved no one.

Then I loved a lesbian.

Now I loved a dead woman.

The sandwich assuaged my hunger. I thought I smelled her perfumed fingers. Then I found it. A damn note scribbled in Lauren's handwriting:

MY DEAR JOHNNY. I CAN'T VERBALIZE JUST HOW MUCH YOUR LOVE MEANS TO ME. I NEVER THOUGHT I'D BE ABLE TO HAVE A NATURAL RELATIONSHIP WITH A MALE. YOU'VE CHANGED ALL THAT. I DON'T KNOW HOW I CAN EVER REPAY YOU--BUT I'M WILLING TO SPEND THE REST

202 ROLAND HOPKINS, Sr.

OF MY LIFE TRYING. I LOVE YOU VERY DEEPLY AND I
HOPE YOU ARE RIGHT NOW ENJOYING THE LUNCH I
ESPECIALLY PREPARED FOR YOU. I PUT IN EXTRA TUNA
FISH. LA DE DA.

I read it over and over through wet eyes. I wasn't enjoying my
sandwich. As a matter of fact, I was choking on it, so I threw it into
the snow.

Every few minutes I checked all around my fort. The serene
silence of snow lulled me into a relaxed state. No sign of life
anywhere. Not even deer or rabbits.

The sun was dipping itself in the sky. During New England
winters, the sun traveled low across the sky, not up and down.

The wind picked up a bit and I began to experience chills.

Maybe my enemies had been tipped off.

Maybe I shouldn't wait.

Maybe I should go in.

Maybe Locke had called the chalet and they were waiting for me.

Maybe a lot of stuff that I didn't know about.

At two o'clock someone walked across the chalet deck. I looked
through my scope. It was a tall dark-haired man with broad shoulders like a football player. I hated to believe it, but it fit the
description Kelly had given me on Locke. Damn. They must've sent
the horse and sleigh down the mountain to pick him up. Maybe they
were getting ready to evacuate Hitler to another hideout--a place no
one might ever discover.

I had to act fast. I couldn't just sit and wait for the obviously
nervous and cautious group to frolic in the hot tub.

I lingered till two-thirty, then slowly left my fort, carrying the
rifle and approached the chalet, which was about two hundred yards
away. The snowshoes kept me from sinking to my waist. It had
snowed at least two more feet since my last encounter with the area.

Within a hundred yards another figure walked across the deck.

I ducked.

No one could see me with the naked eye, but I didn't know what
kind of security they had or if they had binoculars. Someone may
have had me in their sights for the whole trek.

I reached the deck, hesitated and poked my head up. I could see the hot tub, the deck, and a large glass paneled door-entrance to the house.

No one was around.

I pulled myself up and over the railing, then ducked down behind the tub. The motor was off. That told me that I could have waited all afternoon and no one would have bathed themselves.

I crept over to the glassdoors and peered into the house. I saw a large livingroom with cathedral ceiling and massive stone, blazing fireplace.

I attempted a guess at how many people were in the house. Richard, his slut girlfriend, Hitler, Eva Braun, Locke and his three henchmen and maybe some domestic help. A cook and maintenance person? That would be at most ten.

I fantasized bravely walking through the house and picking off everyone in sight. I didn't expect anyone would be waiting for that. Then again, I might succeed in killing everyone but the man I came to assassinate. That would mean failure. That would mean everyone who had died up to now in this caper had died in vain. And, I wasn't about to allow that to happen.

I tried the glass doors. They were unlocked. I slipped into the living-room and ducked down behind a large stuffed couch.

I waited and tried not to breathe loudly.

Several minutes dragged by. I imagined I could hear my watch ticking and my heart beating. Finally, I heard someone enter the room. I held my breath and covered my hand over my loud watch. I caught a sniff and a growl. Damn. A fucking dog. I hadn't planned canine company. I should've recalled that Hitler owned a favorite pet--a German Police Dog--Blondi. Not only had the hoax saved the world's greatest madman and his wife, but his dog also.

I sat as still as possible.

I continued to hear sniffing.

It was coming closer.

I removed my pistol from its holster.

Suddenly a large police dog head appeared from behind the couch. My hand was already raised and I brought the gun butt down hard on the surprised dog's skull. I heard a crack and a split, then saw blood spurting upwards onto the nice beige couch. The dog never knew what hit him and was dead before he folded up his legs.

I pulled his limp, but heavy body behind the couch.

One down, I thought.

My watch read close to three. I wondered if people were eating, especially since I smelled food. My detective instinct at work again. Maybe I would find them all in the diningroom. Maybe not. I decided to wait and the delay wasn't long.

I heard footsteps approaching the fireplace. Then voices. "No hot tub today?" one male voice asked. It sounded pure English, so it wasn't Hitler.

"Turn on the heater. I love it," a woman's voice said. She wasn't German either. It must have been Richard and his tawny girlfriend.

"What about our new guests?" the woman's voice asked. "Do you think they'd like to join us? They look like hunks to me. All those muscles."

"Fuck em," the voice I figured that belonged to Richard said, "I didn't invite them here in the first place and I wish they'd leave."

"Aren't they leaving this afternoon?" she asked.

"They won't tell me. Big FBI guys. Think they own the world. Orders from high up. They have to stay around for awhile and protect Adolf and Eva. They even made me move Adolf and Eva to the guest house out back. Who the hell do they think they are? I brought Adolf here and I'm the one taking care of him and feeding the information to Judge Jackson. Without me, they'd all have nothing."

"You're right dear," I heard the female voice agree. "But if they have to stay, we might as well enjoy ourselves. I think the big blonde one's cutest. Did you see his biceps when he took off his shirt?"

"Look Sally, I pay you enough to forget that whore stuff while you're here. Okay? And if you have to have that big brute, make him pay double, but not in my chalet on my time."

"Oh, you're so sweet to me, Richard," she said. "I won't do anything to upset you. I know my place."

I heard someone open the glass-doors and turn on the hot tub motor. Someone else left the room.

I waited.

The person on the deck returned and then left, also.

I noticed a patch of the dog's blood had splattered on a corner of the couch. Had they noticed it? I assumed negative.

I moved a large pillow and covered over the blood stain. I quickly dragged the dog's body through the glassdoor opening and dropped him off the deck into the deep snow.   He sank, but not out of sight. Should I bury him? Fuck it. I wouldn't be around that long to make a difference. I hoped.

I crept around the outside of the deck to the side of the house. About fifty yards in back stood a stable where they most likely kept the horses and sleigh. Next to it, almost totally hidden in a clump of evergreens, I noticed a small cottage. Could that be where Eva and Adolf resided?

Fifty yards of open terrain separated us.

When I was an impressionable youngster, and ready to give up looking for missing objects, Uncle Bill taught me that 'Everything is someplace'. That lesson inspired me to continue seeking and eventually finding whatever I happened to misplace. That lesson also told me that everyone in the Averly chalet had to be someplace, and I couldn't afford to be seen. At least, not yet.

Paths had been shoveled, but I decided to stay clear of them. The deep snow could hide a moose and it could also hide me. About ten yards from the side of the house grew some low bushes--about four feet high. They could be excellent cover for my approach. It still left about twenty open yards, which I'd have to chance in order to reach the cottage. I still had the advantage of wearing all white, which disguised me a little.

I took a deep breath, said the Lord's prayer real quick. Half of it anyway, got down on my hands and knees and began crawling. The new snow was soft and pretty much covered my entire body. I decided to crawl to the back of the cottage and attempt entry that way. The route turned out to be another twenty feet and another several minutes.

So what?

I wasn't in any hurry. I'd already faced the reality that I would never emerge from the caper alive. Everyone else was dead. Why not me?

Negative thinking.

Change it immediately, I thought. But, I had to be realistic.

I did have a chance.

What did I figure earlier? One in about ten. And the dog was now dead, so my chances had improved to one in nine, or nine to one at Suffolk Downs horse track terms. Were those odds any good? No. I'd rather bet on a favorite. On the other hand, you can't make any money wagering on the favorites, so I'd bet on the long shot.

I should have waited for Sally to be fucking all the FBI guys in the hot tub at the same time, then my chances would've been even better.

Fucking in the hot tub.

Positive thinking.

Good for me.

The backside of the cottage showed no door, but two small windows. I peeked through one.

A bedroom.

Empty.

No. Someone was reclined on the bed. Long dark hair. A woman under a heavy blanket. Maybe Eva taking an after-lunch nap. I couldn't see her face.

I walked to the other window and gazed in through smoky glass. A small living room was highlighted by a blazing fireplace. A hunched-over figure with a book sat next to the sparkling flames. When he turned the page I could see his face. Pale skin, deep dark eyes, wrinkled brow, black hair, firm jaw. Was it Hitler? How the hell did I know for sure. Soft music hummed in the background. I wasn't completely uneducated and ignorant. It sounded like it could have been Beethoven. But, I wasn't sure. All symphonic music sounded alike to me. I'd read that Hitler was a Beethoven fan. Chances were good that I was looking at the Adolf Hitler.

What if it wasn't him?

At first, I froze all over. I felt a chill from my lower back, up my spine to my neck. There he was. Maybe. My prey. Only eight feet away separated by a small window. He was the cause of all my friends being dead. The cause of lots of people's friends being dead. Lots of people all over the world. The cause of Lauren being dead.

I raised my rifle.

Then I changed my mind.

I had to be one hundred percent sure. And besides, if I shot through the window, it would make too much noise.

I decided to walk in the front door, ask him his name and then blow him away right to his face.

Why not?

I carefully made my way around to the side of the cottage and checked to see if anyone was watching.

No one appeared to be.

Then I walked onto the path, onto a small brick front porch and tried the front door.

It was unlocked.

I entered.

The hunched over figure turned around in his chair and looked up at me. He muttered something in German, or what I assumed to be German, waved his fist and made an ugly face. I didn't understand German, so had no idea what he was saying.

"Adolf Hitler?" I asked, hiding my pistol behind my back.

The music continued to filter throughout the room coming from a wooden console record player standing in the corner, a large cone-like speaker on top. "Adolf Hitler?" I asked again and slowly moved myself toward the record player in order to read the label.

He didn't answer, but began to talk louder and frantically waving his hands.

The 78 RPM record spun fast enough so I couldn't read the label without stopping it. I reached in with my finger and slowed the record just long enough to read 'Ludwig von Beethoven'. It was Beethoven all right, Hitler's favorite.

I turned and faced him, now only three feet away. His face snarled up like a dog. Was it Hitler, or, possibly an impostor? A double to fool the likes of me or anyone else attempting an assassination? I had to be judge and jury.

Was I being too careful? Too critical of my own instincts? The longer I waited to make up my mind, the longer my odds of succeeding and getting away alive.

Suddenly I knew.

Beyond a reasonable doubt, I knew. He had calmed down and just stared at me as the music began playing again, almost soothing his ragged nerves. But he wasn't soothed enough. His hands lay in his lap--his fingers uncontrollably shaking. The sign of Parkinson's disease Lou had read to us from the old *Boston Post* newspaper. I recognized the disease because poor Uncle Bill had been diagnosed with it last year. No question in my mind now. I was facing the world's number one murderer--Adolf Hitler in the flesh.

Our eyes met and locked.

Hesitation on my part.

Why?

Was Hitler just a product of our crazy society, doing what he thought was right? What would my father do? Would my mother approve? Uncle Bill would probably yawn and walk away. How about those six million Jews? And then Lauren and Kelly.

Lauren's sweet, beautiful innocent face flashed in front of my eyes. For a split second I weakened the strong, tough look that must have been emanating from my face, scaring the living shit out of this poor excuse for a human being. He must have noticed my weakness. He must have doubted that I was convinced he was Adolf Hitler. No mustache. No shock of hair over his left eye. He was no dumbbell. Hell, he was a Beethoven fan.

He followed my eyes to his hands, which were still shaking, then back to my face, which now showed a new awareness. An awareness that seemed to frighten him enough to open his mouth to call out for help. I couldn't allow that to happen.

I whipped my pistol around in front, pulled a large pillow off another chair, placed it over the barrel and pulled the trigger six times.

Bang, bang, bang, bang. bang. bang.

I saved none of the bullets.

If a guard had been nearby, I was a dead duck.

Hitler's mouth remained open, but no sounds came forth. Slowly blood began dripping from the left side onto his white bathrobe. His deep black eyes stared almost through me, glazed over now with a thin mucous.

Scary.

No wonder people did his bidding. Who'd dare refuse eyes like those?

He had to be dead.

He twitched several times like a chicken with his head cut off.

I couldn't look at him anymore.

All the bullets had found a home in the Fuehrer's gut.

No one came.

The pillowed sounds had obviously been muffled enough so even the woman in the next room never stirred.

I'd completed my job. The job Kelly and I and Lauren had agreed to do. As far as I was concerned the case was closed. I would've loved to kill the FBI men. The way I felt, I would've loved to kill all the FBI, especially the ones who raped Lauren. But, this thing had to end somewhere. Enough blood had been spilled. The man they were protecting was dead.

It was finished.

So I thought.

I reloaded my pistol and slowly and carefully made my way back to my fort. I buried the rifle, snowshoes and bag and smoothed over where the fort had been. Then I clamped on my skis and headed down the mountain the same way Lou and I had done just days earlier. I fell just as many times, but made it to the bottom with my behind still in tact.

My watch said four-thirty. I'd knocked off Adolf Hitler, the world's most heinous murderer, at three-fifteen.

It was about a half-mile to where I'd left Kelly's car and I made it in ten minutes, limping.

No one looked suspicious.

If they'd found Hitler's body, and most likely they had, I was sure the horse and sleigh would show up any minute. I could wait at the mouth of the logging trail and pick them off one by one like sitting ducks, or I could leave and head back to Boston.

After a short debate with myself, I chose the latter. Had I seen the end of Locke and the FBI? I didn't really know. I hoped for their sake, I had. Positive thinking.

My mind couldn't shake the appearance of Lauren's dead body. It seemed to be engraved somewhere deep in my brain. Even Hitler's death didn't help. I couldn't eliminate the thoughts that must have been traveling through her mind as she was being violently raped. Like in the movies, she probably waited and prayed I would ride through the door on my white charger and save her. Unfortunately, in real life, that doesn't happen. In real life, guys like Hitler kill six million Jews and then make deals with their captors for leniency.

I wondered what the Jewish leaders would think if they knew what I knew.

Maybe I'd tell them.

Hell, no one else would believe me.

I wondered what the Russian leaders or Winston Churchill would think about the United States government making à deal with Hitler.

Lots of crazy and uncrazy thoughts flipped through my mind during the long six-hour trip back to Boston.

Chapter 21
CLEANING UP LOOSE ENDS
Boston Post headline, late edition,
Friday, December 17, 1945:
NUREMBERG ATTORNEYS PLEAD
CLIENTS FOLLOWING MILITARY ORDERS
20 TOP NAZIS ON TRIAL

A late December night in the city always brings out the hardy bums and puts away the civilized. Copley Square, bustling during the day, looked more like a city park late at night. The last trolley clanged its bell, while most of the office building lights were dimmed, except for a few tardy cleaning companies. One small light lit the public library steps as the usual action from the Merry-Go-Round room was stilled. The Christmas holidays would come and go this season without much for me to be thankful for.

I parked Kelly's car a block from my office next to a three-foot snow bank which I hoped wasn't covering a fire hydrant. On the other hand, I was sure he didn't mind a parking ticket or getting towed. I looked both ways, as my uncle had taught me. No people. Little traffic. My third floor office showed no activity. I didn't expect any.

I unlocked the front door and entered a neat and clean front room. Rose must have dropped by. She kept it that way when I was away. My private office was also neat and clean.

I stripped, grabbed a towel, walked to the end of the hall and showered. I stood there until the water turned cold, trying to clean all the past several days' activities off my body and out of my mind.

It didn't work, but my skin emerged squeaky-clean. For the first time since finding my friends' bodies, I felt exhausted.

I had been fueled by angry energy.

212 ROLAND HOPKINS, Sr.

I returned to my office, threw on some undershorts and a T-shirt, placed the eight by ten hot tub picture and roll of negatives in my top drawer and reclined on my couch. The other picture I'd sent to myself would most likely be in Saturday's mail. At least I had had the chance to mail my insurance.

I dialed Uncle Bill, waited a hell of a long time for him to answer, then related the entire adventure to him. He remained generally silent until the Hitler assassination part. I heard him groan. "You wouldn't kid an old kidder?" he asked.

I assured him I wouldn't.

"What makes you think they won't retaliate?" he asked.

"The pictures," I answered. "The pictures prove our original theory, which I intend to keep a secret. Nothing will bring my friends back to life and Hitler's dead, where everyone thought he was in the first place. Judge Jackson will have to convict those bastards with the evidence he's already gathered, or find another stoolie."

"Watch yourself, son," Bill said. "I'd let you talk to Rose, but she's fast asleep. I'm sure she'll be there bright and early tomorrow. I got a funny feeling you haven't heard the end of Locke and his crowd. People like him don't just go away that easily."

I told Bill I'd be sleeping at the office, not to worry and wished him a Merry Christmas, still a week away. I don't think he believed in Santa Claus or Jesus.

After tossing, turning and reliving the past twenty-four hours in my mind, I got up, took a swig of scotch, smoked half a Chesterfield then returned to the couch and enjoyed over eight hours of deep sleep.

Rose's phone call woke me. Eight-thirty. "You're there," she said in a shrill, but happy voice. "Hope you noticed I went in yesterday and cleaned up the joint."

"Thanks Rose," I said. "You can come back today. The case is wrapped up and we're all safe again. Any calls when you were in yesterday?"

"Jim Kelly's boss, Chief of Detectives O'Brien. He said Jim had called him from Vermont and he wanted to know what was up. I said I didn't know. Was that the right answer, Johnny?"

"Right," I said. "Good girl. Anyone else?"

"Yeah. Strange couple of calls. When I picked up the phone, they hung up. Just breathing. You know?"

"Okay. Good girl. How about you and I and Bill grab a lobster at Jimmy's Harborside for lunch. You'll like that, sweetheart. And clams. Lots of clams."

"Oh, Johnny. You're so considerate. I missed you so much and can't wait for you to tell me what happened. Is Red coming to dinner with us?"

I couldn't answer. I'd tell her the whole story later. I started talking and hung up in mid-sentence. It was an old trick I'd learned. Rose would think we'd been cut off.

The phone immediately rang. I guessed it was Rose so ignored it. It kept ringing and ringing and ringing. I picked up. "Jonathan Dark, private investigator. This is Mr. Dark speaking."

I heard breathing. It wasn't Rose. Someone was checking on me. Damnit.

I threw on a pair of woolen slacks, white shirt, tie and suit coat. I had forgotten what it was like to be dressed up. I pulled my long trench coat out of the closet, brushed off the dust and doffed my black snap brim. Ready for work again. Jonathan Dark, Private Investigator. The best. I'd even stolen or borrowed, whichever way you wanted to look at it, the Pinkerton logo--an eye--and had it displayed on my front window under my name facing Boylston street. It seemed to be staring at me or warning me.

My first stop, after coffee and donuts at a divey cafe near the Berkeley Street precinct, was a visit to Chief O'Brien, Kelly's boss. He squeezed my hand like a long-lost cousin, most likely believing I was a bearer of good news. He was big, middle-aged, as Irish as Pat O'Brien and even resembled him.

"Johnny my boy, miss you on the force and how's my ace detective, Red Kelly? He sounded pretty concerned when he called. Almost like he was afraid for his life."

I closed the door to his office, invited him to sit down and proceeded to tell him most of the story, leaving out the part about the FBI and Hitler. If looks could kill, the look on O'Brien's face when I told him about Kelly would've done the job. The big man coughed a few times, covered his eyes so I couldn't detect tears and dropped his head onto his desk with a thump. All he muttered was, "shit, shit, shit. My men never think they need back-up." He lifted his head and squinted at me with a stern glare. "Where were you when all the killings took place, Dark? You know how important back-up is."

I wished I'd had a good answer.

I didn't.

"I'm sure you'll hear something from the Vermont police sometime today," I said. "It's been just about twenty-four hours."

"Yeah. Yeah," he grunted. "And you don't have any idea who did it?"

"You'll get a description of me from the manager of the cabins, and if there are any fingerprints, they'll be mine," I answered. "I used an alias. Mr. U.N. Owen. I picked it up from an Agatha Christie novel."

"U.N. Owen," O'Brien said a few times. "Unknown. That's clever, Dark. You're a clever detective, sometimes. Are you sure you don't have a lead on the killers? I never know when you're telling the truth."

"Not right now, chief," I begged off.

"Maybe it's better you don't tell me what you know, Dark," he growled. "The way I feel now, I'd strangle the guy with my bare hands."

And I think he would have.

I placed Kelly's car keys on Chief O'Brien's desk, and as I walked out the door, he was dialing the Vermont State Police.

I next stopped at Mrs. Averly's house in Louisberg Square, taking a cab to the bottom of Beacon Hill and limping to the top. I figured the exercise would clear my head of the horrible thoughts and pictures flashing in and out of my brain.

Too much blood.

Too much death.

The cold wind whipped right through my trench coat into my skin.

I hadn't remembered so many expensive Christmas decorations since the beginning of the war. Every house seemed to have white candlelights in the windows and decorated trees in the yards. The air raid blackouts had killed that type of illumination for the past four years.

Helen Averly was home, seemed somewhat glad to see me and offered tea. I accepted along with three aspirins for my throbbing knee. I hated tea, but figured the heat would warm my cold body.

"I found Richard," I said.

"I know," she replied. "He called late yesterday afternoon from his chalet. He's coming home. Said his company had left. No need to stay. He asked me if I'd heard from you. How did he know about you, Johnny?"

I wasn't ready to tell her about her brother. "How did you answer? I asked.

"I lied to him. I don't like to lie, Johnny, unless, of course, it's absolutely necessary. Why do people have to lie?"

Her Negro butler brought tea and little tiny cookies. For the first time I realized how naive and childlike Mrs. Averly was. Somewhere, down deep in my gut, I felt sorry for the rich bitch and wondered how she would deal with finding out about her brother. Or, if she would ever find out about her brother.

She still resembled Gene Tierney. But, I no longer felt like Dana Andrews. I felt more like the movie bad guys. The assassins. Walter Pidgeon. During the war, he'd starred in a movie in which the plot was to kill Hitler.

He failed.

I didn't. I was the Darkman.

I hoped I'd get over it.

Soon.

At eleven o'clock, after small, nonessential banter, I shook her hand gently and invited her to use my services again, if the occasion ever arose. My lips were sealed about her brother, who probably killed her father. I also kept secret the Adolf Hitler saga. What the hell good would it have done. She'd hired me to find two people and I'd done the job--got paid and see ya later.

I kinda hated to leave.

I finally felt warm, my knee pain abated and I dreaded braving the frigid, wintery morning.

What price bravery?

What price poverty?

I'd have to buy a new and warmer trench coat. I could afford it now, thanks to Mrs. Averly and lots of innocent dead people.

Doloras' kin would have been the next call if I knew she had any kin, and Lauren's kin if she had any or if I knew of any. I would've called on Lou's kin if I knew of any or if I really knew what happened to Lou. What about Kelly's kin?

My visits were over.

My duty done.

For the first time in a week I realized just how exhausted I'd become, mentally and physically. Maybe it was time to consider a new profession. Maybe thirty-five was too old to be running around the country, shooting people, learning to ski and falling in love. All that's for kids and the movies. I had Mrs. Averly's money. I'd pay the rest of my bills, Bill's bills, Rose's bills and take a long vacation. Maybe take Rose with me.

No, I'd take Uncle Bill.

Go to Florida.

Miami Beach.

The horse races at Hialiah. The Flamingos. I'd double my money or lose it all. Bill would love it. Pay him back for all the baseball games he took me to over the years.

I began to feel relaxed just contemplating the trip.

I walked across the Common, up Tremont street into Scollay Square. The only people who ever bothered anyone there were the panhandlers. I had some loose change in my pocket and felt good sharing it with those less fortunate. "Buddy, can you spare a dime?"

Sure I could.

I wondered how many dimes a bum had to beg for before he could buy a cheap bottle of wine. Maybe ten?

I could've been one of these poor souls, I thought.

I walked back into the downtown area. Shoeshine Eddie was practicing his trade next to the active Milk Street newsstand. I placed my shoe onto his homemade box and he began with the black paste. "Haven't seen you around, Johnny. Been vacationing?" he asked.

"Something like that," I answered.

"Guess you found Mrs. Averly's husband. I read about you in the papers. You okay?"

"I guess so," I said and glanced over his shoulder at the newsstand that carried every conceivable paper--even out of town. A headline grabbed my attention from the *VERMONT DAILY NEWS*,

Saturday, December 18, 1945: STOWE CHALET DESTROYED BY MYSTERIOUS FIRE.

I kicked the box aside and plunked down two cents for the newspaper. Apparently a chalet owned by Richard Averly, heir to the Averly Brewery fortune, burned to the ground late yesterday afternoon. Averly's charred body was found in the rubble along with a local waitress, a butler and cook who were in the main house. Two other unidentified bodies were found in a small guest house--a male and female. The male wore false teeth, suggesting that his identity will never be discovered.

I gasped. The FBI had cleaned up any evidence of what I'd learned and what Tony, Doloras, Kelly, Lou and Lauren had died for. No one would ever know or believe or be able to prove it was Adolf and Eva in that chalet, honored guests of Richard Averly and the United States government. Obviously, Hitler had removed his teeth in Berlin and used them for his stand-in. The body found buried at the chancellery would always be deemed his.

So what?

Did I give a shit?

Not really--as long as I was left alone.

Final Chapter
THE KEY TO THE LOCKE
Boston Post headline,
Saturday, December 18, 1945:
MOVIE STAR, AUDIE MURPHY,
ARMY'S MOST DECORATED SOLDIER,
RETURNS TO TEXAS HOME

I had wined and dined Rose and Uncle Bill at Jimmy's for lunch. I was just happy to still be alive. They took turns grilling me on my adventures. I left out the Hitler killing. The fewer people who knew about that, the better. Besides, I'd never be able to prove anything.

Was the man I shot really Adolf Hitler?

Apparently, or the FBI wouldn't have cleaned up so well.

Rose gave me a little package wrapped with a silly bow. "It's not Christmas yet," I said.

"You and Bill don't believe in Christmas anyway. You're both old Scrooges."

I blushed as I unwrapped it. A gold plated watch with an inscription on the underside. TO THE BEST BOSS, WITHOUT WHOM I'D BE AT A LOSS. I didn't know she was an accomplished poet.

She gave Bill a bottle of vodka and a box of oranges. So much for his fooling us.

Uncle Bill handed me an envelope containing tickets to a Boston Bruins hockey game. Bill was a good friend of Milt Schmidt, the Bruins star center.

He gave Rose a pearl necklace. He might have wanted people to think he was a Scrooge, but this proved differently. Uncle Bill, in reality, was just an old softy.

I couldn't detect if the pearls were real or not. I think you're supposed to bite them--but then I didn't know what that might prove--so I didn't. And I also couldn't imagine where he came up with the cake to buy any kind of nice jewelry, real or fake. When Rose excused herself to powder her nose, Bill revealed his bookie friend had sent him back my overpayment after reading about my involvement in the Provincetown shooting. I guess people would now begin to take me for a real-life tough private eye.

That would be okay with me.

"Thanks, you guys," I said. "I bought you nothing."

They understood.

We all got mildly loaded, had a grand old time and I put both in a cab, Bill back to the apartment and Rose to the office.

I stopped at the Berkeley street precinct to see O'Brien on my way back to my office and dropped the Vermont newspaper on his desk. "This pays off a few debts," I assured him. "Not all, but a few. That's all I can tell you. I wish I could tell you more. But I can't."

He didn't understand, but I appreciated the fact he didn't push. "Kelly has a mother who lives on the north shore. Revere. I called her already. We're going to help arrange a funeral for Tuesday."

"I'll be there," I said, my head bowed. "I'll even say a few words, if it's okay with you. Red was my best friend and I feel I somehow let him down."

My watch read almost four o'clock when I arrived at my office building. The sun had already dropped in the sky and the day was slowly becoming night. It was Saturday and I didn't expect any new business, but I wanted to check the mail for the manila envelope I'd sent myself. When I arrived, Rose displayed a real odd look on her face. Somewhere between terrified and frightened. "You got company, Mr. Dark," she whispered. She never called me Mr. Dark unless something was wrong or she was pissed at me. I knew I'd done nothing recently to piss her off, unless it was my lack of a Christmas present at lunch.

She put up four fingers and then made a real ugly face like a King Kong. I think she was trying to tell me that four gorillas were in my office.

"Thanks Rose," I said in a loud voice. "I don't want to be disturbed."

As I walked by her desk, I picked up her pencil and scribbled on her pad: CALL CHIEF O'BRIEN. GET HIM OVER HERE, PRONTO.

I opened and closed the door to my office. Four large, thick-necked men sat in various parts of the room. They could have been linemen for the Boston Yanks football team, which was owned by Kate Smith--also about their size.

The tall blonde on the couch, facing my desk, I assumed was Erv Locke. "Welcome gentlemen," I said. "Come here to hire my services?"

I removed my coat and flipped my hat toward the rack. It missed. So much for being a smart-ass.

"Don't make any dumb moves," Locke said. "This gun in my lap ain't no pea shooter."

I sat in my desk-chair across from Locke, my lower body hidden from his view. "Drink gentlemen?" I offered. I started to open my side drawer.

Locke jumped up and aimed his pistol, equipped with a silencer. "I told you to watch your moves, Dark" he barked in an officious tone like he was used to being obeyed.

"It's only a bottle," I said, waved it in front of him and poured a half glass of scotch for myself. "Join me?"

The three goons looked at Locke. He nodded negative. "No thanks," he said. "And no thanks for them, either. We're working."

"What gives me the honor of your presence?" I asked in a flippant manner.

"Don't be a 'wisenheimer', Dark. You've embarrassed a lot of top-ranked people. We got orders to search your office for a certain picture and some negatives and then silence you for good."

At least Locke didn't mince words. I admired honesty. The prick planned to kill me.

I carefully reached behind my back, removed my rod from its holster and placed it in my lap. The desk still hid my activity. "You can gladly have the picture and negatives, but I don't think it wise to kill me."

As I opened the top drawer Locke jumped up again, pointing his gun in my direction. I removed the negatives carefully and tossed them gently across the desk. He sat back down, and looked them over, lit a match and watched them go up in flames on my coffee table. Obviously he liked playing with fire. He opened the envelope, and studied the eight by ten glossy. "You got nothing here," he said with a sly grin.

"I don't agree," I said with the widest smile I could muster up from a fearful face. "We figured out who they were and so would a lot of other people."

Locke sort of shrugged his shoulders. "Well, it's all up in smoke now. Where's the big photo? The one Kelly told me you mailed to yourself?"

"I haven't checked my mail yet today. It's probably there. I assume you bribed Kelly by telling him you'd spare his life if he told you about the pictures?"

"Close, Dark. I promised him I'd spare the dame and he bought it. We were Marines together, you know. Marines are tough and he was willing to give his life to save your girlfriend."

I felt my finger tighten on the pistol trigger, recalling how Kelly had told me of the trust he had in Locke because of the Marine camaraderie. But, I hesitated. Behind Locke's back, through the milky glass partitions between the offices, I spotted Rose's silhouette. When and if Chief O'Brien showed, I'd see his too. I'd have to stall.

To the right of my desk blotter pad and next to the telephone stood a new, funny looking contraption that Rose had coerced me to buy from a cute, but pushy salesman last summer. Ten dollars down and two dollars a month for I don't know how long. It was like a walkie talkie that the soldiers used in the war. The salesman called it an intercom, dated Rose for two months afterward and then took off. I never used it. When I wanted Rose's attention, I just yelled through the glass. The moment seemed to have arrived to test it. I slid my hand toward the box-like object, hopefully unseen, and pressed the ON button.

"So your Marine buddy Kelly gave you the information and you killed Lauren anyway?" I said, and leaned my head as close to the intercom as possible without appearing contorted. "No blood loyalty between old Marine friends?"

"That's right," Locke boasted. "We were allies during the war, Enemies now. Besides. I was just following orders."

I was getting tired of hearing that line as an excuse for everything, and I was having a hell of a time holding back my anger. "Were you following orders when you raped the girl?" I said, and wished I hadn't. My stomach flipped over and I almost lost everything I'd ingested at Jimmy's Harborside Restaurant. That would look messy on my office floor.

"The girl was a fucking lesbian," Locke said, then scanned the faces of his goons, flashing a toothy smile. "No loss to the world. Right boys?"

I felt the heat work its way up my spine to the back of my neck. I wondered if the hair back there was standing on end or if hair actually did stand on end when someone was experiencing hate or fear. Uncle Bill once explained about the seven deadly sins and why they were called such. Hate was a big one. 'If you hate someone else, you only hurt yourself', he said. Right now I hated Locke with every bone in my body and he didn't seem to feel a thing.

"Did Kelly tell you that we sent an envelope to J. Edgar Hoover?" I inquired, wondering if he actually believed we had sent it or had forced Kelly to admit we hadn't. I grabbed a stale Chesterfield out of my silver cigarette case, not offering one to anyone else, lit it and blew some rings. One of the goons looked entertained.

"Waste of a stamp," Locke said with a satisfied appearing smile. "Hoover knows what's going on. He even sanctioned it. Besides, he's as queer as your late girlfriend."

I wondered if he was lying. I'd never heard that Hoover was a homo. He wasn't married, if that meant anything. But neither was I. I wondered how many people labeled me as a homo. "I thought you worked for the FBI and they protected the freedoms of the country's citizens," I said, stalling for time and hoping to glean a little more information, all the time talking as close to the intercom as possible, without appearing too obvious.

"I do. But a separate branch. CO branch. Covert Operations with its own commander and staff. Hoover knows about it but isn't involved. He keeps his distance, just in case we get nabbed. So, I'm afraid the picture you sent him will be filed under W in the waste-basket and won't keep you alive. Sorry, Dark, I have to admit, you were a fair adversary."

"What about chief prosecutor Jackson at the Nuremberg trials?" I asked. "We intercepted some correspondence from him about Richard Averly's informant."

Locke didn't seemed concerned. "He doesn't know who the informant is either, and frankly, I don't think he cares."

I glanced though the glass into the front office, hoping to see more than Rose.

I didn't.

"That was a coup I helped pull off," Locke puffed out his already large chest. "Richard Averly spearheaded the plan to smuggle Adolf, Eva and his dog out of Berlin right under the Russians' noses."

Locke removed a handkerchief and wiped his nose. He sneezed loudly and wetly. "Damn snowstorm," he said. "Hate winter weather."

"So you're saying that Jackson knew nothing about what you and I know about. Right? What about President Truman?" I asked, still stalling.

Locke put away his hanky. "That fool? He had his hands full deciding whether to nuke the Nips. He knows nothing about what went on with the Nazis. Can you think of any reasons why you shouldn't join your nosy newspaper friend, my buddy Red Kelly and your lessie girlfriend?"

My mind spun. Locke really pissed me off. If he was attempting to get me to lose control, he was slowly succeeding. "Well, since you're going to put me to sleep anyway, and you insist the pictures aren't insurance on my life, you got nothing to lose in answering a few other questions?"

"Shoot," Locke said. And he didn't know how close I came to doing just that as I still held my 38 in my right hand aimed under the desk at his groin. Locke sat directly in front of me with his back to the glass partitions. His gun rested on his lap, not his hand. One goon sat beside him. Another in a chair near the window to my left and the third on the other side of the room on my right. None of them exposed guns, but, I knew they were there--somewhere. If and when I pulled my trigger, my bullet would have to pass through the front of my wooden desk and may miss its target. One of the six shots would find a home and I may even have time to get one of the goons. The chances of getting all four was somewhere between none and none. Not quite as good odds Bill and I get at Suffolk Downs, if I ever see Suffolk Downs again. My only ace in the hole was Chief O'Brien, who, I assumed was on his way across town. I sort of hoped this would be like a Hollywood movie when the cavalry rode in at the last second and saved the day. The day being me. Just last month I'd seen a movie at the Old Howard about General Custer. I think it starred Errol Flynn. Unfortunately, the calvary rode in too late.

Locke wiped his nose again. It was beginning to turn red. He glanced at his three cohorts as though he needed approval to continue, which I knew he didn't need.

"Then Mrs. Averly's clean?" I said loud enough into the intercom. Something inside of me wanted her to be innocent.

"Clean, naive and stupid," Locke said. "But pretty. I'd go for a piece of that. Wouldn't you Darkman?"

I didn't like his toothy grin or the grins on his goons.

"Richard's smart," Locke said. "His sister's dumb and the father even dumber. Richard set up the whole deal with Hitler. The fake suicide, the getaway, everything. Smart man. Smart double agent. Worked for us during the war."

"Whose side was Richard on?" I asked, really wondering who double agents actually worked for.

"Both. He got paid by both, worked for both and was loyal to both, when necessary."

"And this government didn't care that Hitler got smuggled into this country?" I asked, again my mouth close to the intercom.

Locke was wiping his runny nose. "Richard sold my boss on the idea that Hitler's *Final Solution* was misinterpreted by some of his mad officers who diabolically released hydrogen cyanide into the showers filled with unsuspecting Jews. Millions of them. Hitler swears that it was Himmler's idea and he knew nothing about it. That type of information is being fed to the Nuremberg prosecutor. All very inside and secret data which will ultimately hang them all."

"You believe that shit?" I asked, feeling my stomach beginning to turn over just thinking about the ovens that had been uncovered in recent months at Nazi prison camps.

Locke sneezed and I wondered what the odds were that he'd choke on his own snot. "It made it easier for us to believe Hitler didn't know," he said. "And, besides, I don't get paid to think one way or the other. I was informed that the surest way to convict those twenty Nazis on trial at Nuremberg was with the information gathered by us from Adolf Hitler."

Somewhere along the trail I was taught that there were at least two sides to every story. Sometimes more. Locke had his side. Hitler had his. I had mine. Too many innocent people dead and still dying had theirs. I leaned toward the intercom, glancing again though the glass.

Nothing yet.

I snuffed out my cigarette and lit another. Locke rose and grabbed a pile of mail off my desk. "Maybe the picture I'm seeking is in here." He thumbed through a bunch of bills, a few circulars and then found an eight by ten manila envelope postmarked Stowe, Vermont. Shit. He'd found it. My insurance policy.

"What's this tiny morsel?" he smiled, ripping open the envelope and removing the glossy. "Ha, ha. If Kelly told me the truth, and I believe he did, this is the last bit of evidence." He glared at me, lit a match and watched the picture smolder in his hands. "Sorry, Dark. The best laid plans, you know."

Somehow I had to continue to stall. "Do you expect me to believe that President Truman, FBI Chief Hoover, and chief prosecutor Jackson didn't know the identity of their informant?" I asked, watching the picture reduced to ashes.

Locke made a disagreeable face at me. "Dark, don't be so stupid. I don't care what you believe and don't give a shit what they know. I told you that Hoover knew we had an informant but didn't want to know his identity. It's Jackson's job to convict these twenty bastards. People compromise everyday. You know that. Not just in wartime. How many police cases do you think are solved by cops making deals with robbers and lawyers?"

I knew he was right. But, I was more interested in who knew and who didn't. "You're right," I agreed. "But I can't imagine that the

President okayed the escape of Adolf Hitler. That wouldn't enhance his popularity with our allies."

Locke scratched his head. "Do you think Truman knew his A Bomb would kill that many people? The first one turned over 70,000 innocent Japs into dust. All he knew is that the bomb would end the war and save a lot of allies' lives. An evil means to an honorable end. I would say Truman buys the fact we're receiving important information from a high ranking official. I was told that he didn't want to know anything else. Just like Hoover."

"So all the people getting killed around here are okay as long as Jackson gets his information?" I said.

"The means to an end," Locke said, and chuckled. "Don't blame me. It's not my fault. I don't call the shots. Just follow orders."

"You said that too many times," I said. "Would you jump off a bridge if they told you to?"

Locke squinted. "I have my limits," he said.

"Don't you have a conscience, Locke? Don't you have any feelings for your Marine pal, Red Kelly."

My trigger finger was actually beginning to itch. He was using the same excuses for his crimes as the Nazis were using for theirs. But I controlled my instinct to blow Locke's fucking head off. At least until he'd answered one more question.

One of Locke's goons reached for a cigarette from my silver box. He found one, lit it and made a face. I hoped it was real stale.

"Any other questions, Dark?" Locke pulled up his sleeve and looked at his watch. "It's getting late. My stomach is growling. Time for dinner."

"What happened to Lou Mills?"

"That jerk?" Locke said. "You played right into our hands on that one. By the way, the guy up on the mountain--Hans Kaufman--he was one of ours. He got careless. You croaked him. Right?"

"Something like that," I answered. "He drew first. Even winged me." I rubbed my shoulder where Hans' bullet had found its mark. "I'm sure he'll turn up in the spring thaw."

Locke smiled as though he didn't care one way or the other. "Meat," I heard him mumble.

"What's that?" I asked.

"Meat," Locke repeated. "Hans was just meat. A piece of meat. Frozen meat by now." He let out a loud laugh.

It was nice to know I was dealing with someone with a sick sense of humor. "What about Mills?" I asked again.

"You guys are so dumb," he said. "Red Kelly and I waited for him inside the Boston Post building while my three partners waited just outside. Al--he pointed to the goon beside him on the couch--slit his throat. Real clean. Then we dropped him into Boston harbor for fish food. You may never find him."

I looked at Al. He was flashing a satisfied grin, attempting to blow smoke rings.

"We just follow orders, Dark, and get paid real well. I bet you follow orders. Like at the chalet. You were just following orders. Right?"

"Wrong," I said. "That was my idea and my own orders that I could take or leave. And I gladly did it for free."

I lit another cigarette, this time offering the box around to the company. Al took a stale Pall Mall. "In my line of work, I can accept orders or reject them," I said. "You might say that I follow my own conscience." I stared at Locke when I mentioned conscience.

"Trying to tell me you never killed anybody?" Locke said with a big fucking grin splitting his ugly puss. "What about my monocle man in Provincetown?"

"Just in self-defense," I answered. "And I wondered if he was yours."

"So you shot Hitler in self-defense?" he sneered. "What did Hitler do, threaten to spit on you. The poor old guy had Parkinson's disease so bad, he could hardly hold a pencil, let alone a weapon. You blew away an unarmed man, Dark. Six bullets right into his unprotected gut. Where the hell do you get off judging me?"

He was right. What was the difference? I felt I was doing my duty as a loyal American. Maybe Locke was doing his duty as a loyal American. Maybe Hitler was doing his duty as a loyal German. Maybe all those Nazis being tried at Nuremberg were doing their duties as loyal Germans. Who makes the rules? I didn't know. My head was swimming in pools of doubt.

I'd shot Hans after he'd taken a shot at me.

Legitimate self-defense.

I'd assassinated Hitler in cold blood.

And I'd yet to execute Locke for murder.

Would all three be deemed justifiable homicide?

I wasn't a lawyer, but it sounded good.

I asked my one final question. "Whose idea was it to rape the girl?"

I took turns staring deeply into each of the four faces and noticed the silhouette of Rose's head quickly turn. I hadn't told Rose and Bill everything. I also saw the outline of a large figure hunched over Rose's desk, hopefully listening to every word on the intercom.

Locke's face became serious. The others just smiled. "Who says she was raped?" Locke finally said.

"I checked her body real close," I said through clenched teeth. "She was raped, and you know it. I just want to know who's idea it was. You could've just shot her and left her to die. I doubt anyone ordered you to rape her."

The four men exchanged culpable glances. Locke began nervously biting the cuticle on his thumb. "It was no one's idea," he said. "It just happened. You know. Four guys and a naked girl. The spoils of war."

"The war's over," I said, gritting my teeth tighter. "Don't you read the papers?"

"The war is never over in my business," Locke announced and puffed out his chest. "Forget about the girl. I told you before. She was just trash. We had a book on her. She was a lesbian, running around with that other dike, Doloras. You saw what Richard had done to her."

"Same scenario as his father?" I sort of asked.

"Same scenario," Locke admitted. "Foolproof. Soak everything in alcohol and push the car off the bridge. Just another statistic. Another alcohol related accident. Stowe was an unfortunate fire. Too bad for Richard. He'd served us well, but with Hitler dead, he ceased to be of any use to our agency."

I wondered what people like Locke did with old girlfriends or ex-wives.

Behind Locke's head and through the milky glass I could see not only O'Brien's large figure, but two other figures wearing officers' caps. Even though my swimming head ached, I sighed relief.

The cavalry had arrived on time. They must have read the script. I placed my attention back to Locke and the silencer that sat on his lap. I knew that Rose and Chief O'Brien had heard enough confessions to wrap up every loose end. We didn't have the name of Locke's immediate superior, but I sensed that even if Locke knew, he'd swallow a cyanide pill before revealing. He was that type of soldier. Good ally, bad enemy.

"No one ordered you to rape that girl," I heard myself mutter. "No way was she the spoils of war or the spoils of anything else."

As Locke wiped his red nose and flashed a toothy grin, he mouthed the word MEAT. I felt myself losing my composure and I was aware of tears beginning to roll down my cheeks. "Lauren wasn't trash. She wasn't meat," I heard myself hollering, out of control. "She was an innocent human being. And I loved her. You bastards killed and raped the woman I loved. That was your mistake. The last mistake any of you mugs will ever make."

I think Locke could tell by the fiery look in my eyes and the rising tone of my shaking voice that he suddenly wasn't as safe as he had thought. He quickly glanced over at his three accomplices as though four to one odds wasn't quite enough against someone whose adrenaline was obviously beginning to flow rapidly.

"Let's finish this jerk and his chubby secretary and get the hell out of here. It's late," Locke said.

I noted his hand move toward his gun.

"Too late for you," I yelled and squeezed my trigger.

The sound of the shot shattered through the room, but totally missed its target, since I was shooting from under the desk and through some thin plywood.

The office door flew open and Chief O'Brien jumped through, gun in hand with the other two patrolmen right behind him. Locke's face froze when I shot. His twisted mouth dropped open in amazement. The hand on the silencer stopped moving long enough for me to fire again.

Missed again.

I fired again, and again, and again and one more time for good measure.

The last two shots found a fleshy home. One in his mouth and the other somewhere near his balls. What could have been more appropriate?

"That's for Lauren," I heard myself mumble, incoherently.

The three goons never put up a fight, immediately throwing down their weapons when seeing that their boss had been taken out of action and three cops standing in the doorway.

How did I feel?

My third kill this week.

Did it cure my hate?

Did it bring Lauren back?

None of the above. I felt nothing except tired and dirty. To me, Locke was just a big piece of meat.

"That was quite a show you put on for me, Dark," Chief O'Brien said, approaching my desk where I remained seated, frozen in shock. "I'm not sure I understand everything, but maybe I'll take these guys to the precinct and question them to fill in the missing details. I think I can get them to sing."

Chief O'Brien noticed my silver cigarette case and reached in. "Mind if I do?"

Nodding to the negative, I reached into my pocket. Ignoring O'Brien's puzzled look, I offered him a fresh Chesterfield.

"Thanks," he said. "You know what's funny, Dark? If anything can be found funny about this whole mess."

"What's funny?" I asked in a droned tone.

"I thought the war was over."